ACTING

FROM THE

ULTIMATE
CONSCIOUSNESS

ACTING

FROM THE

ULTIMATE
CONSCIOUSNESS

ERIC MORRIS

Published by:
Ermor Enterprises
8004 Fareholm Drive
Los Angeles, CA 90046

Distributed by SCB (800) 729-6423

Library of Congress Cataloging-in-Publication Data

Morris, Eric, date.
Acting from the ultimate consciousness/Eric Morris.
p.   cm.

1. Acting.   I. Title.
PN2061.M588   1988
792′.028—dc19   87-22338 CIP
ISBN 0-9629709-1-3

Book design and composition by The Sarabande Press

Printed in the United States of America
5   6   7   8   9   10

In memory of Brooks Clift, a dear friend for all too short a time. I hope he is in a better place.

Acknowledgments

My deepest gratitude to Scarlett Gani for her tireless efforts in the editing of this text and her constant support and advice. This book could not have been written without her help!
And to Anna Ivara, who coined the phrase "ultimate consciousness."

CONTENTS

CONTENTS

INTRODUCTION

♦ *Acting from the Ultimate Consciousness* is the fourth in a series of books on acting—a particular system of acting. The approach is based on the Stanislavsky Method, but only in terms of the basic theories. The process explored in my books is a complete one. It addresses the actor's instrumental needs as well as providing him with a specific craft. In my other books, *No Acting Please, Being & Doing,* and *Irreverent Acting,* I deal with the elimination of acting obstacles and with a specific craft process for fulfilling material. While the first two books mainly address themselves to the actor's instrument, exploring hundreds of exercises and techniques designed to free that instrument of blocks and obstacles, the third book, *Irreverent Acting,* devotes itself entirely to the process—the craft of acting—discussing, exploring, experimenting with the specific techniques and approaches that take the actor to the fulfillment of the obligations of material.

In this book, I have attempted to explore and document work that I have been experimenting with for many years, in my classes and as a director. These areas are seldom, if ever, confronted in the actor's training or in acting texts. The book starts with *consciousness*—what it is and how to elevate it. Consciousness is the prerequisite to the *ultimate consciousness,* an incredible state, which when attained by an actor is electrifying both to him and the audience. Since the unconscious is where the greatest part of all talent lives, the process of reaching and communicating with it is totally explored through techniques that create a liaison between consciousness and the unconscious.

In addition to taking this esoteric journey, the book deals with *ensemble,* the highest state of creative relating on the stage, a place most actors strive to reach. Ensemble is explored pragmatically through exercises and approaches which take the actor to the threshold of incredible involvement experiences. *Characterization,* a process that has become as complex as the structure of the brain, is demystified and put into a perspective that any actor can understand and apply. The text continues into unexplored areas, teaching the actor how to *chart* and keep *journals,* so that he can document the process of his craft and have a blueprint to follow from scene to scene. In the final sections, *rehearsing* is explored. How to rehearse in the different mediums, film and theater, is explained, and an example is given of ten complete rehearsals between two actors who are building the realities that will fulfill the obligations of a specific scene. For years, I have heard actors and directors complain that they did not know specifically what to do in a rehearsal. These ten samples take them step by step from one rehearsal to the next.

This book stands entirely on its own and can be used separately from the others. However, it can best be realized, particularly in specific craft areas such as *obligations, choices* and *choice approaches,* when used in tandem with *Irreverent Acting.* All four books complement each other and comprise a compendium of acting that will serve the serious actor for a lifetime.

ACTING

FROM THE

ULTIMATE
CONSCIOUSNESS

I

CONSCIOUSNESS

The first thought I had after titling this book was that the title sounded somewhat esoteric. The work is extremely pragmatic and does not border on the mystical or the parapsychological. *The ultimate consciousness* is just a term I use to describe a phenomenon—which I will get into later—wherein unconscious impulses are being communicated to or fed into conscious behavior.

BEING, IRREVERENCE,
AND THE ULTIMATE CONSCIOUSNESS

The three stages of BEING, *irreverence,* and *ultimate consciousness* form a chronological chain of interrelating behavioral states, which hopefully set up a foundation for reaching an exciting level of theatrical life that is being supported by the purity of unconscious impulses.

BEING—which is explored in great detail in my other book, *Irreverent Acting*—is a state wherein the actor is in touch with everything he feels, on a moment-to-moment basis. He is experiencing a truthful flow of impulses, which he expresses freely, and is comfortable doing no more or less than what he feels. This state is the prerequisite to an organic creative process and must be reached before the actor can take the next step.

There are a great number of techniques for getting to a BEING state, but in addition to the work that he must do systematically to arrive there, the actor must also progressively encourage a growing consciousness toward BEING in his life. The BEING state is a place of truth, from which the actor can stimulate the truth of the character in the piece. On the creative journey, while exploring the choices that will fulfill the various obligations of the piece, the actor is *irreverent* to the material, expressing all the impulses stimulated by his choices while attempting to find the "yellow brick road" to the fulfillment of the piece. This irreverent state is a *must* if the actor is to service the piece

19

organically. If he then establishes a BEING state, and from there is totally irreverent in the exploration of his choices—provided that they are intelligent and dimensional—he may hope for some contact with the unconscious, which will affect his conscious behavior in the scene and thereby enable him to achieve an *ultimate-consciousness* state.

Before I define the concept of the *ultimate consciousness*, let's talk about consciousness: What is it? Where does it come from? And are you born with it?

Everybody is born with consciousness, but the level to which we develop it is entirely dependent on our upbringing and our exposure. Some people are born to parents who are already aware and who transfer that awareness to their children, who, in turn, go further in their own quest for consciousness. Other people develop the component parts of consciousness on their own. Whatever stimulates curiosity in a child, whatever it is that makes a person look more deeply into the eyes of another, whatever makes one ask questions and seek knowledge—these are the elements which help develop consciousness. Like a muscle in the body, consciousness is developed and exercised. Once the awareness is piqued, a hunger to stretch the consciousness is created.

THE COMPONENTS OF CONSCIOUSNESS

No doubt you have all seen people who seem totally unaware of what is going on around them: they stand in a pathway oblivious to anyone wanting to pass or so close to you that you can feel their body heat, or they sit there eating lunch as if in some faraway world of their own, and so on. It makes you wonder what causes such insulation and lack of awareness. Besides the fact that these people can be a nuisance, the more important reality is that they miss experiencing life and the world around them! Was it fear, insecurity, or shyness that caused such withdrawal in the first place? Whatever it was, it can be a lifelong liability.

To the actor's creativity it can be fatal! Besides needing to be aware of the world around him, the actor must also be fed by external and internal stimuli, which constitute the foundation of the impulses which shape his behavior in a scene. Therefore it is mandatory that the actor be highly conscious and accessible to the objects in the world around him.

Consciousness is made up, in part, of curiosity, sensitivity, awareness, perception, interest, and a feeling for life itself. The desire to experience, to know, or to find out about things stimulates consciousness. Where do these qualities come from, and how are they created?

Usually they are born in childhood, particularly if they are encouraged. Parents, teachers, peer groups can encourage or stifle curiosity. It can become a subject of ridicule to be too curious or sensitive. The "free" schools around the world are famous for encouraging consciousness and individuality. The public schools, on the other hand, are more interested in maintaining discipline than in opening the mind. Education, particularly on the higher levels, encourages the use of the mind and stimulates curiosity as well.

As his consciousness is expanded, the person (actor) begins to communicate with the world and himself on a greater number of levels. He acquires an awareness of his own body and its state of health, as well as a growing knowledge of how he feels, not only in the moment but also about an infinite number of things and people he comes into contact with. This elevation of consciousness forms the bridge to the unconscious. The more open and available the actor is to conscious stimuli, the more accessible he becomes to the flow of unconscious impulses and signals. Therefore, expanding one's consciousness is necessary not only in order to be affected by the impact of internal and external stimuli, but also to create the opening through which communication from the unconscious can occur. It is this "unconscious communication" which yields the most exciting life on the stage. The truly inspired moments that an actor experiences come from the unconscious well of his being.

Since one cannot usually communicate consciously and directly with the unconscious, it is important to establish some other kind of communication with it and to encourage a conscious openness for unconscious impulses to flow into behavior. There are a number of exercises and techniques for establishing such communication, and we will explore them later in the chapter on the *ultimate consciousness*.

HOW TO DEVELOP CONSCIOUSNESS

After you have identified what consciousness is, what being a conscious person means, the next step is to break down the elements or qualities of consciousness and to begin working on creating these elements and expanding the already existing talents you have for consciousness.

Curiosity, imagination, awareness, sensitivity, perception, interest, knowledge, concern (for life, others, the world) and an *affinity for all life* are the major ingredients of consciousness. You might begin the journey to consciousness by taking an inventory of yourself: how many of the above ingredients do you possess, and how developed are they? It is important that the actor spend time each day to develop his instrument. His daily work schedule can include time spent in instrumental areas as well as working on the craft. He could do some sense memory, relaxation, and sensitizing; he could deal with material, prepare for rehearsals, log his journal, and so on. Besides doing this daily "homework," the actor also spends a lot of time traveling from place to place, as well as countless hours waiting in offices, restaurants, and other such places. These are the times when he can work on his consciousness.

A good place to start is with curiosity: you can pique and elevate your curiosity by asking questions about the people and the things around you. Wherever you are, there are hundreds of objects that can be explored. Ask questions about everything, even things that don't interest you. If you arbitrarily get involved with objects or people that hold very little interest, you will be surprised to learn that you soon develop curiosity, involvement, and indeed interest. By encouraging yourself to do this, you will stretch your curiosity, and you will soon find that you are much more interested in everything.

DEVELOPING CURIOSITY

While waiting for a friend to arrive for lunch, glance around the restaurant and *wonder* about the decor, the kinds of people around you, the sounds and smells, the table setting and the china. Who selected them, and why? Was it a woman? a man? Who chose the color for the walls? Was it done by a professional decorator, or was it a family decision? How do they keep the carpets clean? What does the kitchen look like? Do they take as much pain with the places that aren't seen as with the ones that are? What about the waiters? Are they all of the same sex, or are there both men and women waiting on tables? Are their uniforms the same? What individual touches has each waiter added to his dress? Is there background music? And if so, what is it? Is anyone paying any attention to it? What kind of lighting is there? Is the room color coordinated, or do things clash with each other? What kind of people eat here? Suppose it is lunchtime: are these mostly clerks, blue collar workers, or executives? Are there many different kinds or types of people? The cost of the food determines the class of people who eat here! What is the ambience of the place? Is it pleasant to be here? Or is there an unpleasant din of mixed and uninterpretable sounds? Glancing around the room, can you determine which of these people are on a time schedule and which are not? How can you tell? Is it by the way they eat? talk? How many of the people who are here seem happy?

The questioning process can include literally thousands of questions and can go into every area imaginable. Start the process with the things that interest you first, and then encourage yourself to go to less interesting areas. Stretching your curiosity develops awareness and perception. Each time you do this kind of exercise you are elevating your consciousness. Carry your curiosity into every area of your life. Since this exploration can be done silently, you can do it anywhere and at any time, undetected. A very good time and place to exercise your curiosity is while riding in a car or bus. It is at that time that we are assaulted by a myriad of sensory stimuli: sounds of all kinds, people in other cars or buses, shops along the side of the road, banners, advertisements, billboards, people waiting at bus stops, school yards filled with children, shoppers, trucks—open or closed and marked with the logos of a thousand kinds of businesses—trees, mountains, cloud formations, the clarity of the air, people dressed in a large variety of clothes of different colors, and so on.

Once you begin to tickle your curiosity with this kind of exploration, it becomes a habit, and you will soon do it without even thinking. It is at this point that you stimulate a permanent expansion of your consciousness. When you truly become a curious person, the world expands; it holds so many delights and surprises! We as people were born with a natural curiosity. Children are always asking questions like Why do birds fly? Why don't we? I believe that curiosity would continue into adulthood if it wasn't discouraged by impatient parents and teachers. Even if you have lost that wonderment, it can be reclaimed! Apportion your time so that you can do a variety of consciousness-raising exercises, and before you know it, your curiosity will be functioning full time.

DEALING WITH THE IMAGINATION

I grew up in a time without television. There was, however, radio! It was a little boxlike object, which sat on a shelf and either made music or "talked"! I remember my whole family huddled around the kitchen table listening to radio shows in silence and sometimes in suspense. The popular shows of that era were *Mr. Keane, Tracer of Lost Persons; Lights Out; The Hermit's Cave; Lux Radio Theatre;* and a host of daytime after-school shows for younger people.

We sat enthralled as we heard the sound of footsteps going up to a room where a frightened woman was huddled, shuddering under the blankets, while with each footfall *it* came closer to her room, the room with the squeaking door. As the door slowly and noisily creaked open, there was a scream, and then . . . the commercial message! I remember those shows and that time as a special and important time in my life. It was a time when I shared a closeness with my family and exercised my *imagination!* We saw that woman in that blue room with printed wallpaper. She had long, flowing red hair, freckles, and a pug nose. The tears were streaming down her face, and she was terrified. Each of us probably imagined a different monster climbing those stairs, and each of us was as frightened as she was. It didn't matter that in a studio somewhere there were four or five actors standing in front of a microphone, with a script in their hands, while a sound-effects man created the footsteps and the squeaking door. All that mattered was that we were given the opportunity to supply the reality through our imagination.

It was also a time of *storytelling*. My father sat in the "big chair" many a night and told stories, which fascinated me, about the days in Russia before the revolution, when Cossacks rode through his little village, brandishing swords and lopping off the heads of the people who unfortunately got in their path. He described in frightening detail the pogroms, when the Cossacks attacked a village and killed the Jews. He talked about hiding in the basement under many garments, and about how he narrowly escaped during many of these pogroms. I will never forget the story about the "sainted" man who came into my father's place of business and asked for alms, and, after my father had given him something, how the man blessed him and wished him a good life. My father's eyes always filled with tears when he told that story, and I always saw in detail the features of that "sainted" man. I could almost smell the vodka on the breath of the Cossacks as they pillaged the village; I could hear the sound of the air splitting when they swung their swords.

I used to look forward to those stories. They were the treat of the evening and usually occurred after dinner and, unfortunately, just before bedtime. You can be sure that my dreams were full of Cossacks chasing me down the streets of Chicago, as I dodged the automobiles and taxicabs. It was wonderful to imagine things that you could not see, to create your own pictures from the sounds you heard. Today, everything is created for us. The only things on the radio are music and news. So where does one go to stimulate the imagination? How do we create a society of actors who have a well-developed ability to use that wonderful tool? We must train it, work to stimulate it! We must make it part of the training process. Just as you can pique and elevate your curiosity, you can also challenge your imagination.

Fantasies

If you are not accustomed to fantasizing, then you must consciously decide to spend some time each day in fantasy—as an exercise. You can fantasize about anything—starting with who and what you are in the world and changing your role every day. In fantasy you can be on a desert island with anyone you care to be there with. Try to encourage sensorial responses to your fantasy suggestions. It makes the fantasy richer while at the same time elevating your sensorial abilities.

Example:

"I am sitting at this sidewalk café, and I am sipping an espresso. Little do these people know that I am not what I appear to be! I am not of this Earth; I am a visitor from a place many light-years away . . . I am not even of their form; I have a different shape and size, a much larger and more developed brain—or information center—capable of thinking on many levels at the same time. I can transport my thoughts into other creatures' minds so that they will do as I want . . . You see, I made that female over there take a sip of her drink! . . . I am inhabiting this shell *they* call a body, but I can leave it anytime and move invisibly around this place, unseen and undetected. At this very moment I am receiving the thoughts of every human being here. I think I will change their attitudes about each other and watch the fun that follows."

That was a stream-of-consciousness fantasy that I made up as I sat at the typewriter. No matter how cliché or unoriginal your fantasies are, they are valuable in stimulating the imagination. As soon as you depart from the conventional, as soon as you create any thought which is not rooted in reality, you are stretching the imagination and training it to function and create worlds that are different from this one.

You can have a fantasy without disrupting your living routine. You can daydream while eating breakfast, or you can become the monarch of some mythical kingdom while driving to work. Before you get out of bed in the morning, you can design and execute a delicious fantasy; before falling asleep at night, you can traverse continents. Besides being a necessary component of consciousness, imagination is a gift of life to be enjoyed. It is also a very important component of the actor's instrument. It is not possible to be a good actor without a good imagination.

Making up Stories about People and Things

Another good imagination exercise is the creation of a scenario about, and surrounding, real events. It is somewhat like a fantasy involvement; however, it differs from it in that you imagine things about people you don't know, creating, as it were, a life story about the person sitting across from you on the bus, or supplying a place with a history that has been totally manufactured by your imagination. It is somewhat like writing a script. You supply the names, dates, and pertinent facts in a person's life, creating his character through your imagination. In reality, the person you are using might be the antithesis of the character you have created, but that is all right!

I have a whole list of exercises in my other books to which you can refer. Unleash your imagination! Be courageous! There aren't any limits to the kinds of stories you can create.

Example:

I do this frequently while having breakfast or lunch. Almost every day I have at least one meal at an outdoor restaurant on Sunset Boulevard. I eat there because the food is good and also because there are a lot of different kinds of people who "fall into" the place. Not only is the variety of types interesting, but it also affords a great opportunity to "people watch," which is one of my greatest pastimes. I try to be unobtrusive while creating my little scenarios:

I see a little man sitting at a table in the back. He is furtively darting glances around the restaurant. I notice that he has been distractedly rolling his napkin between his fingers. There is no doubt that he is uncomfortable and extremely nervous. From the way he is dressed I can tell that he is attempting to be as unobtrusive as possible. That is a person who has something to hide! He is waiting for someone who has not yet arrived, to pass some important information that he is selling to a foreign power. He is in actuality a scientist working at Rocketdyne and building very important guidance units for NASA. The information he is selling is highly sensitive classified material. I glance around the parking lot to see if I can identify his car. He is probably driving a very expensive Mercedes—which would certainly blow his cover! . . . Unless he was smart enough to have thought of that and rented a car. I wonder what makes a man of his stature betray his country. Is it just the money? or is it the intrigue? I notice that he reaches down to pat his pants pocket every so often . . . Maybe he has a small pistol! Wow, what if the police cornered him here? Would he shoot it out with them? There might be danger to us, the innocent people who don't know what's going on here. He gets up. Where is he going? (I follow him with my eyes as he disappears into the men's room. I wait nervously for his return.) Has he gone out the back? No, here he comes. What is that he is carrying? It looks like a toolbox! It is a toolbox! As he walks out of the restaurant and into the parking lot, he waves to the owner, who smiles at him, and he promptly jumps into a pickup truck, which is tastelessly painted lime green and sports a sign announcing "Joe's Carpentry," with a huge telephone number beneath the name.

If I had been doing an observation exercise I would certainly have noticed the man's hands, which were surely not the hands of a scientist. But when you do an *imagination* exercise, you suspend logic and deductive observation for the pure theatricality of making up stories, no matter how bizarre.

Another variation of this exercise, which is also a good rehearsal technique, is for two actors to invent a story: one actor begins, stops at a crucial point, and the other actor picks it up from there, taking the story into any direction in which he decides to go. The two actors go back and forth like that until the original story has been so modified by the startling changes in direction that it has become an entire collection of stories.

Imagination is an integral part of consciousness and should be exercised each day. It can really be a lot of fun.

HEIGHTENING AWARENESS

It might seem that the word *awareness* is a synonym for *consciousness.* Awareness is actually only a part of consciousness, but an important one.

You might be thinking, I am aware! I know what is happening around me. Awareness is linked to curiosity. If you elevate your curiosity, you become more aware. At first, you must consciously decide to "pick up" on the things around you. Asking questions is a great technique. You might also look at an object and encourage your eyes—like a radar scanner—to dance all over it. Encourage yourself to respond with feelings for the object you are scanning. While resting your hand on it, explore its texture. Learn to sense the presence of things behind you. Dissect single sounds, and identify the parts of those sounds. Become aware of temperature and changes in the direction of the wind. Become increasingly aware of *energies*—the energy in a room or the energy of another person. Energies are something that you sense, feel. We have all been in the presence of a hyperactive person: there is an energy emanating from him. Being in the presence of someone who is putting out a lot of "negative" energy also has a definite effect on most people. There are all kinds of energies, and as you become more sensitive, you become much more aware of them. Most people respond to them without knowing exactly what it is that they are responding to.

Awareness is a state of BEING. It can be developed to a very high level. When that occurs, the individual experiences life on a much higher level of responsiveness.

Awareness is sensorial. You become more aware through the use of your senses. So utilize the senses to practice awareness. In the process of daily practice, you might start by isolating your senses. You might decide to deal only with *smells* today; so all day you exercise the olfactory sense, smelling and breaking down all the odors you come into contact with. The next day you can explore the auditory area, listening and responding to the world of sounds. After you have completed this isolation of your senses, you can put them all together and practice sensorial awareness with all five sensory areas. In a very short time you will feel the changes taking place. Your entire being will become a "Geiger counter" of the energies around you.

ENCOURAGING SENSITIVITY

Most of the elements of consciousness dovetail into each other. Awareness leads to being more sensitive to the objects around you, and since you relate on a conscious level to more things around you, it follows that you become more "feeling" about those things.

Here is the dictionary definition of *sensitive:*

"Capable of perceiving with, or as if with, a sense or senses; responsive to or affected by something; responding markedly to small changes of condition or environment; responsive to the feelings, attitudes of others; expressive of small changes of feeling; easily hurt, damaged, or irritated; quick to take offense; touchy . . ." etc.

From the above definition one would understand sensitivity to be a combination of availability, affectability, awareness, responsiveness, sensory awareness, and a heightened level of emotionality.

There are a variety of techniques which stimulate sensitivity. For the senses, an excellent exercise is *Sensitizing*, which is explained in great detail in my other books. Sensitizing is the process of isolating each sense and concentrating in each area until that sense is more accessible. For instance, if you were sensitizing the auditory area, all your concentration would go into listening to sounds—their intensity, origin, and component parts. You would "live" in your ears until you began to hear even the most subtle sounds. By doing this process with all five senses, you heighten your sensitivity and make your instrument much more available to being affected by external stimuli—which in turn stimulates emotional responses.

Using the Personal-Point-of-View Technique

Finding out how you feel about everything is part of being sensitive. A Personal-Point-of-View workout puts you in touch with how you feel in relation to everything around you, so in truth it is a very good technique for elevating your awareness and piquing your curiosity, as well as an excellent sensitivity exercise.

Example: (This exercise can be done silently or out loud, in a stream of consciousness.)

"I am looking around this room. How do I feel about the room itself?
I like it! . . . I feel comfortable here.
"The couch—what do I feel about it?
It's sad, isn't it? . . . It needs some attention . . . I guess I feel attached to it.
"How do I feel when I look out the window?
I love the view! . . . It sends me on a high! . . .
"I am looking at the telephone on the desk. What does that make me feel?

Ooh! I feel ambivalent about the phone. It obligates me! Sometimes I wish it didn't exist!"

(In response to all of the above questions you should encourage yourself to express the full measure of your feelings, audibly.)

"I hear a fire engine on the street below . . . How do I feel about that? I hate noise . . . it's unnerving! . . .

"I'm looking at the plants . . . I wonder if they are aware of me. How do I feel about them?

I love the plants . . . They feel like family . . . They have been here a long time . . . I feel attached to them!

"I see the house next door . . . What is my point of view about that? They built it too close to this one! . . . I'm angry at those people! . . . It's an ugly house . . . I wish those trees would grow and hide it from view! . . ."

The exercise may continue for quite some time, covering a wide range of objects in and out of the room. If done every day, this technique increases your sensitivity by making you more aware of the existence of things, while at the same time putting you in touch with how you feel and helping you to express those feelings.

Sensitivity means becoming sensitive to others as well as yourself. Being a *conscious person* means having a relationship to the world and beyond, feeling hurt for others who are hurting, being sensitive to the conditions of different people around the country and around the world, being sensitive to injustice, and having feelings about righting wrongs! These things are all part of sensitivity and consciousness.

BECOMING PERCEPTIVE

Being perceptive means knowing, having insight, having awareness to a keen degree. Perception constitutes a deeper level of observation. It is the ability to see into things and often understand what motivates behavior. Some people seem to have a natural ability to look more deeply into things than others. Perception and selfless awareness seem to run hand in hand.

Here again, the way to become more perceptive starts with questioning — asking questions about what you see, what you hear, the things you come into contact with; wondering, exploring, deducing, interpreting behavior; picking up on the most subtle change of expression in someone's eyes; watching life's dramas play themselves out right in front of you; being a humble student of human behavior and learning from your observations.

Deductive Observation

This is a technique that promotes perception. It starts with observing people and reasoning with the information you acquire through these observations. At the beginning of this process you deal with simple observations and deductions, but these get more complex as you grow in your ability to see and understand more things. Find a place where there are a large number of people: you can maintain your anonymity by being a part of this sizable group, and at the same time you have a lot of choices to choose from. Start with the obvious: "He has a briefcase and is dressed in a business suit; therefore he must somehow be involved in the world of business." Very obvious observation, but it is a starting point! To that first observation you can add the following deductions: "His briefcase is vinyl—not leather; his suit is not in style—it looks as if it is a couple of years old; he is eating fast-food in a place which is not too great; so . . . one would get the impression that he holds some kind of subordinate position in some company." (In fact, he might be an eccentric millionaire, but the observations certainly do not support that.) "He seems well-groomed—which suggests an interest in himself and in creating a good image. He is fidgeting and seems into himself—which is a sign of anxiety. It looks as if he is waiting for someone. He keeps turning around to look at the entrance. There is a sadness about him. He is fiddling with his food: either he doesn't like it, or he is not hungry. There is a time concern there, because he has looked at his wristwatch at least three times in the last two minutes. He is not aware on an expanded level, because he seems interested only in what concerns him: the small space around him, the plate of food in front of him, his wristwatch, and the entrance to this place. He hasn't noticed me, and I have been watching him for ten minutes. He might have blue-black color blindness, since one of his socks is navy blue and the other is black! . . . But that might also be a result of his having been in a hurry this morning. He has a slight twitch around the upper part of his mouth and a couple of other physical tics that indicate some insecurity."

This observation-perception exercise could go on for hours, and if the subject continues to hold your interest, maybe you should stay with him; however, if you get bored or simply run out of things to deduce from, you might want to do the same thing with someone else. This is a very good technique for developing your perception, and you can do it anywhere.

There are a number of other good exercises for raising your level of perception. Observe, Wonder, and Perceive is very helpful in a number of areas. (You can find an elaborate description of this technique in chapter 3.)

The root of perception is *interest*. If, for example, someone were threatening your life, brandishing a knife and walking toward you, I am sure that you would perceive every move, change of expression, and attitude of the attacker.

Your level of perception in a case like this would be ultimate! Wherever there is interest or whenever something is at stake, a person will instantly become perceptive. When dealing with another person—when something meaningful is at stake or there is a need for a response—the tendency is to search for any evidence of what you are looking for in that person.

The key then is *interest*—stimulating an involvement and looking deeply into another person, asking questions, deducing, wondering, and so on. A wonderful word is *why*. Asking why something happened or why someone responded that way calls for an answer, and with the answer comes understanding. Perception is a wonderful gift. It allows a person to taste the wonders of the world, which are invisible to most people.

DEVELOPING INTEREST

Most of the components of consciousness are linked to each other. Curiosity stimulates interest, which in turn elevates perception, which creates an understanding and a feeling for life and all living things.

The enemy of interest is self-involvement! When a person's scope of awareness extends only a few feet from his body, he sees very little. One does not wake up on a special morning and say to oneself, Today I will become interested in the world and everything in it! No, interest has to be practiced and developed just like any other ability. As people, we tend to take for granted life and its gifts—health, intellect, the abilities of the senses, talent, and the capacity to use that talent. In the same way, actors expect that the only thing needed in order to act is to have talent and that that will be enough. Untrue! We must work at life as well as at developing our talents. If we don't care for our health by eating properly and exercising, we lose it; if we don't challenge our brain, it petrifies; without sensory awareness and stimulation the senses become dull and unaffectable; and so it is with any talent. You must work on yourself every day of your life!

Any discipline must be accompanied by good working habits. If you establish a routine that you can follow, it soon becomes a part of the way you live each day of your life. I have seen too many actors get gung ho for short periods of time and then give up on the practice. A way of work must become a way of life! The entire concept of consciousness is a living process and must become integrated into every living moment.

The component parts of consciousness can be integrated into a way of functioning, a style of life. Almost everything we learn to do starts with a conscious effort before it becomes second nature. Interest too can be excited and developed. One way you can expand your consciousness is to ask questions about almost everything you come into contact with. At first, the questioning process will probably be arbitrary, but as you continue with it, your interest in things will grow, and so will your knowledge. As you become interested in behaviors, animals, objects, colors, style, architecture, weather, and so on, your knowledge will expand and in turn further stimulate your interest. It is like building a pyramid of involvement: awareness leads to curiosity, which in turn arouses interest, and that supplies greater knowledge.

Most people are interested only in what directly affects them: the kinds of clothing they wear, a particular kind of automobile, the way people respond to them, and so on. This is a self-involvement type of interest, which limits the world to a very small circle around the person. Start your journey by exploring things that do not directly relate to you! Ask how things work, even if at first you don't care. Ask your friends how they feel, and really listen to what they say. Pursue their response; go deeper into the exploration of people you know. Extend your curiosity and interest to people you don't know, and look for the elements, features, behaviors that you might find interesting in everyone. Speak to people you meet. Ask questions.

I fly from coast to coast every other week, which means that I spend approximately twenty hours a month in the air. Whoever is sitting next to me always has a story, a life, a profession, and it is all extremely interesting! Every flight I take becomes an incredible learning adventure. People are delighted to talk about themselves and what they do, and if you express an interest in them, they will tell you almost anything you want to know. I don't of course mean private things! I mean things that you can ask about without prying into their personal lives. It is amazing how much you can learn about the world just by asking questions and listening. Listening is a major tool of consciousness and can be developed into a very high art form.

When a person starts to become really conscious, he is often overwhelmed by the increased awareness of how much there is to see, feel, experience, and know in the universe. Before becoming conscious—conscious on a much higher level—most people function inside a familiar perimeter, and with this limited awareness they are comfortable in the predictability of their lives. If a tragedy occurs, they are immediately thrust into a circumstance where they are forced to become conscious, but after dealing with it they usually return to their former place of consciousness.

Increasing Interest by Listening

The school systems—particularly in the lower grades—are geared toward the "three R's": reading, writing, and arithmetic. These are the major learning areas. The schools do very little to teach a child how to *listen* or really *think*. Listening becomes something we all take for granted: "Listen to the teacher's instructions; listen to what she is saying; listen for the bell signaling the change of classes . . ." This kind of listening can be called "hearing listening": you listen in order to hear, and not to explore or learn on a deep level. Ask yourself a question: Do I enjoy listening? You might immediately answer by saying, Yes, of course I enjoy listening . . . to music . . . to a voice that means something to me . . . But that isn't what I am talking about at all! I mean that listening to almost anything can be a meaningful experience. When you read a statement in print, it says what it says. You may interpret it in a number of different ways, but you can't hear exactly what the person was feeling when the statement was made. Listening can tell you a great deal about what is being said. It often lets you know what the person feels in the statement or what is behind the making of that statement; it helps you in varying degrees to understand the personality of the talker, to know how deeply he is connected to what he is saying, whether there is humor in his statement, how much emotional connection he has with his voice, and so on. You can even hear falsity in his voice.

Start your education in listening by becoming aware of your ears. Listen to sounds around you. Dissect those sounds, and listen for the component parts of every sound you hear. Sensitize your ears; live in them! Try to hear what you cannot hear. Stretch your listening so that you may soon hear things that didn't seem to be there a short time ago—the subtleties in a person's voice or the faint whisper of an emotion under a word.

By now you must realize how all the components of consciousness are linked to one another. By sharpening the listening tool, you will not only elevate your interest, you will also greatly increase your perceptions. So begin to listen for meaning or for logic and to acquire a deeper understanding. Listen for content, and put together all the information you hear so that it is understandable. Allow the hearing of stories to excite your imagination and create pictures for you. When you listen to music, separate the instruments; ask yourself what it is you are hearing—how many different pieces and how they blend. Listen to what is called silence, and find out that it doesn't exist: you can always hear something anywhere.

So listen! Ask yourself what sounds mean! We don't always know where a particular sound is coming from. Thunder can sound like a number of things: the rumbling of the earth at the beginning of an earthquake, large cannons off in the distance, or someone moving furniture in the apartment above you. The backfire of a truck might sound like a gunshot, but if you listen—and if you have listened—you can easily distinguish between a backfire and a gunshot; they have an entirely different sound. In fact, if your interest has taken you into the area of firearms, you can also tell the difference between a pistol shot and the sound a rifle makes when it is discharged. There are so many things that we don't hear or perceive but that are available to us if we only listen. There are famous actors who do voice-overs for commercials on television. You never see them in the commercials; you just hear their voice. But if you are a "listener," you can immediately recognize the voice and identify the actor.

Interest is definitely elevated by listening and learning; the more you learn about anything, the greater your interest level in that particular area.

Stimulating Greater Interest by Questioning

Asking questions seems to be a part of our lives. We start to do it as very young children. We ask questions every day; however, what kind of questions are they, and how deeply do we pursue our curiosity with each question?

If you remember, most primary-school teachers grew impatient with our questions. Their attitude toward a child's curiosity seemed abrupt and discouraged further questioning. We learned from those disapproving responses and the ridiculing laughter of our peers to curtail the need to know the answers to our questions. On into adulthood we carried the belief that to ask too many questions might appear stupid or ignorant or just plain "uncool"; so we stopped! When you stop satisfying your curiosity, you begin to lose it. After years of that kind of stifling, it doesn't seem to matter anymore why things are or why they do what they do.

Starting right at this moment you can remove those membranes from your curiosity! As part of the process of expanding your consciousness you must begin to ask questions and learn or relearn how to do it. As a child you were perhaps involved in question and answer sessions with your father that went very much like this cliché dialogue:

"Why do birds fly, Daddy?"

"Because they have wings."

"Yes, but why do they have wings?"

"Because they were born that way."

"And why were they born that way?"

"Because God wanted them to have wings!"

"Why didn't God give *us* wings? . . ."

The questioning would go on until "Daddy" would get too impatient and frustrated to continue to answer, and the final response might sound something like this: "Just because, that's why! So stop asking so many questions!" The sound in "Daddy's" voice was harsh enough to communicate the warning that you'd better stop at this point and that it wasn't "right" to go on asking any more questions. So the next time you wanted to know something from the point of its genesis, you might have thought better of going beyond the first question.

34

A few years ago I had the pleasure of visiting Connecticut in the fall, just as the leaves on the trees were turning into a breathtaking rainbow of colors. I remember riding in the car with my friends who lived there, and commenting with a childlike excitement on almost every color I saw. Besides the glee and awe that I was experiencing, I had an immense curiosity about the phenomenon of this wonderland I was in: What caused the leaves to change colors? How did they know one season from another? What was the scientific explanation for the change? Why were there so many different colors? Even on the same tree the colors of the leaves varied—why? Some of the trees seemed to be in an advanced stage of changing colors while others retained a lot of their summer green—why? What kind of trees were these? Were they indigenous to the East Coast? Why was it that some species didn't change colors?

I expressed a good number of the above questions to my friends, and they were either kind enough or good enough hosts to answer as many of them as they could. They told me that when the temperature drops in the fall, it affects the sugar content of the leaves and that in the process of dying they lose the properties that make them green in the spring and summer. That answered only one or two of my questions. I continued to ask the others anyway, hoping to either get some satisfaction or figure out the answers for myself. At this point you might be thinking, Why couldn't he just have enjoyed the beauty of the environment and let that be enough? To that I say, I *did* enjoy it, enormously, but even more because of my curiosity! The pleasure I experienced because of my interest was intensified by my looking at and seeing more of the terrain and really noticing each tree and the blend of contrasting colors. If I hadn't been intensely interested and curious, I would have seen an overall canvas of color splashes and not the extreme details which heightened my experience and pleasure! The process of asking deep and varied questions starts with giving ourselves permission to do just that.

I have had the fantasy of going back in time to a much earlier period in history, before all of the incredible technological changes of the twentieth century had taken place. It always occurs to me that, even though I have experienced television, automobiles, and atomic energy, I wouldn't know how to explain them. Could I tell the scientists of yesterday how television worked, what the function of an internal-combustion engine was, or how the atom was split? We have a tendency to accept these wonders and leave the workings of them to those who created them. But wouldn't it be tragic to indeed go back in time and be helpless to communicate these breakthroughs because of our ignorance and lack of consciousness about our world? Even though you might never be able to tell those ancient scientists how to construct a cyclotron, it would be nice if you could supply enough scientific theory to save them scores of years of fumbling around in the dark.

Why do birds fly? How do they fly? Have you ever really watched a bird in flight? What keeps it aloft? How does it change directions? When it soars, how is that accomplished? Did we imitate the birds? How much of our modern-day flying came from the birds? If there hadn't been any birds, would men have ever flown? Would they have wanted to? What keeps an airplane that weighs four hundred thousand pounds aloft? How is it that birds' wings flap and airplane wings do not? The questions can go on indefinitely, coming from a very real curiosity. Imagine the number of things on this planet that you could explore, find out about, and become *interested* in!

CONSCIOUSNESS THROUGH KNOWLEDGE

A very big part of consciousness relates to knowledge, knowing about things. We are all ignorant about some things; no one can know everything. You can, however, expand your knowledge infinitely by using some of the techniques already discussed. There is an old saying, "The truth shall set you free!" So will knowledge. Being informed, knowing about things can save your life! Knowledge can save you from being victimized. The knowledge of how to use tools can make life easier and more enjoyable; knowing protocol can enhance an experience while saving you from embarrassment; a knowledge of history and art can make a trip to Europe an experience you will never forget; psychological understanding can lead to fulfilling relationships. Education is a lifelong involvement, and the expansion of knowledge is directly linked to the elevation of consciousness.

Acquiring Knowledge

You learn something new every day. Without your even trying, things come in. Bits of information overheard from a conversation taking place at another table in a restaurant, or when changing channels on your T.V., implant a fact about the unexplainable mass suicide of the lemmings. While passing a building under construction and offhandedly noticing a bricklayer at work, you acquire information and knowledge that you didn't have before. Knowledge can also be collected during recreational involvements, such as reading for pleasure or watching a play or film. It is impossible not to learn something all the time. This is what I call "contact learning." It is very valuable, but it must also be accompanied by "conscious learning." "Conscious learning" comes from active investigation, exploration, and desire: you set out to learn something or find out about something. An example of "conscious learning" is the reading of an instruction booklet for a new computer that you have just purchased. Everything already discussed in this chapter is a prerequisite to the acquisition of knowledge. In short, knowledge can be gained through almost every activity in your life.

You can, however, insulate yourself from learning through a lack of awareness, curiosity, perception, interest, sensitivity, concern, or imagination,—in short, any of the components of consciousness. The same rules apply to the acquisition of knowledge as to the improvement of your abilities in any of the other areas. You must make a conscious decision to educate yourself beyond where you are at this moment, and you must embark on a journey toward learning. Read more; listen more intently as well as deeply; watch people, animals, nature; read the ingredients of everything you put into your body; question everything; explore; use your senses as you never have before. Increase your knowledge of other countries and other cultures; know what is happening in the rest of the world; read newspapers—a variety of them; listen to the news; digest a variety of newscasters' commentaries; listen to the President's addresses; avail yourself of political speeches. Seek out film documentaries in a large variety of areas; take classes in subjects that interest you; learn to do something that you would never have thought of doing before. Travel as much as you can; seek out great teachers in any field and challenge them; watch experts at work and question their techniques. Feed the spirit! Trust what you already know, and use this available knowledge to acquire more. Listen to personal criticism, and use what is valid as a catapult to a higher level of excellence. Get hungry and stay hungry for knowledge about anything, because that hunger will make you broader and richer of mind.

Besides the fact that all this knowledge will add another facet to your consciousness, it will also pay off in big dividends in your acting. The educated actor is a multi-dimensional actor, who has more information to use in interpreting the play, in making decisions about his creative responsibilities to the piece, as well as in selecting exciting choices in hopes of fulfilling those responsibilities. The more you know, the more options you have in the creative process. *Consciousness is the antidote to mediocrity!*

CONCERN AND AFFINITY FOR ALL LIFE

Conscious people seem to have a heightened reverence for life. Most educated and informed people put a high price on human life. No life is "cheap"; each has a relevance to the meaning of the entire universe, and no one has the right to arbitrarily take the life of another.

There is a definite connection between having a sense of one's own personal value and having reverence for other forms of life. If a person considers his own life as important and meaningful, it follows that he respects other lives on the same level. Some people have a high regard for life from a very early age. They are born with, or develop, a sensitivity toward other living creatures that stays with them all through their lives. Possibly, it comes from a connection with the "universal consciousness." There is a direct connection between consciousness and the feeling of reverence for life. As you elevate your awareness and sensitivity, you start to feel more for others. With this growing sensitivity and concern you begin to feel and understand the injustice in the world; you begin to care about what is happening in South Africa and in other places where human rights are being denied. You develop points of view that you begin to activate in expression. You attempt to do something in response to these wrongs: you write letters to your political representatives, or you boycott the products of dictatorships. You feel strongly about what is happening, and it adds a dimension to your consciousness. A sense of morality develops—principles that were subordinated until now. This affinity for life begins to infiltrate your behavior and expression. People around you call attention to these added dimensions of your personality. You seem to feel more deeply and to respond more fully to nature and to the trials of your friends. You carry these added elements into the roles you play, and with the growth of your consciousness there is an obvious expansion in the usage of your talent.

There is something I have done all my life, which relates to a concern and an affinity for life: whenever I see someone being mistreated or hurt in any way, I ask myself how I would feel if that were me! What if I lived in a country where I was a second-class citizen who was discriminated against—a place where I could be thrown in jail for not carrying identification? Since all of us can relate to what affects us, asking these types of questions is one way of developing an understanding and an affinity for others. Another way to add to your concern for the world is to expose yourself to these unpleasant things from which you may have heretofore shielded yourself. Encourage yourself to watch the injustice, to see the atrocities man has heaped on his fellow man. Stop covering your eyes, and look at these things. Be shocked, be appalled by it all, and above all feel the concern that these things will bring up.

I am sure that you have known people who seemed aware, perceptive, and even somewhat sensitive, but who had very little concern or affinity for the rest of humanity. These people are in a state of *limited consciousness!* They have developed some of the parts of consciousness but failed for one reason or another to reach the others. On the stage, this lack of humanity leads to actors without "soul" or pathos in their work, actors who are proficient but cold. You have all seen such actors, who, but for the absence of that cupful of humanity, could have been stars! As happens when anything is done incompletely, if one doesn't achieve full and complete consciousness, one remains limited in certain areas of impressive and expressive experience. There is a natural arithmetic to the universe, and it states that wherever an imbalance exists, there is a corresponding subtraction of quality. In a sense we must accept that we "pay the piper" for all that we do and all that we leave undone.

When a person has worked on all the component parts of consciousness, these parts begin to dovetail into each other—much like tongue-and-groove boards fit together—and the parts create the whole. Know, for example, that when you are working in areas that elevate your interest, you are also building a foundation for the development of your concern and sensitivity.

With the gift of life comes the responsibility to stretch your endowments to their individual limits. One who does not reach beyond his grasp hasn't really experienced the potential of life, and the greater tragedy is that some people live a whole lifetime and never become conscious of that fact!

The conscious person becomes the conscious actor, and an expanded state of consciousness not only creates the opportunity for a connection with the unconscious, but it also makes for a better actor. A complete actor is one who has higher degrees of affectability and sensitivity, knowledge that he can use in every piece of material he approaches, a fuller and freer imagination, as well as a greater ability to involve himself with the world and the people in it.

The realization of consciousness builds a bridge to the unconscious. As the actor reaches a heightened degree of affectability to external stimuli, he becomes equally able to be affected by internal impulses, some of which are unconscious. These unconscious impulses filter up through the conscious veil into conscious impulses, and the actor begins to feel the thrust of inspired emotions. If these unconscious impulses continue to flow through the conscious veil, the actor will light a fuse which may possibly ignite into an explosive *ultimate-consciousness* experience of a high degree.

It is very important at this point to restate something about how and why you must develop your consciousness. Aside from obviously improving the quality of your personal life, this process must be undertaken if you are to become an artist. There are many competent journeymen actors who are galaxies away from artistic achievement. To reach the kind of depth, feeling, and compassion, as well as the threshold to ensemble work that are needed in acting, you must attain a very high level of consciousness. In order to do that, you must add the exploration of consciousness to your daily work program by consciously putting aside periods of time each day to deal with one or more of the component parts of consciousness. For example, as you practice sense memory, you are developing one of the elements of consciousness—namely curiosity. Your imagination is greatly expanded in the sensory process also. An actor must work all day, every day of his life, if he wants to achieve the level of a creative artist. As you work, what started out being conscious becomes automatic; and as consciousness grows, you become integrated with the process, so that this is the way you function in life. You don't even have to think about it anymore. The journey toward consciousness begins at birth, where your consciousness is limited to the delivery room. From that moment forward, it goes on expanding to encompass the entire world.

2

THE
ULTIMATE
CONSCIOUSNESS

Ninety-five per cent of our talent comes from the unconscious, and only a fraction of that talent lives in the conscious part of us. We are constantly being fed by the unconscious: thoughts, impulses, unpredictable responses that seem to come from nowhere. However, as nature has constructed the human being, we are not fully in contact with the unconscious until we are asleep, at which time it takes over and expresses itself in our dreams.

The unconscious is very imaginative and creative. It creates scenarios that are full of sensory delights or horrors. It is also our greatest teacher, since it is in our dreams that we are informed of the truths in our lives. Carl G. Jung and Sigmund Freud did a great deal of work in the area of dream interpretation. The work that I am involved with in relation to the *ultimate consciousness*, however, has very little to do with interpreting dreams or reaching a psychological understanding of life. Those concerns are certainly very important, and we would all be richer and better adjusted psychologically if we did understand and work with our dreams in that way. My emphasis, however, relates to *acting*. My entire exploration of the unconscious is designed to create a connection between the conscious and the unconscious parts of ourselves, for if we accept as the truth that the major portion of our talent lives in the unconscious, then we must find ways to contact it and draw the most from it! We must create a liaison with it so that every time we act we can "plug into" that bottomless well of creativity.

The unconscious communicates with us many times a day, mostly in subtle

40

and undetectable ways: we have a thought triggered by someone's response, and that thought seems to have a wisdom or knowledge that goes beyond our consciousness; our intuition tells us things constantly; we have instincts of all kinds and flashes of insight, which usually fleet from our memories, just as our dreams do shortly after we wake. Unfortunately, it is all like smoke: you grab it only to discover that when you open your hand, it isn't there. I think it is on the very highest level of importance that the artist explore and seek a connection between the conscious and the unconscious parts of his being. The unforgettable moments on the stage are those when the unconscious seems to seep into our acting.

THE ULTIMATE-CONSCIOUSNESS EXPERIENCE

There are various levels or degrees of experiencing the unconscious on the stage. The experience I will describe is the ultimate of these. On a scale of one to ten it is definitely a ten!

While on stage, the actor has a certain awareness of where he is and what he is doing. The creative process of using choices and choice approaches demands a certain level of intellectual guidance; but if he is ideally involved in his process, his awareness that he is on the stage acting is relegated to what I have termed "the eleventh level" of his consciousness. What that means is that he is totally involved in the moment-to-moment realities of the character, responding to the way he is affected by his choices, the other actors, and any external stimulus or internal impulse taking place in the moment, and that his awareness about acting, being on stage, the next line, what he must do next, and so on exists only far below the surface levels of his consciousness. It exists on the eleventh level of consciousness as it were. On the other ten levels the actor is functioning with total organic involvement in, and responses to, the realities stimulated by the choices and the moment.

In this state there is some communication with the unconscious. Depending on the impact and meaningfulness of his choices and on his involvement with them, the actor will call up a certain amount of unconscious support for the life that is taking place on the stage. If, however, the stage involvement exists only on a surface level of consciousness, the actor cannot expect very much backing or inspiration from unconscious sources.

Two things become quite clear. The first is that, if he wants to experience communication with the unconscious every time he acts, the actor must have a technique, a craft, a process on which he can depend to stimulate a high degree of reality, and with which he has attained a certain degree of mastery. Secondly, he must have additional techniques that will build that bridge between the conscious and the unconscious. These techniques are what a large part of this book is about.

The ultimate unconscious experience is essentially unpredictable. The actor doesn't know when or if he will step over the line, and he knows even less what the ingredients for stimulating such an experience are. It happens infrequently, and most actors have never had it. When it does occur it is an unmistakable experience. It is like being taken over by some mysterious force or energy. You feel inspired, exhilarated, involved on a deeper, more meaningful level than ever before. Every thought of the play, or the choice, or your process in the moment disappears, and you are transported by this emotional energy that is deep, varied, colorful, and totally unpredictable. It is as if an invisible force has become the character, and the life of that character and of the actor truly become one! The words of the play flow with an ease and a truth you have never experienced before, and the moment-to-moment life is as unpredictable to the actor as it is to the audience. The impulses are deeper, fuller, and more dimensional than they have ever been, and what is at stake for the character in the play becomes so for the actor. If the character is fighting for survival, the actor feels that same urgency. The reality is ultimate. For as long as the experience lasts, it is the most fulfilling involvement you have ever had. It is like catching the tail of a comet and riding it through the universe!

I have seen it happen only a few times in my entire life: twice on television and once in the movies. As an actor I have experienced *ultimate consciousness* about six times in my entire career.

Once you have had such an experience, you never forget it, and you strive and hope for a reoccurrence. To witness it happening to another actor is almost as incredible as experiencing it for yourself. As it begins to happen, it seems to lift the actor and the audience out of the suspended level of theatrical disbelief and into total reality—something like watching the first man being rocketed into space. It lifts the audience out of the theater and away from any awareness of watching a play or film and into a kind of spectator-of-reality state. It is what theater should be! If only that phenomenon could happen more frequently! Stanislavsky said that the audience pays for two minutes of exciting theater, not two hours, and that if a play can supply those two electrifying minutes, the audience will feel as if they have received their money's worth! He was probably referring to some such experience of his own. I think that it is possible to have experiences of the unconscious of varying degrees every time you act! I am also convinced that the *ultimate-consciousness* experience can be stimulated much more frequently than it is, and that the way to make all of this possible is to take it out of the realm of accidental occurrence and into that of practiced process by exploring the ways, the techniques and exercises, that would make it commonplace and not the rare exception!

Suppose you could go to the movies or to plays and be transported each time to a level of experience like the one we have been discussing. Let us further suppose that there is a way for actors to make acting that real, that exciting, and that important. *There is!* With the development of the *ultimate-consciousness* concept and with the realization of techniques that can and will stimulate that kind of unconscious power every time you act, we can look forward to a new breed of actors on the horizon!

I have been working with the concept on and off for about ten years. At first I was obsessed with the idea of finding a way to promote the *ultimate-consciousness* experience with some kind of regularity. It seemed to me that there must be a way to pique or trick the unconscious into cooperating. I knew of course that the unconscious could be reached through sleep or hypnosis. I became a kind of self-styled modern-day Edison looking for a way to make an "electric light" in the area of consciousness, only to become frustrated time after time with attempts that worked on the level I wanted them to only once in a while and without control or consistency. I gave up the pursuit many times, only to come back to it armed with new thoughts and exercises. What I didn't realize in all of my experimentation was that I was looking for a "glory hole," an incredible stash of gold nuggets worth a fortune, while all the time I was picking up gold dust along the trail! For a long period of time I started every class with an *ultimate-consciousness* workout. We would do a wide variety of exercises designed to elicit that wonderful response. Only a couple of times did actors reach that level; however—and it is an important *however*—every time we did such exercises, there were meaningful results for a large number of the actors in my classes. People would report experiencing deep emotional responses and sometimes unsettling and unexplained feelings coming from a very deep place in their being. When one of these preparatory exercises was followed by a monologue, the actor would fulfill the monologue on a much more important level than ever before. Suddenly, the work would take on a dimension and a meaning it had not had prior to the *ultimate-consciousness* workout. After each exercise I asked these actors to share their experience, and usually more than half of them would report that they had felt deep and complex responses, which had impelled them to more exciting behavior.

I was aware that something important was taking place, but I was still stubbornly looking for that ultimate of all experiences. Time and again I would retell of my *ultimate-consciousness* experiences, holding them out like a carrot for people to reach for. I knew it was possible to experience moments like those on the stage, so why not look for ways to make them happen all the time? I got discouraged many times and would then stop doing any exercises related to *ultimate consciousness*. Then something would happen in a scene or a monologue in class which seemed to have an unconscious origin. I would interrogate the actor: "What did you feel? Was that moment different from the moments preceding it? . . . What did you do just before that happened? . . .

Was it the choice? Did you change the choice or the approach any time before that? If so, describe it!" I would seize on any evidence of an unconscious occurrence like a bloodhound hot after a scent! I gathered fragments of information every time these experiences happened, only to add to my confusion and frustration.

There were some common patterns and consistencies among all of the actors who reported on their work, and these always seemed to lie in the area of the depth of their involvement and the unique impact of their choices. It was certainly something to go on, so I pursued that evidence. Many of the exercises I structured had to do with very deep involvements and primal experiences. I pushed my actors to dig deeper for more meaningful choices. There was definitely some success with this work. What I had neglected to realize all this time was that in every other aspect of the work that I taught there was the element of conditioning, the conditioning of a complex instrument which had to be trained to believe in and answer to emotionally appealing choices, the day-by-day repetition of techniques that trained it to respond (e.g., the Sense-Memory process, which depends on repetition and the schooling of the senses to react to imaginary stimuli). This conditioning process was accomplished over a fairly long period of time, depending on how much work the actor did outside of class. It reminded me of that old joke: "How do you get to Carnegie Hall?" The answer: "Practice, practice, practice!" So it was with the accomplishment of a process, a craft of acting. This realization renewed my excitement with the *ultimate-consciousness* exploration, and I am at this moment working on more approaches to the unconscious. The key, however, is to include a *daily involvement* with the approaches and techniques that promote the connection.

What also became quite clear to me was that the *ultimate-consciousness* experience was a climactic experience; that while it was extremely exciting and desirable, it was only the consistent connection between the conscious and the unconscious that could establish a flow of unconscious impulses and create the dimensional fabric of an entire performance; and that the possibility of achieving these heightened experiences of the unconscious was multiplied many times by having that consistent connection. If you can for a moment compare a technically presentational actor to an actor who functions from an organic origin and really experiences on some level the emotions of the character in the play, you will see that the differences between them, in terms of reality, are tremendous! Imagine the same organic actor supporting his reality from the wellsprings of his unconscious every moment he is on the stage! I am sure that the difference would be just as profound.

PERSONAL EXPERIENCES
WITH THE UNCONSCIOUS

Long before I became involved in the search for the *ultimate consciousness*, I was acting—at first in school and later in professional environments. Even though I went to good schools and to a university that had quite a reputation for turning out fine actors, I didn't know what the hell I was doing on the stage. My head was filled with ponderous "Method" theories, which served me better when I talked about them than when I attempted to apply them to my acting. In spite of my practical ignorance I would sometimes do pretty good work. That was usually accomplished when my head wasn't full of intellectual concepts, which did more to derail me than to help me. There were moments on the stage when I would get inspired and when a certain emotional acceleration would take place. These moments were very satisfying, even though I didn't understand where they came from or how to repeat them. I really don't know whether they were connections with the unconscious; more likely, they were involved conscious responses to the other actor or to something else that had affected me in the moment. It was much later that I had my first real experiences with the unconscious.

I was studying acting with Martin Landau, a person who helped me enormously. He encouraged me to give up my intellectual involvements with acting and supplied some incredible tools to stimulate reality. All of this training took place at the same time as he was helping me to strip away many of my instrumental obstacles. For a long time I struggled with my problems, succeeding in small ways with the work. I had given up what I thought I could do for something that I could not yet do, so I was in a state of transition to another place, and I felt as if I were in limbo!

In my beginning scene work the kinds of comments I received from Martin were: "Eric, that isn't even good bad English acting!" I would have been terribly hurt and offended except for the fact that he was right! From that point on, the journey took me into using more and more of what I felt in the moment, and consequently my work began to improve . . . *slowly!*

About a year and a half down that "bloody" road, I had my first *ultimate-consciousness* experience. I was doing a scene from Tennessee Williams' *Summer and Smoke* with an actress by the name of Kay. We—the characters—were arguing. I was working for the physical manifestations of her behavior that were rejecting me—"selectively emphasizing" what I saw in her eyes, the disgust I heard in her voice, the way her lips curled at the edges with distaste for me—when all of a sudden something happened that I had never experienced before: anger rose in my body like hot liquid erupting from the center of the earth! I felt hatred for her as I had never allowed myself to feel before; she embodied every woman who had ever rejected me, who had ever hurt me, who had ever been insensitive to me. I exploded with a flow of dialogue that took on all the meaning Williams might have intended, and possibly a bit more. I forgot that I was acting and felt what the character felt. The place became real; the relationship acquired an urgency. When the scene was over, I didn't feel the need for a critique: I knew that something special had happened, and I also knew that I had crossed a line as an actor that I would *never* have to cross again.

That was twenty-eight years ago, and the experience still burns clearly in my memory! At the time, I didn't know what had happened or what had caused it. Of course I knew that it was directly related to the choice, but what I came to understand later convinced me that it was the first of three *ultimate-consciousness* experiences that I had in that class. With the knowledge that I later acquired about piquing unconscious responses, I figured out what had caused the experience. At that time in my life I had a track record of very little success with women. I felt generally rejected by them, and I was deeply concerned and hurt by this. I had a very strong agenda, which even affected my dreams frequently. As a result of my choice, I had inadvertently sunk a shaft into the core of an unconscious turmoil which was only too ready to erupt, and it had! Many times I had heard Martin Landau quote Lee Strasberg saying that most of our talent lived in our unconscious, but at that time it had seemed to me little more than an additional piece of information.

My second experience with unconscious responses occurred many months later. I was working on a scene from *Desire Under the Elms* with an actress by the name of Marsha. We had been working on that scene for quite some time—as a matter of fact I had already used up four actresses on it. I was doing Eben, and she was playing Abbie. I had been having considerable difficulty with the scene, and the critique was always the same: "You are doing some nice work, but I don't believe that you are a farm boy! You don't have that connection to the earth; you seem much too sophisticated!"

I am a very stubborn person, who never gives up on anything, and while it might sound as if I think that that is a good quality, it has caused me a lot of grief over the years, as well as incredible rewards! I tried a large variety of choices while working on that scene and finally decided to work for the sense of an animal. The animal I chose to use was the gorilla. That was the choice that made the difference! It grounded me; I became more visceral in behavior and more of the animal that Eben is connected to. Working to create a sense of the gorilla stimulated other impulses apart from the character elements: it made me feel more "territorial," protective of what was mine. I became more aggressive, and my responses were more impulsive. The scene began to take shape, and I began to fill Eben's shoes. There wasn't any more of the prior criticism. On the contrary, I was praised for my connection to the character. I felt very good about the discovery of the animal choice, and—after having attempted the scene over thirty times—I felt victorious.

It was later, however, that I experienced the connection with the unconscious. One evening, while I was repeating the scene, something took hold of me. I was working for a sense of the gorilla, as well as for some sexual choices in relation to Marsha, and emphasizing her available behavior of competitiveness and challenge. In the scene as written, Abbie is attempting to seduce Eben in order to get control of the farm they live on. She is brighter than he is and manipulates him sexually. He feels that the farm has been taken away from his mother to begin with and that it is rightly his. He is torn between his feelings of possessiveness and of revenge against his father and his helpless attraction to Abbie. The scene is loaded with intense ambivalence. Abbie uses his love for his mother as another way to manipulate him. It becomes a conflict of wills, with the sexual impulses getting stronger and stronger.

That evening, while working with my choices, I was transported into a place where I truly felt my existence was at stake. All of a sudden I began circling Marsha. I really felt like a cornered animal. The intensity of her looks frightened me, but at the same time the challenge was exciting and sexual. I felt that this was a battle to the death! The stage disappeared, and I was suddenly alone with her, and I wanted her! I wanted her on my terms, and I was going to take her. The words of the scene flew from my lips as if they were occurring to me at that very moment. Everything was at stake for me—my manhood, my pride, my possessions, my very survival! It was a very complete experience, and again I needed no critique. It was apparent to everyone that something important and unusual had just taken place.

Much later, when I understood more about responses from the unconscious, it was fairly simple to figure out what had happened: the combination of the animal, the sexual desire, and the challenge of wills had elicited very deep and "primitive" feelings. Marsha had a natural competitiveness with men—or at least with me. We argued in rehearsals! There was always the issue of who would get his way about how to approach the scene, about when to rehearse, and so on. The choices I had used to create a strong sexual attraction, combined with the animal impulses stimulated by working for the gorilla, were enough to reach into the unconscious and trigger a primordial and instinctive response. Wherever it is that we came from, our origins are somewhere imprinted in the inherited unconscious memory of us all, and when something penetrates our protective shield, that unconscious memory is freed to gush into our consciousness. I believe that one of the "buttons" to the unconscious is the use of primal and primitive preparations. At the time I was doing that scene, the unconscious connection was made by accident. It was a lucky combination of choices and available realities that had pushed me into that experience. Understanding and knowledge can take this out of the realm of accidental occurrence and make it possible for the actor to repeat it.

The third and most important experience of the three took place about a year later. I say *most important* because it was the fullest *ultimate-consciousness* experience I have ever had. The scene was from *Dark of the Moon*. I was working on the character of the Witchboy. It was the final scene where Barbara Allen dies in his arms and he is going to have to return to being a witch.

There are a great number of obligations in the scene: he is grief-stricken over Barbara Allen's death and terrified about going back to the life of a witch. In the scene he hears the witches coming for him in the form of eagles, and at that point he releases the body of Barbara Allen and experiences an incredible combination of terror, helplessness, and overwhelming grief. His behavior at that time is intense and out of control. I knew that what I needed was a powerful choice that came from a deep place, a place where my greatest fears lived. I searched for several weeks during the rehearsal period and finally came upon an experience that I had had many years before. It was a very disturbing experience, which I still believe to have been supernatural.

My aunt lay dying in a hospital. There were two of us in her room with her: her daughter and I. She seemed to be fighting with someone, or at least she was arguing with some imagined presence. I stood there holding her hand. She was conscious and coherent but heavily sedated, and I thought that the conversations she was having were a result of hallucinations stimulated by the drugs. At one point her daughter was called away to answer a phone call. Suddenly, the room got cold; the light seemed to grow dim as if the sun had disappeared behind a cloud, but there was no sun that day: it was overcast, the shades were drawn, and the lights were on. I felt a presence in the room. An eerie, intangible, undefinable entity had come into that space. Suddenly, at that moment, my aunt sat bolt upright and shouted, "No, I won't go!" She clenched my hand with what seemed to be superhuman strength. I knew right then that the "Angel of Death" was there! I knew it; I felt it with a kind of instinctive knowledge. I had never experienced such terror, such helplessness. I was afraid for my aunt, and I was afraid for myself. I didn't know what to do, and in that moment I also knew that I could do nothing! It was a moment that seemed out of time, out of place, as if it were existing on another plane—a surrealistic moment when time seemed to stand still and everything ceased to move. Then, suddenly, the room was filled with people—doctors, nurses, orderlies, etc. . . . Later the doctor said that my aunt had come very close to dying in those short moments when we were together in that room. To this very day, forty years later, I still get chilled when I think of the experience.

It was that experience that I used as a choice for *Dark of the Moon*. I re-created it by approaching it as an "affective memory." I worked for my aunt, the room, the light in the room, the odors, the colors, the sounds, and the chill of that presence beside me on that day. As I worked for the choice that night in class, I felt an incredible change taking place. I began to feel that presence again. I felt that same helpless terror; only this time I imagined that *It* had come for me! I looked for a place to run to, but there was no escape route. I lost all reason and whimpered like a child. Rational thinking was out of the question! Time seemed to stop as it did in the original experience! I lost all awareness of the stage and the scene and crossed that line into *another level of consciousness.* The experience was so powerful and absorbing that immediately after the scene I had no recollection of my behavior. I can honestly say that it was the richest experience I have ever had on the stage. It is what we all want as actors!

It wasn't until I started to explore the *ultimate consciousness* that I was able to put together the ingredients of that experience and to understand why it had catapulted me into the unconscious the way it had. At the time of the scene I knew something wonderful had happened, but I really didn't go beyond crediting the choice for the results. Later on, I understood that the original experience had affected me on such a primal level that it had pushed buttons that connected to my unconscious. My intrigue with the occult, the fascination I have always had for the supernatural, the terror I feel toward all unexplainable things, my natural fear of death, and my feeling that it comes in the form of an emissary (I grew up with the old-country superstitions about this "Angel of Death"—called "the Malchamovis"—indelibly impressed upon my imagination, and I must have dreamt about the passage to the other world many times while growing up)—all of these elements had come together to pique a response from the unconscious that had transported me, the actor, into the land of the *ultimate consciousness!* It is hard to imagine how many choices of this kind an actor has in his repertoire of experiences, but I do know that there are more than one!

Over the years I have had many fleeting tastes of unconscious life—in a scene in a film, in a moment of relationship while doing a television show, and so on. Most of these responses from the unconscious happened unexpectedly; however, upon examination after the fact, each seemed to be the result of a meaningful choice, of an impulsive reaction to a stimulus supplied by the other actor, of something which had touched a buried memory or an undefinable feeling from a time in the past. Sometimes these *ultimate-consciousness* experiences were the result of an anger or a rage that had ignited a fuse which burnt deeper into the unconscious than I could understand. As time went on, I learned to accept these wonderful and unexplainable flashes, even though I had no control over when and where they happened.

It has only been in the last seven or eight years that I have learned how to communicate better with the unconscious. I believe that there are ways to pique and control the flow of unconscious responses into conscious behavior. Contrary to what I originally expected and wanted, I now feel that the process of establishing a relationship between the conscious and the unconscious is a conditioned process; that while the *ultimate-consciousness* experience is still not a decided-upon event, the actor can enrich and deepen his life on the stage enormously by doing a great deal of work in this area; and that the *ultimate-consciousness* kind of actor will stimulate that ultimate experience much more frequently than an actor who does not delve into the unconscious! With practice and repetition an actor can create a communication with the unconscious that will supply the kind of inspiration and excitement which live only there.

As I have already mentioned, there are many levels to *ultimate-consciousness* experiences, and those I have described are at the top of the scale; but for the sake of clarity and because the total experience is so intense, I will refer to all experiences where the unconscious flows into conscious behavior as *ultimate-consciousness* experiences.

THE CONSCIOUS-UNCONSCIOUS CONNECTION

As I said earlier, creating a liaison with the unconscious is a matter of seduction and conditioning. The first step is to make a *conscious* decision to communicate with the unconscious, by becoming aware of its existence, of the way it functions while we are awake, and of what impulses can be traced to unconscious sources. As with all other explorations, here too you start with questions—inventories exploring the manifestations of unconscious impulses. Many times a day we have "feelings" and thoughts that seem to come from nowhere, intuitions and recollections of things in our past, which spring up because of an odor or a sound or some subtle or subliminal stimulus. We often wake up with a mood that colors our behavior for the whole day. It is important that you start to investigate these feelings, moods, thoughts, and so on. Ask yourself what you are feeling (personal inventory) and where that feeling is coming from. Most of the time, especially in the beginning, you will not be able to identify the cause or the origin of a particular unconscious impulse. There will be times, however, when you will be able to trace a response to something that you can remember from your past. There are scores of stimuli that hook into our memory banks and unconscious areas.

In a movie I was watching on television a while back, there was a character who was using a whip in one of the scenes. He would pull the whip back over his head and with a flick of his wrist crack it through the air, and it would make the sound that a whip makes as it is suddenly jerked backwards. I listened to that sound for a minute or so and was transported back to the circus at the stadium in Chicago. I smelled the unmistakable odors of sawdust, cotton candy, horses, and so forth; I began to experience that same internal excitement I used to feel, mixed in with the anticipation of seeing the clowns, the high-wire acts, and all the other wonders of the circus for which I would wait all year. While sitting in my chair in my library and watching the old Western, I was taken to another time and place, rich with feelings and thoughts that had been locked in my unconscious for years. The memories were conscious, but the feelings, the excitement, and the return to childhood impulses constituted what I think is that "connection" with the unconscious. The experience happened by accident, as most such experiences do. There are, however, ways to encourage these connections to happen much more frequently.

Try to become more *conscious* of your feelings across the board! There will be something different about a response from the unconscious: it will be more dimensional, possibly somewhat mysterious in its essence. Be careful not to interfere with it by questioning the response or feeling while it is happening. Allow it to run its course of expression, and then question it! If you identify the stimulus as I did with the whip, it will be easier to go back to it and to the surrounding stimuli it brought up and to explore this experience of the unconscious more thoroughly. With this kind of exploration you are building that "bridge" from the conscious to the unconscious by deliberately working with stimuli that push those unconscious buttons. Each time you get involved like this you add building material to that "bridge."

The sensory process, which I describe in great detail in all of my other books, is a very good approach for piquing responses from the unconscious. If you are working with or for an object that has strings attached to the past and that is very rich with emotional impact, there is a likelihood that you will stimulate unconscious impulses, which will flow into your conscious responses to that object. Affective Memory is another useful technique, which I will get into later in this chapter.

The Personal-Inventory exercises also put you in touch with how you feel in the moment. As you become increasingly conscious of the unconscious you might add other questions that trace the origin of your feelings.

Example:

"How do I feel? . . . I feel . . . a little out of touch at the moment . . . How do I feel? . . . I feel a little sad . . . I'm not aware of why, but I feel a little down . . . How do I feel? . . . I'm looking out the window . . . I see all the trees and the lake . . . I feel nostalgic too . . . ."

At this point you might add another type of question to the Personal-Inventory process:

"What and where do these feelings come from? . . . What stimulated them? . . . Was it something internal or external? . . ."

There is a chance that you will know the answer, but if not, continue to do the exercise, and explore the origin of the feelings that you have hooked into. In the above example there is a possibility that the sadness and nostalgia, if related to a prior experience in the same or a similar environment, could create a connection with the unconscious. Oftentimes it is a combination of elements that piques a response from the unconscious. If the temperature, the exact time of day, the position of the sun in the sky, the shadows being cast on the deck in front of you, the time of year, and the odors indigenous to that time match the environmental stimuli that were part of an emotional experience in your past, it is possible for you to relive an entire unconscious response to that event replete with the attitudes and emotions that you had at the time. Unfortunately, we experience thousands of these "feelings" without knowing what they mean or what they are related to. In order to become more conscious and to establish that conscious-unconscious connection, the actor *must* do something to promote an awareness of these fleeting "feelings."

PERSONAL INVENTORY III

In my other books there are detailed descriptions of Personal Inventories I and II. For the sake of clarity and distinction I will now refer to this new kind of exploration as Personal Inventory III.

The approach technique for doing all of the personal inventories is the same:

"How do I feel? . . ."
The response:_____
"How do I feel? . . ."
The response:_____

—and so on. You include all the distractions that occur while you are asking those questions.

When doing Personal Inventory II, you add: Am I expressing what I feel, and if not, why not, and what can I do to express it? In Personal Inventory III, you also explore the origin of certain specific feelings that you suspect are anchored in unconscious agenda. When you feel something that seems deep and cannot be explained, if you intuitively sense that there is a well of unexplained impulses beneath what you are feeling and expressing, then you should investigate that possibility by adding questions to the conventional personal-inventory process.

Example:

"How do I feel? . . . O.K., I guess . . . I feel rested today . . . I feel lazy. How do I feel? . . . I don't know! . . . How do I feel? . . . I feel good . . . I mean, I feel O.K. . . . maybe a little anxious! How do I feel? . . . I feel a little irritated . . . anxious . . . Why do I feel anxious? . . . I don't know! . . . I'm not all that anxious, either. How do I feel? . . . I guess I feel a little out of sorts . . . yeah, that's it, I feel out of sorts! What is stimulating that? . . ."

(The origins of the irritation, the anxiety, and the overall feeling of "out of sorts" could be investigated through the use of Personal Inventory III.)

"I don't have a clue! . . . I'm looking around the room, and there isn't anything I see that makes me feel anxious. How do I feel? . . . I feel a little frustrated! . . . What's causing that? I think I feel frustrated because I don't know what is stimulating this anxiety that I feel . . . How do I feel? . . . I'm curious about the feelings I have . . . I wish I could find out why I'm irritated! . . . All right, I am going to break it down into each sense . . . What do I smell? . . . I smell the pine trees, the wood smoldering in the fireplace . . . I smell the air and the odor of the lake . . . How do those odors make me feel? . . . I feel fine about them: they make me feel good! What do I feel in my body? . . . I feel good . . . healthy . . . My clothes feel loose and comfortable; the chair I am sitting in feels good . . . What do I taste? . . . Is there an unusual taste in my mouth? No . . . there isn't . . . There is the aftertaste of the coffee I drank a little while ago; I taste a little sourness just barely there. What do I hear? . . . I hear an airplane high up in the distance . . . I hear the breeze blowing on the drapes . . . I hear a bird occasionally chirping as it flies by the open window . . . I am aware of the music coming from the stereo in the corner . . . It is soft and barely audible . . . What is it I hear? . . . It sounds like a fifties song . . . As I listen to it, I begin to feel an increasing level of anxiety! . . . What is that all about? . . . I don't know . . . I like fifties music! . . . How do I feel? I'm curious about how and why I feel this way . . . (Listening to the song more intently) What is it about that particular song that makes me feel this way? . . . I don't think it's the song at all . . . Does that song remind me of anything? . . . I can't specifically remember an experience. I wish I could remember the exact year when I listened to it! . . . Do the words mean anything special? . . . (Listening) No . . . or at least I don't think so . . . Does it relate to a particular place? . . . I used to listen to music on the car radio . . . at home . . . sometimes at school in the lounge . . . (At that point I feel something specific happening, almost as if I had pushed an important button in my brain.) Yes . . . I remember . . . there was always music playing in the background in the Student-Union lounge where I would go to study for tests." Just as I realize that, my anxiety level rises to a high pitch, and I identify the specific emotional life going on inside me as the same feelings of fear and anxiety that I experienced all through my school years when I was studying for a test: I would become anxious and irritable and feel that there wasn't enough time to do everything I needed to do. I felt inadequately prepared to take and pass the test no matter how much I had read and prepared throughout the semester.

So on a less-than-conscious level I was responding to that background music from the fifties, which had keyed into an unconscious memory of those times at the Student Union when I was preparing to take a test. Without my conscious knowledge I was being affected by that subtle and almost inaudible music, which was stimulating a very discernible emotional response. This kind of thing happens all the time and many times each day. By becoming more sensitive to the unconscious influences in our lives, we can establish a conscious awareness that will lead to communication with the unconscious. If we pursue the experience beyond the recognition stage, we can really delve deeply into the unconscious, thereby building a more solid bridge between it and our consciousness.

At the point in the Personal-Inventory exploration when you have identified the origin of your feelings, you can ask more questions about the time, the place, and the stimulus relating to the original experience.

Example:

"What kind of room is this? . . . (Answer the question sensorially.) What is the color of the walls? . . . (Sensory response) Where is the music coming from? . . . What does it sound like? . . ." etc. . . . etc. . . .

The questions should cover as many areas as possible—including your dress at the time, other people that you remember, smells, other sounds, the specific books of study, and so on.

If you involve yourself in this process repeatedly and whenever you experience a response from the unconscious, you will progressively establish a strong connection with the unconscious, which will do a number of things for your acting: first, it will enable you to become aware of areas and choices that you might use in your work; secondly, it will allow you to go deeper into impacting emotional areas; and—possibly the most important of all—it will stimulate a much more consistent flow from your unconscious into your conscious behavior in a scene. When that happens on the stage, the life is fuller, more dimensional and unpredictable, and the actor is much more available to *ultimate-consciousness* experiences.

This is a cumulative process: each day that you work on your instrument or your craft, you are adding layers of growth. By working each day with consciousness and the unconscious, you are paving a road that can be traveled every time you act. When the actor achieves a constant connection with the flow from the unconscious, he becomes a multidimensional artist. He achieves what people call "depth," an inspired quality of life on the stage. I wonder how many more wonderful artists would exist on this planet if we knew that it was possible to work toward, and achieve, that kind of brilliance, rather than believing that it is a fortunate accident or gift of birth to possess those uncommon qualities.

There is a very popular concept among actors and other creative artists. It is believed that if you can act, then you act! That is absurd! It is like saying that if you have the talent to be a surgeon, all you need to do is appear in the operating room and go to work on the patient!

There are an enormous number of techniques and approaches that I teach and write about. It would be preposterous to consider working to perfect or use them all at one time. But does that mean that they are unimportant to your work as an actor? Of course not! All of the instrumental and craft exercises and techniques are there to be used as they are needed, much as a carpenter chooses to use a saw when a hammer won't do. The daily work of the actor is designed to help him master all of the techniques existing in this process; and while clearing the instrument of all obstacles is of the utmost importance, so is building that bridge to the unconscious. To be successful at anything you must have some organization. If you can *organize* your day so that you use the time to your greatest advantage, you will be able to find the right opportunities to work at becoming more conscious and at making those connections with the unconscious.

TECHNIQUES FOR MAKING CONSCIOUS CONNECTIONS WITH THE UNCONSCIOUS

DREAMS

When we sleep, our unconscious is awake, and it essentially takes over. It creates the dreams and nightmares we have, teaching us lessons through the symbolic information yielded by those dreams. Many books have been written about dreams and how to interpret them. Freud and Jung are possibly the most famous for working in this area, but there have been others.

Dreams teach us the greatest lessons in our lives. If you can comprehend and interpret the information in your dreams, you will learn and understand what you are doing and what you must do in order to grow and to change your life. Most of the time, however, we do not even remember our dreams after we wake up and consciousness takes over. It is rare for most people to recall a whole dream or the specific details of a dream unless it has had a tremendous impact on them. For our purpose, dream interpretation is secondary. It is wonderful for you to understand your dreams and to help yourself with that knowledge, and I encourage you to explore that ability; but here the emphasis is on establishing a greater connection with, and greater use of, the unconscious, and for that purpose it is important for you to become increasingly aware of your dreams, to remember them, and to emotionally relate to them.

Becoming Increasingly Aware of Your Dreams

We dream several times each night, even though sometimes we don't remember dreaming at all. The first step in becoming aware of your dreams is therefore to decide consciously that you are going to do just that. Before going to sleep tonight, make a strong decision that you are going to be aware of dreaming. Know that you will dream, and insist on being aware that the dream is going to happen. The second step is to remember your dreams, and it also depends on wanting to remember them and making a commitment to doing so. The third step is to attempt to re-experience some or all of the dream while being in a conscious state.

Remembering Your Dreams

There are a number of reasons to remember what you dream. One of them is to create a growing communication with the unconscious. Another is to learn from the dream by interpreting its message; and yet another is to use the dream.

There are a number of ways in which you can use your dreams in your acting and in the process of becoming an *ultimate-consciousness* actor. First, the unconscious is rich with potential choices that you can use to deal with and fulfill material. As you become more conversant with your dreams, you discover a multitude of new choices to explore. The second—and perhaps more important way to use your dreams—is to work to re-create and re-experience them while in a conscious state. After you are fully awake and have a solid memory of many of the components of a dream, you can work to re-create those elements in much the same way as you re-create any imaginary stimulus. But before we get to that technique, I want to discuss some of the ways by which you can insure remembering what you dream.

The moment you are awake in the morning and are conscious of the world around you, catch the threads of the dream that you have just had. Try to recall as many details as possible. The dream will disappear very rapidly, so become accustomed to working fast. As you condition this early morning activity, you will be able to hang on to more and more of your dreams. Another technique, which isn't quite so imaginative, is to use a tape recorder and to teach yourself to awaken when you become aware of just having had a dream. Record everything you can remember at that moment, and listen to it in the morning. It will probably sound somewhat disjointed and a little incoherent, but I'm sure it will make enough sense for you to get something out of it that you can use. A pencil and paper might do just as well, except that I have found it difficult to read my handwriting the next morning! You can also use the tape recorder after you awaken in the morning, thus making sure that you can return to the dream later in the day or even at some future time. Whatever process you use, it is very important that you establish a memory of your dreams. As you ensure the habit of remembering and recording them, you will condition yourself to retain your dreams much more frequently and completely.

Encouraging Yourself to
Re-experience What You Dream

Although the evident value of the dream itself is not to be denied, our purpose for dealing with dreams in this context is primarily to establish a connection with the unconscious. When you break a dream down into its separate parts and then attempt to restimulate your emotional response to each stimulus in the dream, you are connecting the threads of your unconscious with your conscious state. The more often you do that, the greater becomes the tie between the two levels. There are a couple of ways to re-create a dream. The first is just by remembering it and encouraging a moment-to-moment emotional response to the memory. If you do that immediately after a dream occurs or after a particularly impacting dream experience, the re-creation could be almost as vivid as the dream itself. The other way to re-experience a dream is to re-create it sensorially. In order to accomplish this successfully, you must be proficient with the technique of Sense Memory. Using Sense Memory will restimulate the actual response to the objects and the stimuli in the dream, and, as a result, the reality level will probably be greater.

Using Sense Memory to Re-Create a Dream

The Sense-Memory process is executed in the same way as when you are practicing with an object, asking questions about the object as it relates to the senses. The major difference is that here you are attempting to re-create elements of a dream—which is something full of symbolism and of objects that change shape and meaning without warning. If you have recorded or written the dream down, you can be much more specific about the details and objects in it, not to mention the chronology of events.

Start by dealing with the place where the dream is occurring, beginning with sensory questions relating to that place.

Example:

"Where am I? . . . (Answer the question visually. Since a dream happens when you are asleep, you can approach the sensory questions and responses with your eyes closed.)

"What does this place look like? . . . (Respond visually with the inner eye.)

"What color are the walls? . . . (Also a visual response. Attempt to see the colors, sizes, shapes as they were in the dream; and if they are distorted or different from what they might actually be in reality, try to accept the distortions as the reality of the dream.)

"Where am I in this place? . . . (Respond with whatever senses are called for as a result of that sensory question.)

"What are the sounds I hear? . . . (Respond with the auditory sense. Attempt to hear what is there.)

"Where are the sounds coming from? . . . (Another auditory question. Respond with that sense.)

"How many different sounds do I hear? . . . (Auditory response)

How do I feel? . . . (Sensory and emotional response)

Who else is in this place? . . . (Sensory response)

Where is that person? . . . (Sensory response)

What is he doing? . . . (Sensory response)

What does his face look like? . . . (Sensory response)

What do I see in his eyes? . . . What color are his eyes? . . . How is he changing? . . . Whom does he look like now? . . . Do I know him? . . . How is he dressed? . . . What sounds is he making? . . . What else is happening in the room? . . . Who else is here? . . .

"It looks like a different place now . . . How has it changed? . . . How am I dressed? . . . What is that odor? . . . (Respond with the olfactory sense. Smell it!) Where is that smell coming from? . . . What is happening now? . . . How do I feel? . . . I hear someone crying . . . What does that sound like? . . . Who is it? . . . Where is the sound coming from? . . . Is it me? . . . Where do I feel those sounds in my body? . . . Who is that child directly across from me? . . . He looks familiar . . . It's me . . . I'm ten years old and he . . . I . . . am crying . . . What do I look like? . . . How tall am I? . . . What is the color of my hair? . . . What does my face look like? . . . What sounds am I making? . . . Whom or what am I relating to? . . . What do I hear him . . . me . . . saying? . . . He is speaking to me . . . asking me to take care of him . . . me . . . What do the words sound like? . . . How does he . . . I . . . look when saying those words? . . . Someone has just entered behind him . . . me . . . Who is it? . . . What does he look like? . . . How tall is he? . . . How is he dressed? . . . He has a blank face . . . What does that look like? . . . How do I feel, watching all of this? . . . He is forcibly holding the child . . . me . . What do I hear? . . . I feel helpless . . . I can't move . . . I feel stuck to the floor! . . . What does my body feel like? . . . I hear myself screaming . . . but no sound is coming from me! . . . What does that feel like? . . ."

The process can continue for quite some time, and you can ask many more questions than the example indicates. Be specific in each area of exploration, and allow yourself to stay with any group of sensory questions that feel right. Remember that a dream is quite different from the conventional reality of life and that you must make a conscious adjustment to accept the unpredictable changes that occur without logic or reason.

The more you practice the process of re-creating your dreams, the better you will become at it. Re-experiencing the dream won't be exactly the same as having it, because the conscious mind is now involved in the process, and it is much more logical and rational than the unconscious. As you repeat each dream, its meaning and message will probably become clearer. Just doing this will build that connection with the unconscious, and along with that will come a better memory of what you dream. In a short time you will begin to notice a change in your work on stage. At first, you will experience just a deeper feeling of inner life, but later, as you establish a better connection and a greater level of trust, you will begin to experience more impulses and a greater dimensionality and unpredictability in your work. Best of all, you will have created a foundation for the *ultimate-consciousness* experiences to occur.

The Sleep-Wake State

The time at night just before you fall asleep and the time in the morning when you are not in a deep sleep but are not yet awake are what I call "the sleep-wake state." These are times when you are very much in touch with your unconscious. It is then, in that preconscious place, that you can participate in your dreams with some amount of conscious control and awareness. It is also a special time when you have the capacity for extrasensory perception. I have had clairvoyant experiences during those preconscious morning states, where I knew what would happen later in the day, and several times in my life those fleeting premonitions have come true. Whatever the powers of the unconscious are, it is then that we are the heirs to those powers. The first step is to become aware of these special times. Just before you drop off tonight, make a conscious effort to note that moment or two when your thoughts wander into unexplainable journeys; wake yourself up and quickly grab the threads of what just happened. Continue to explore these little sojourns into the world of preconscious fantasies and dreams. The phenomenon of waking up is different from that of falling asleep: in the morning these "journeys" are more like real dreams, while at night they are not like dreams at all, but more like fantasy trips.

The Night State

Besides providing the valuable opportunity to experiment with the conscious-unconscious connection, this involvement is a lot of fun. Going to sleep at night takes on a new dimension. It becomes an adventure into the wild unknown of the unconscious imagination. At first, just wake yourself up after each "going under," and try to put the disjointed elements together to make some sense out of them; or just wake yourself up and don't attempt to understand anything at all—just enjoy the experience. After a few such explorations, start to inject thoughts into the involvement. Think about being on a safari in Africa and walking through the bush, for example, and let yourself fall off to sleep while exploring that fantasy. Continue to change your story, and see what happens.

By injecting these fantasies you can see what the unconscious will do with them, while at the same time programming yourself for a possible response from the unconscious stimulated from a conscious place. After a period of time, you will find that this process is very much like working the muscles in your body. You progressively establish a greater communication with the unconscious so that when you act and are working for a choice that will make an impact, that choice will not only affect you on a conscious level, but it will also pique unconscious responses more readily than usual. Since the greatest part of our creative talent lives in the unconscious, elevating the unconscious into consciousness puts us in touch with that wellspring of talent; and because of the new conditioning, the exception becomes the rule: inspiration from the unconscious becomes a much more commonplace event, which leads to an abundance of exciting life on the stage.

The Morning State

In the morning you are still asleep and possibly dreaming. As you get closer to consciousness, you become more aware of the preconscious zone you are in. As that awareness occurs, try to remain asleep instead of jarring yourself into consciousness. Suggest to yourself that you know that you are dreaming or musing, and participate in the dream. Be a part of the "action," and at the same time become a bystander to that action. Stay involved as long as it is possible to maintain the preconscious state. When you become more conscious of being awake than asleep, languish in this elevated level of awareness as long as possible also. There are a variety of levels of preconsciousness, and each one has its rewards. While you may be too conscious to dream in a more highly elevated state of preconsciousness, you will still be experiencing that connection with the unconscious, which should be savored as long as possible.

So much of your success with both of these preconscious states depends on decision, discipline, and repetition. If it were a simple thing to communicate with the unconscious, we could do it easily. Nature, however, has separated the unconscious from the conscious, and in order to take advantage of the treasures locked in the unconscious, we must diligently and patiently pursue any opportunity to uncover them.

Becoming a Spectator in Your Dreams

In addition to the preconscious states, we must also consider the unconscious state when we are really "under" and dreaming. At that time, we are, for the most part, totally involved in our dreams and not at all conscious of dreaming. There are times, however—and we have all experienced them—when we are aware that we are having a dream. It is then that we can become both participants in the action of the dream and spectators to the drama involved. This phenomenon usually occurs by accident when there is an element of consciousness involved. Why it happens or what causes it to happen, I don't know! I imagine that it depends on how deeply one is "under." For our purposes it isn't important to understand the workings of any of this. What *is* important is to find techniques to communicate with the unconscious and to reap the rewards of becoming an *ultimate-consciousness* kind of actor.

If before going to sleep every night you accept that you are surely going to dream and decide to be aware in your dreams, there is a possibility that you will become increasingly better able to know that you are dreaming when you are. Suppose that the next time you begin to dream, you have an awareness that this is a dream: at that exact moment acknowledge, Yes, I am dreaming, and I will watch and enjoy this as if it were a movie! Just watch at first, but later, as you become more able to know that you are dreaming, you may want to participate in the dream. For example, in the middle of a nightmare, while being chased by some faceless monster, you may become aware that, This is indeed a nightmare! At that moment you can participate in the action and allow yourself to feel the exhilaration as well as the fear. You may even enjoy the chase a little. What you are trying to accomplish by doing all this is to integrate the conscious into an experience of the unconscious.

Nightmares affect the entire nervous system, the heart rate and blood pressure rise, and the entire experience may be totally exhausting. It is said that nightmares are the expression of our deepest fears and terrors, and I am sure that they have a function in taking the pressure off by releasing those fears so that they don't fester. It is extremely important for our psychological health to dream, and it is therefore essential, no matter what our reasons are for interfering with the dream process, that we do not disturb nature's intentions. However, I am confident that dream participation will continue to be the exception rather than the rule.

Manipulating Your Dreams

Once you gain some experience watching and participating in your dreams, you may want to begin to manipulate them somewhat. If the conscious part of your brain has enough power, you might consciously suggest other responses and actions in the dream. For example, the faceless monster in hot pursuit could suddenly trip and fall and become unable to keep up, or you might suggest to the part of you that is creating this nightmare to hide around the next corner or to turn abruptly and knock the monster down. There are an infinite number of ways to create a new scenario for any dream. You can become quite creative with your suggestions. There will be times when some particular conscious input might jar you awake. If that happens, go back to sleep with the decision to pick up the dream where you left off. You will probably be able to manipulate in some way any dream in which you can participate. You can add people to a situation, change the environment, decide not to feel what you are feeling; you might want to challenge someone's behavior, refuse to understand something and ask for an explanation, and so on. If your attempted manipulations are unacceptable to the unconscious, you will more than likely awaken or stop dreaming. Don't expect to be able to do all of this every time you dream. The phenomenon is rare, but the more you commit to having it happen, the more frequently it will!

To recapitulate: First acknowledge that you are dreaming. Once you know that, allow yourself to watch the dream. After doing that several times, begin to consciously participate in the action, and after some experience being a participant, slowly begin to suggest changes and additions to the action of the dream. Make sure that you don't lose sight of the purpose of your experiments. These involvements can be entertaining and educational, but the purpose is to establish a growing communication with the unconscious.

There are a lot of people who do not remember dreaming at all. They have some recollection that they did dream, but the dreams remain vague and out of reach. Others remember every part of their dreams and can describe them in vivid detail and color. Why some people are more in touch with their dreams than others is somewhat of a mystery. If you are one of the lucky ones who remember their dreams, it will be easier for you to participate in them and to manipulate and use them as a source of rich choices in your acting. If, on the other hand, you have difficulty recalling any or all of the parts of a dream, the techniques discussed in this chapter can help you strengthen this ability and teach you to use your dreams to make yourself a more complete and dimensional actor.

If you are thinking that dealing with this area and all of the techniques for relating to and using your dreams seems far afield and very different from any of the acting techniques you have ever been exposed to, you may be right. You may even feel that this kind of involvement is esoteric or psychological and wonder what any of it has to do with the wonderful world of imagination, pretending, and fantasy—not to mention the nuts and bolts of doing your job on the stage! You may be asking yourself, What about that wonderfully simple reality of *just acting*? Why is it necessary to do all of this "Method" stuff when in reality acting is a talent, and if you have that talent, you just act? There is a wonderful story about Sir Laurence Olivier and Dustin Hoffman, when they were making *The Marathon Man*. There was a scene in the film that called for Dustin Hoffman's character to be extremely fatigued and under stress from having stayed up all night. Hoffman supposedly did just that and also some other important work to fulfill the obligations of his character in the scene. Upon seeing him in the morning, Olivier commented that he looked terrible and asked what he had been doing to look so bad. Hoffman told him of his process and that he had been up all night to stimulate the reality in the scene, upon which Olivier exclaimed, "Have you ever tried acting?"—or so the story goes. Olivier's response is a typical one for any actor who is not oriented or committed to a "Method" process. While there is room for many techniques on the stage, and while talent is definitely talent, the truth remains that creating reality is the goal of every committed actor, and if creating that reality is based on a specific process, then the actor must engage in that process.

I am very aware of how full and extensive all the elements of my process are. I am also aware of the complexity of the work and of how many instrumental exercises and techniques, as well as craft approaches, are involved. At first, when you look at it from the ground up, it may all seem overwhelming, but it is a day-to-day involvement—putting one foot in front of the other. Before you even realize it, you have traveled quite a distance on this journey. If you structure a daily work schedule, you have ample time to do everything that is necessary to become a *master craftsman* and even have time left over. Every day of your life will pass anyway. Those days will turn into weeks and the weeks into months and years, and only you can decide whether those weeks and months will be filled with the activity of becoming an artist or just another older person! The work you do in the dream area is done for the purpose of creating a relationship with the unconscious and strengthening it so that you will be able to cross that line into the *ultimate consciousness* much more frequently. Working with your dreams, becoming more conscious of them will insure that your unconscious participates more fully in your acting. Dealing with your dreams is just another way of getting the unconscious to yield its "gold" into every role you do. There are other techniques for reaching the unconscious, and we are about to embark on the exploration of those.

INTUITION

The dictionary definition of intuition is: *"Knowledge discerned directly by the mind without reasoning or analysis; a truth or revelation arrived at by insight."* This definition suggests that intuition comes from a place other than consciousness; but if that is true, then where does it come from? Most people think that it is some kind of unexplainable talent or gift that is given to one at birth. "He or she is a very intuitive person," they say. Intuition has always held some mysterious property, and few people question its existence or accept the possibility that it can be trained or influenced. Let us for one moment conjecture that intuition is just knowledge—the kind of knowledge that is acquired through schooling, reading, listening, and experiencing—only it is not acquired consciously, but unconsciously; and when we experience a feeling which we accept as an intuition or an insight of some kind, it is really just the realization of another kind of knowledge, which has come into consciousness from the unconscious. If that is true, then we can say that at those times we are once again in direct communication with the unconscious.

Have you ever had an intuitive feeling that something was going to hap-pen—not a national disaster, but, for instance, that someone would do a certain thing at a certain time? If you analyzed the feeling in an attempt to trace the origin of the intuition, you might find that what you had was really a subtle perception based on a series of experiences involving the person and the events in question.

As I explained in the first chapter, consciousness is very closely related to the unconscious, and being a highly evolved and conscious person means that you have elevated your perception to a very high level. Again, let us speculate for a moment: suppose that perception constituted a direct connection to the unconscious—was at least one of the ways in which the unconscious acquired its education. Being a perceptive person would then be another way of communicating with the unconscious! As a result of our perceptive inputs, the unconscious spews out intuitive responses at a very healthy rate many times a day.

Of course, some of these intuitions are not earth-shattering, but they are intuitive responses nonetheless. Many of them pass without recognition or notice and consequently are not consciously dealt with. If in your quest to become an *ultimate-consciousness* actor you add to your daily work plan an involvement with intuitive responses, you are then taking another path on the journey into the unconscious. What must you do? How do you relate to intuition? Isn't it something that happens quite by accident? Do you just sit and wait for intuitional inspiration? No, you do not! You start by treating the intuition like a normal occurrence—one that happens quite often but usually goes unnoticed. You start to acknowledge your "feelings."

Example:

You are having lunch in a restaurant somewhere, on a nice, sunny spring day. In walks a middle-aged man who seems shy and introverted, but at the same time you sense that he is extremely lonely. You know intuitively that he is going to sit down at the next table, even though there are many empty tables farther away. You also intuitively feel or know that he is going to strike up a conversation with you. Something tells you these things—and, lo and behold, that is exactly what happens! How did you know this? Was it a coincidence, a lucky guess, perception, or was it an intuition you had the moment you saw that man come into the restaurant? You don't have to break down the components or analyze the event; all you have to do is to begin to trust the feeling and accept it as part of your communication with your unconscious.

Strengthening Intuition and Learning from It

Start by becoming aware of these intuitive impulses; honor them and encourage yourself to have them. When you feel something, explore the feeling. In the example of the lonely man in the restaurant, you might have pursued the intuitive flash by asking more of the feeling:

"When is he going to speak to me? What is he going to say? Will he come up with some lame excuse to talk to me, such as 'Do you have the time?' or will he be up front with his desire to converse? What else might he say?"

If you follow up on an intuitional impulse, you will essentially be accepting the intuition and at the same time encouraging it to function better. You don't have to wait for the intuition to happen; you can encourage it to work, as one primes a pump to suck water. Include it as part of your daily practice as an actor. When arriving at a particular place where you have never been before, ask yourself what you intuitively feel about the place, what that pretty girl behind the desk is going to say first, what might happen in this office in the next few minutes. Some of what you do might fall into the category of playing with a crystal ball, but the process is designed to excite the intuition. Sometimes it will respond, and sometimes it will all be conjecture. No matter! Keep doing it.

Besides asking yourself what you feel about this or that, also ask yourself what impulses you are having and cutting off before ever expressing them. Many intuitive impulses pass right by us without being expressed or even acknowledged. How many times have you had the impulse to say something to someone and let the moment pass without fulfillment? Some of those impulses came from your intuition. Often you meet someone that you immediately mistrust, and yet the person has not done or said anything to warrant your distrust; it's just a feeling you have, but it turns out later that your intuition was correct. How often have you said, "I wish I had gone with my impulse to go there or to do that" or "If only I had trusted my intuition, I wouldn't be in this mess"? You strengthen your intuitive powers by using and encouraging them. Keep asking yourself, What do I feel about that? . . . about him? . . . about this situation? . . . Do I sense danger in this move? . . . and so on.

Using Impulsivity to Encourage Intuition

There are a number of impulsivity exercises that I do in my classes, and most of them are used to encourage impulsive responsiveness as an antidote to a dependency on the intellect, logic, or premeditation. These techniques can also be used to exercise the intuition; all that is necessary is to make a simple adjustment in the exercise. In addition to expressing every single impulse that you have, also ask yourself, What do I feel about this? and about that? . . . How does that affect me?

The Disconnected-Impulsivity exercise is done this way: dealing with the moment-to-moment impulsive reality that you are experiencing, and including the environment as part of the exercise, you express moment-to-moment all the impulses that occur, as fast as they do.

"Window . . . see sky . . . floor . . . I feel empty . . . books on shelves . . . mystery . . . Alfred Hitchcock . . . see door . . . leave . . . enter . . . Sunshine Boys . . . funny movie . . . can't help . . . jump down . . . song sing I wish I knew the answer . . . nice place here . . . want to succeed . . . see clouds . . . pretty . . . I'm tired . . . don't want to think . . ." etc. . . . etc. . . .

The exercise can continue for quite some time and include both internally and externally stimulated impulses. Using the same structure, you can add other questions, questions that will stimulate an intuitive flow. Insert these questions between the impulsive responses of the conventional impulsivity exercise:

"How do I feel about this place? . . . What do I feel about that person? . . . What might happen here? What was this place before? What are the energies in the room? . . . What are these people thinking about? . . . What kind of experience is this going to be?"

If you intersperse these kinds of questions into the exercise, you will tempt your intuition to become involved. Trust is a major ingredient for elevating the intuition into your consciousness. Encourage yourself to trust even fleeting intuitional impulses.

Exercising Your Intuition
on the Stage

One of the reasons for encouraging moment-to-moment life on the stage is that there is a real connection between *going with the moment* and communicating with the unconscious. Logically speaking, it is easy to understand that if there aren't any obstacles to expression, the impulses will flow more freely. In addition, there will be an increased possibility for unconscious impulses to ventilate themselves in conscious expression, and with the flow of those unconscious impulses you can expect some intuitive life. Far too often these intuitive responses are unnerving to the actor. They don't seem to service his concept of the material, so he short-circuits them; but along with them he may indeed inhibit the possibility of having an *ultimate-consciousness* experience.

Behavioral leadership and conceptual involvement will certainly inhibit the flow of organic moment-to-moment impulses; but the reverse is also true: if the actor services the moment and honors what he feels, he will establish a flow of emotional reality, some of which comes from unconscious sources. Intuition is encouraged to function if one allows oneself to trust that whatever happens will be acceptable. Trust is a major ingredient in creating reality and inducing intuitive flow.

There must be a place to experiment and fail! If every time an actor acts he must be "good," he will never take the risks necessary to grow. So in order to establish a level of trust in expressing moment-to-moment impulses, the actor can practice at home or experiment in the laboratory (class, workshop) or in rehearsals.

There are several ways to stimulate trust in expression. I have already mentioned the impulsivity areas: there are numerous impulsivity techniques, which you can locate in all of my other books, where they are discussed in great detail.

Expressing Impulses in Sounds and Gibberish

Whether in a rehearsal or in a classroom, you can start working on a scene or monologue by creating the realities through your choices and approaches and expressing your impulses in sounds or gibberish. The sounds become the expression of the impulses stimulated by the choice you are working for, and if that choice was originally selected to address the responsibilities of the material, then the emotional life will essentially parallel that material. If the actor allows each impulse to be expressed through either sounds or gibberish, the life will be much more intuitive and impulsive. With the omission of words, concepts are also eliminated, and the actor is free to honor his moment-to-moment realities and thereby create a structure of *trust* in his work.

Inner-Outer Monologues

Another good technique for establishing trust in your impulsive flow is the inner-outer monologue. It is done simply by going back and forth between the written material and the reality of what you feel in each moment.

Example: (monologue from I Never Sang for My Father, *not verbatim)*

MONOLOGUE: "I left my father's house that night forever . . ."

INNER LIFE: I heard myself say that line . . . I feel awkward . . .

(The actor carries the preceding impulses into the next line of dialogue.)

MONOLOGUE: "I took the first left and the second right, and this time I went all the way to California . . ."

INNER LIFE: I feel a little better. I'm looking around the room . . . searching for something to grab on to . . . I feel a little confused . . .

(Carries the life into the next lines.)

MONOLOGUE: "Peggy and I visited him once or twice, and he came to see us . . . and finally he came, and we put him into the hospital . . ."

INNER LIFE: It's funny; when I say those lines, I think of my own father, and it makes me sad! . . . I wish he were still alive!

MONOLOGUE: "The reason we gave him and the one he could accept was his swollen ankles, but the real reason was . . ."

INNER LIFE: I wish I had been able to say so much more to my father while he was alive . . . Why do we always wait

until it's too late? . . . Wow, I'm really being affected
by the words of this piece! . . .

The above process continues throughout the entire piece, as you go back
and forth between the written words and your moment-to-moment inner life.
If you carry the emotional life from the inner monologue into the written
piece, the written words become the expression of your inner truth, and you
encourage yourself as well to free and trust your unconscious life and your
intuition.

It is very important to accept that it is all right to express any impulse, even
if it is not right for the material. If you really violate the logic or the author's
intent, you can always make an adjustment with your choice. It is also
important to note that, more often than you might imagine, the life that is
expressed impulsively is not only acceptable for the material, but may even
bring to it a more exciting and multidimensional reality than the author
originally conceived. If the actor never forgets even for a moment that he is an
actor, then all of life can be used as the playground, the training ground for
using the multitude of techniques that stimulate a greater level of consciousness, a freer instrument, a fuller grasp and mastery of the craft, and the
conditioning of a conscious-unconscious relationship that will lead to *ultimate
consciousness*.

Intuition is not some mystical gift given to some and withheld from others.
It is more than likely unconscious knowledge that has been acquired in this life
from instinctive places and that rose into our conscious awareness because of a
closer connection with it. The greater the connection, the more intuitive the
flow.

EXERCISES THAT PROMOTE
ULTIMATE CONSCIOUSNESS

Just as in any of the other areas of instrument and craft, here too there are
exercises and techniques, which work to connect the conscious with the
unconscious. Most of these approaches are to be practiced regularly and must
be repeated often. Some of the following techniques can double as preparations for getting into a scene.

THE PRIMAL MOAN

I have used this technique as an instrumental exercise for many years, for the
purpose of getting actors more deeply into emotional experiences. It is a
marvelous way to break through the obstacles that stand in the way of really
deep feelings. An exciting bonus of the exercise is that it also piques uncon-

scious life. I have seen actors do incredible things immediately following a primal-moan workout! In addition to the size and depth of the emotion it produces, it often brings out dimensions and colors that no other exercise stimulates. The emotion, the sounds, and the color of expression often seem inspired—as if they came from a very different place. Both the immediate responses to the exercise and the acting work that follows are full of *ultimate-consciousness* life.

To do the exercise, lie down and assume the fetal position—on your side, curled up into a ball with your hands between your thighs. Begin to make a sound that comes from the deepest place in your being. Hold the sound as long as you can on a single breath, and repeat it again and again. It should be a very deep, moaning sound, a sound that might emanate from a very deep pained place. It is not unusual for the exercise to stimulate heavy sobbing. If this occurs, just accept it and go with it! The more affected an actor is while doing this technique, the more successful he is with the process. It should last for about five minutes, although it can be done for shorter or longer periods of time. The sounds must be supported by emotions, or the exercise is not being done properly.

This particular exercise should not be done arbitrarily. It is also not the kind of exercise that you might repeat daily, the way you deal with your dreams. As an instrumental approach, it should be done to crack through resistance or to attempt to go deeper when you feel blocked from the source of your emotions; as an *ultimate-consciousness* exercise, it can be used as a preparation leading to a monologue or scene; if you are experimenting with the conscious-unconscious connection, you might want to try a primal moan to plummet down to a deeper level of life. It can also be used in combination with several other exercises to create a "piggyback" effect (I will get into that later). Because the exercise is loud and must be done lying down in what must look like a very strange position, you can't do it in an office before going in on an interview or on a soundstage just before, or in between, takes; the right time and place must be selected.

While doing the exercise, try to get deeper into your emotions, encourage the sound to have some kind of vibrato, and when you begin to be taken over by the exercise, surrender to every emotion that you are experiencing. When you finish, lie there for a moment or two, and then sit up very slowly. You will probably feel a little strange and disoriented; that's not something to be frightened of—it is normal! Don't pull yourself together; instead, capitalize on the life that has been stimulated by the exercise, and begin working with a choice and a piece of material. Whatever your choice approach might be, include all the emotional impulses piqued by the primal moan.

Several things will probably happen as a result of the exercise: you will be infinitely more available emotionally; you will be much more responsive to any choice that you are working to create; and—most important of all—you will be experiencing at least some unconscious support of your conscious behavior. How much of, and how full, an *ultimate-consciousness* experience it might be is dependent on many things: where you are emotionally when you start the primal moan, how available your unconscious is at that particular time, what experiences you have had leading up to doing the exercise, and what your general connection with your unconscious is. If you "dry up" while in the midst of rehearsing a monologue after doing the primal moan, just go back to it and repeat the process.

PRIMITIVE ABANDONMENT

This is another good primal-type exercise. It can be done by itself or immediately following a primal-moan workout. Both of these exercises hook into unconscious impulses. Both of them stimulate unexplainable impulses that can be very exhilarating. A Primitive Abandonment is done much like a conventional Abandonment, except that you can do it in a lying, sitting, or standing position. When the exercise is done properly, it looks like someone is having a tantrum—an uncontrollable physical fit accompanied by large animal sounds. The body undulates and shakes with rhythmical animal beats and energy until the whole experience feels like some savage ritual from the deepest, darkest parts of the jungle! It is done for as long as necessary to stimulate a completely abandoned state, both physically and emotionally. It should give rise to a primal, primitive, basic feeling in the actor. Besides the evident freedom produced by this technique, there should also be a heightened feeling of sexuality and aggressiveness and a connection with unconscious impulses, which will flow quickly into conscious responses. Like a Primal Moan, a Primitive Abandonment should not be done arbitrarily, but for a specific purpose. It too is used as an instrumental exercise to unclog the actor at those times when he is encountering a lot of obstacles in himself.

There are a variety of ways to do the exercise: you may want to start slowly, just by creating slow rhythmical movements, undulating in every part of your body while encouraging a beat—a primitive beat that is very animal-like. This can be done in a small space, or you might be impelled to use a large area as you move around. The slow rhythmical undulation should progressively build into a more frenzied abandonment, culminating in very large sounds, movements, and animal-like behavior.

Another way to approach Primitive Abandonment is to start with very large expression, throwing yourself around on the floor, writhing and flinging your arms and legs in all directions, while at the same time matching this wild movement with sounds and rhythm. In both cases you end up in the same place: wild, animal, primitive, and impulsive!

A third approach to the same technique is to adopt the physical attitude of a wild animal and then, using the general movements of that animal, accelerate them into a frenzy, as if the animal were truly going wild. It is not important that you really get an organic sense of the animal, as you would if you were working with an Externals choice approach; what is necessary is to stimulate movements and sounds that are animal-like and that fit the animal that you have chosen to "imitate." If, for example, it is a gorilla, you would begin by assuming a simian position (close to the ground), start to move as a gorilla does, make apelike sounds, and then exaggerate them to a very large degree until it became a wild and abandoned experience. Again, all three of these approaches lead to the same goal. The variety gives you a choice, and, besides, some approaches work better than others for particular actors.

Sometimes it is advantageous to do a Primal Moan just before a Primitive Abandonment. Using these two techniques in combination with each other can yield some very exciting results. If you choose to try this, come directly out of the primal moan into the primitive. Don't pull yourself together before starting the second part. Whatever that button is that opens the doors to the unconscious, it seems somehow connected with the animal in us—the primitive, instinctive parts of our being.

The primitive exploration has many bonuses: besides piquing the unconscious, it stimulates a heightened degree of sexuality and aggressiveness, violent impulses of various natures, and a directness that is very necessary to acting.

When approaching the Primitive-Abandonment technique, be sure that you clear a large space, removing all furniture or other objects that can become dangerous to you when you are in the midst of all of the violent movement. If you are aware of the dangers of colliding with solid objects before you begin the exercise, then there will be no risk of getting hurt while doing it!

After you have finished the Abandonment, you might want to go directly into dealing with a piece of material, or you may choose to let the exercise "settle." Whatever the case may be, encourage an unbroken flow of expression following the exercise. Do not pull yourself together or interfere with any of the impulses wanting to be expressed. Allow everything you feel to run its course, and be vocal in your expression! If you want to deal with a monologue, you could just carry the existing behavior into the lines—which would most likely not be right for the material—or you could begin working on an interim preparation or choice to affect the existing life and take you closer to the responsibilities of the piece. Doing material immediately after such a workout is a good way of determining what the exercise did for you. Of course, you will be *irreverent* to the piece, but if you give yourself that permission for the sake of the exploration, you will discover what link, if any, you have created with the unconscious.

SWITCH-TRICK EXERCISE
IN FEAR AND TERROR AREAS

This technique is approached in the same way as a conventional Switch-Trick exercise. You start to encourage impulsive responses to arbitrarily suggested stimuli. The suggestions should come in rapid-fire succession and if possible be supported by some sensory-involvement process. The major difference between this and the conventional Switch-Trick exercise is that here you selectively emphasize stimuli that frighten or terrify you! The suggestions should be filled with your real fears and with what nightmares are made of. They can be expressed out loud or silently, but the responses should always be audible.

Either in a sitting or standing position, start with very impulsive suggestions of things, people, places, and conditions that terrify you.

Example:

"It's dark; I can't see anything; I feel surrounded by dangerous things that want to hurt me. (Switch!) A man with a knife coming at me. (Switch!) There's a snake at my feet! (Switch!) An ugly monster behind me . . . (Switch!) Spiders crawling all over me! (Switch!) I'm drowning . . . going down . . . can't breathe! (Switch!) I feel the presence of unseen evil spirits! (Switch!) The walls are closing in on me! Closer . . . closer . . . closer! (Switch!) I'm being swallowed by the ground under me . . . like quicksand. I'm going down faster and faster!"

Your suggestions here are of a very personal nature. You should use those things that are the most impelling to you in fear areas. The exercise can be as short or as long as necessary to accomplish the desired goal. Once you begin to respond organically and your suggestions become less arbitrary, the flow of impulses will reach a high level of emotionality and hopefully elicit unconscious responses. At this point you might try working for a choice that is connected to the material you are attempting to fulfill; but if the exercise has had a very large impact on you and it seems impossible to jump directly into working for a choice, then it might be necessary to let the stimulated impulses run their course before starting with a new stimulus.

The Switch-Trick exercise is a marvelous way to hook into the unconscious and to make connections with primordial impulses. Under very frightening or stressful circumstances, something happens to us: we acquire powers, strengths, intelligence, survival mechanisms, and insights, which help to protect and save our lives and which originate in our unconscious. This exercise connects us to those powers. If, in addition, you are suggesting stimuli that come from the world of your dreams and nightmares, then you are dealing with a direct link to the unconscious.

THE ULTIMATE-CONSCIOUSNESS TRIO

This is a combination of the Primal-Moan, the Primitive-Abandonment and the Switch-Trick exercises. These three work very well in combination. They should be done in the order given and one immediately following the other. Start with the Primal Moan, and at the point when you feel you have reached the summit of that exercise, go directly into the Primitive Abandonment. You will begin to know when to go to the next exercise by what you feel. So when you sense it is right, go into the Switch-Trick part, carrying the life over into the beginning suggestions. You will be amazed at the kind of things that spring out of your mouth and at the incredible thoughts and impulses stimulated by the prior preparations.

If you are successful with the trio, you can expect to stimulate very theatrical emotional responses and life, while at the same time making an important connection with the unconscious. As you begin to work in other choice areas, you should become aware of the depth and quality of the resulting life. The choices that you use should dredge up fuller and more dimensional responses and make you infinitely more impulsive.

ANIMAL EXPLORATIONS

A very important prerequisite to having deep and organic experiences on or off the stage is to get out of your head! Whenever an actor short-circuits himself, it is usually the result of some kind of intellectual activity. If, in the midst of a scene on stage, an actor comments on what he is doing in the moment, he immediately interrupts the flow of his involvement in, and responses to, what he is feeling and expressing. A running commentary on what he is doing or feeling keeps the actor from any connection with authentic and organic moment-to-moment impulses, not to mention the wall it builds between the conscious and the unconscious. Whatever he does, the actor must find ways to connect with the flow of organic reality.

Working with animal movements and sounds directly links us to the animal in all of us. It takes us out of the intellect and stimulates primal feelings and impulses, and it also creates a foundation for unconscious life. Again, let me remind you that this is very different from working with an animal to attain a full and organic sense of it as you do in the Externals-Choice-approach area. This involvement is much more general and arbitrary and does not depend on the achievement of accuracy with the animal. It is done exclusively to stimulate primal and primitive responses and, hopefully, to connect with the unconscious.

There is a considerable amount of freedom in this exercise. You can choose a specific animal or use a conglomerate of several. Start by assuming some kind of animal stance—a position on all fours or a crouched simian attitude. Begin to move about rhythmically the way the animal does, slowly at first, so that you might ease into it, and then increasing the speed and size of the movement. Add sounds as you begin to feel more comfortable. Relate to objects and to the environment from that animal place, and increase the fervor of the exercise until you get to an abandonment level. Continue the involvement long enough to experience impulses that are definitely animal. When you *feel* like an animal and have stopped thinking and commenting, you have achieved your primary goal. Do not snap out of the exercise abruptly; instead, let the impulses you have stimulated by this process run their course and slowly become more "human" in quality. You can do animal explorations as a preparation to doing a scene or as an *ultimate-consciousness* workout or for both reasons. Besides separating you from your intellect, it really creates a connection with your unconscious impulses.

The sounds of an animal can be very provocative. I personally have had a great deal of success with the sounds that a lion makes. While working with animals at the zoo, I became fascinated with the lion, more for the sound it made than for its movement. The sound seems to come from a very deep place in the animal's body. It starts from the abdomen and seems to rumble through the body, up to the throat, and out of the mouth. It almost looks as if the lion is about to regurgitate when he is manufacturing the sound. I found that when I was working with that sound for a period of time, I began to feel very animal-like! In addition, I became aggressive and primitive. It is usually better to combine the sounds with the movement of the animal; however, on some occasions the sounds alone may work quite well. In circumstances where you have very limited space and cannot move around, picking the right sound may do the trick.

Start making the sounds of any animal that you are familiar with, and vary them in your exploration. Go from one animal to another, experimenting with the various choices to see which sounds yield the best results. If you start at a low volume, increase it as you go along, so that at the culmination of the exploration you are making a lot of noise. If you choose animals that make more subtle sounds, try to experience those on a very deep and visceral level, and repeat them until you begin experiencing the animal feelings that they have stimulated. At this point, try an impulsivity workout, expressing moment to moment whatever you feel. Doing this on the heels of an animal workout, or of any of the *ultimate-consciousness* exercises, is a good way to measure the impact of the exercise on the unconscious.

If you haven't had any experiences with animals or if you haven't observed them, begin the exploration of the sound and movement by making general animal growling sounds and jumping around in tempo. This will excite whatever primitive impulses are buried inside. Animal explorations are rich with results and usually open the capillaries of the unconscious.

"I'M FIVE YEARS OLD AND I . . ."

I use this exercise in my class for a variety of instrumental and craft reasons. It is also, however, a wonderful way of communicating with the unconscious. Repeating this technique opens up your memory, while at the same time it frees a plethora of forgotten emotions. As we live from day to day, we experience an enormous amount of feelings related to the impact of people and events in our lives. As we grow up, those experiences are filed away in the memory banks of our unconscious and stored there for our entire lifetime. In unlocking those experiences by recalling them, we bring up not only the components of each experience, but the emotional reactions we had at the time. It is possible that those emotional responses were not even expressed then and that by reliving the experience we are able to express emotions that we were too inhibited to expose twenty years earlier! With the expression come impulses that are solidly ensconced in the unconscious. As the actor does the exercise, this unconscious life filters in, and if the connection is solid, it will probably carry over into a scene or monologue, thereby setting the stage for an *ultimate-consciousness* experience.

The exercise is done verbally and audibly, beginning at the age of five and continuing into the teens and older. You start by saying, "I'm five years old, and I . . ." filling in the blank with whatever occurs to you from that age period and staying with each age until you run dry and cannot remember anything more or you feel that you have expressed all the significant things. You then move on to the next age: "I'm six years old, and I . . ."—and so on.

Example:

"I'm five years old, and I . . . am sitting on the floor . . . I'm in kindergarten . . . I'm five years old and . . . the teacher's name is Mrs. Anderson . . . She doesn't like me . . . She makes me put my bubble gum on my nose . . . I have it there all day! . . . I'm five years old, and my best friend is Bobby Snell . . . I'm five years old and I hate school . . . I want to play the triangle, and Mrs. Anderson makes me play the sticks . . . I hate her . . . I have bad dreams about her . . . I'm five years old and I . . . live on

Fillmore Street . . . There's a train that runs across the street . . . I chase it and scream to the engineer to throw us chalk . . . I'm five years old, and I saw *Frankenstein,* and I can't sleep because I know the monster is in my closet . . . I cry, and my brother Phil turns on all the lights and opens the closet door and shows me that the monster isn't there . . . I'm five years old, and I worry a lot! I'm five years old, and my brothers and sisters are so much older than me . . . I'm five years old, and I don't think I'm smart like they are . . ." (You can go on with this age or you may elect to go to the next level.)

"I'm six years old and I . . . am in first grade! . . . I feel smarter now . . . My teacher's name is Miss Bryant, and she is beautiful . . . and I think I will marry her . . . She likes me . . . she smiles all the time . . . I think she is smiling because she likes me . . . I'm six years old, and I hate recess because I get hurt in the school yard every day . . . All the kids are bigger, and I fall a lot . . . I'm six years old, and I have lots of toys . . . I play outside until the cold comes . . . then we play inside . . . I'm six years old, and I . . . have a scooter . . . I call it The Red Rocket, and everybody wants to ride it. I'm six years old, and my father is old . . . I wonder how he got that old . . . My mother is too . . . I pretend that my sister is my mother . . . and that's what I tell all the kids in school . . . I'm six years old, and I . . . want to be an aviator! . . . I'm going to fly airplanes . . . I fly little balsa-wood gliders off the roof of the building I live in. I'm six years old, and I . . . listen to scary shows on the radio . . . I sleep in the same bed with my sister Helen, and she listens to the radio with me . . . She told me that if I slept close to the wall a hand would reach out and get me, so I traded places with her! . . . I'm six years old, and I laugh a lot . . . I'm six years old, and I have a dog . . . His name is Marchy . . . He goes to the bathroom on my bed! . . ."

Continue the exercise for as long as you wish, allowing yourself to express all the emotions that are stimulated by it. Be aware of large changes at certain times in your life. Some actors start out carefree, until, at a certain age, they hit upon some major trauma that changed the course of their entire life. If you discover such a juncture in your own life, explore it thoroughly, since it might be very rich with suppressed impulses. Be sure that you respond in the *now,* and not retrospectively: "I'm six years old, and I *have* a scooter," not, "I had a scooter." If you deal with the exercise in that way, you will re-experience the life as it happened, here and now!

This technique yields wonderful results in connecting with the unconscious. I have personally experienced amazing things as a result of it, and I have seen other actors do the same. Try it just before doing a scene with another actor. Do the exercise, and begin working for a choice. Your responses will be deeper and will reveal more vulnerability and more facets of emotional life. If you practice this exercise repeatedly, you will establish a connection with your past. It will help you become comfortable digging into past experiences, and, as a bonus, these will in turn filter into your dreams, making them richer.

Making the techniques in this area part of your daily workout will help you build that bridge to the unconscious, and even without *ultimate-consciousness* experiences, the content, depth, and variety in your acting will make you grow as an actor beyond description. If the unconscious becomes a consistent part of your acting, you will be infinitely more impulsive, unpredictable, and irreverent.

AFFECTIVE MEMORY AS A TOOL
TO STIMULATE THE UNCONSCIOUS

I spend considerable time describing Affective Memory in my other books, specifically in *Irreverent Acting*. It is the twelfth choice approach and is primarily used as a tool to re-create experiences from your past so that you can achieve the emotional results you need for the scene you are attempting to fulfill. Mostly, it is used to reach areas of emotional life that are not available through other, conventional choice approaches. It also helps the actor to develop a richer and fuller substance in his acting.

The real bonus of Affective Memory is that it pries open the steel doors to the unconscious. By setting up the circumstances for sneaking up on an emotional response, the actor, if successful, piques and liberates the unconscious life locked up in the specific experience that he is trying to re-create. The result of a successful affective-memory involvement can be startling. It can actually take you back to the original experience, making you relive it just as it was the first time and feel things that you have not felt in a very long while. If, for example, you had a stammering problem as a child and the experience that you re-created happened in that time frame, you might really re-experience stammering. If the exercise is successful enough to put you back there, all that you were will exist now! The potential of this connection is staggering! Not only could you as an actor stimulate life and responses beyond which you have already grown, but you could also open a bottomless well of unconscious impulses that have been locked away for twenty years or more! The rich fantasy life that you allowed yourself as a youngster, but that you no longer subscribe to; the fun; the willingness to pretend, to believe the unbelievable, to wonder if Santa Claus really exists, to believe before questioning, to be in a time of your life when it wasn't embarrassing to cry in public or to be childlike—imagine freeing all those wonderful things just by doing an Affective-Memory exercise!

Affective Memory is done by using Sense Memory as an approach technique. After identifying the specific experience that you want to re-create, you start by sensorially exploring and creating all the objects and stimuli that existed around you, possibly hours before the actual event itself. For example, if the event you are focused on occurred early in the evening, you might begin by asking yourself questions about the early afternoon. All the elements that you re-create must lead to the actual moment or moments of the experience. In a sense, you create everything that surrounded the experience and then sneak up on the moment of encounter!

Start with the place and the time, and ask sensory questions that will create those realities for you; then go to the people involved and create them in specific detail. Create the time of day, the year, the temperature, the way you were dressed, the objects around you—in short, everything! Ask all sensory questions in the here and now, and respond to them in the same manner.

Example:

Let us say that the event in question is the funeral of your father. The actual moment or moments that you wish to re-create are those after the eulogy, when people started to leave the cemetery and the casket was lowered into the ground. It was then that the grief and remorse took you over, that you felt so much pain and loss that it was almost unbearable! Those are the moments that you wish to re-experience.

You might start the exploration with your first waking moments on the morning of that day, as you saw the ceiling and became aware of your bedroom and the objects that surrounded you; or you might start with the cemetery just before the funeral. Wherever you decide to begin, do so by creating the components of the environment, asking the questions in the here and now:

"What do I see in front of me? (Answer the question visually, with the sense itself.) How far away is the canopy? (Respond sensorially.) What are the colors of the chairs in front of me? (A visual response) What does the ground look like? . . . (Visual response) What is the texture of the ground? the colors? . . . Is there grass? How long is it? What are the variations in the textures and patterns of the ground? Can I see the coffin? . . . How far away is it? What is its color? What is the shape of the coffin? How is it adorned? What is it sitting on? How would it feel to touch it? (That last sensory question is responded to with the tactile sense: you attempt to feel the texture in your fingers and hand.)

"What is the temperature? . . . Where on my body do I feel that temperature? What does the sky look like? . . . Color of the sky? . . . Are there any clouds? Is there any wind? . . . Where is it coming from? . . . Where do I feel it on my face? . . . How am I dressed? . . . As I look at my pants . . .

what do I see? What is the color of my trousers? . . . Texture? . . .
Material? . . . How does it feel to my fingers? . . . on my thighs? . . . As I
touch my shirt . . . what do I feel? . . . How does the collar feel on the back
of my neck? . . . As I look at it, what is the color I see? . . . Do I feel the
jacket on my shoulders? . . .
"Is there anyone else around? . . . Where? Who is it? . . . How far away
from me is that person standing? . . . What does he look like? How is he
dressed? What is the shape of his face? Can I see the color of his eyes
from here? . . ."

You may ask dozens of questions in each area. Go back and forth between
the senses and employ as many of the five senses as necessary. The number of
sensorial questions you ask is dependent on how many are needed and how
specific you must be in order to create the reality. You must actually see, hear,
feel, smell, and even taste the stimuli that make up the experience. The reality
must be complete if you expect the moments of the experience to recur. The
Affective-Memory process comprises the entire experience. The hope is that
you will feel the same things you felt at the time. If that happens, you will
surely unlock a treasure of unconscious life. In fact, it might even transport
you into an *ultimate-consciousness* experience. The first time you attempt an
Affective-Memory exercise in a certain area, it may take you several hours to
realize the total experience, but after several repetitions you will be able to re-
create it in a much shorter period of time.

CHOICE HUNTS

This is a technique that enables the actor to discover new choices to use in his
work. Many of the exercises and techniques have a double or even triple
purpose. This one, in addition to locating choices out of our past, often piques
important unconscious life. Unlike some of the other *ultimate-consciousness*
exercises, it is more of an exploration than anything else. While a primal moan
will definitely elicit a large and deep emotional response, a choice hunt may
not. It all depends on what you stumble into on the journey. This process will
involve you very deeply with the past experiences of your life and will liberate
hundreds that you might have forgotten. It is like taking a journey into the
past. The trip will lead you into a variety of emotional areas, and even if you
don't have significant experiences of the unconscious while on a choice hunt,
you will certainly discover the keys to the doors of your unconscious. Each
time you do this exercise, more choices and experiences will become available
to you. A choice hunt is not only designed to find compelling choices; it is also
intended to stimulate emotional life. As you follow the path of your explora-

tions, you must encourage each experience to come to life, and you must respond to the elements and objects in each part of your life.

The best way to approach this technique is to lie down and close your eyes, but you may also do it in a sitting position. You must, however, keep your eyes closed. Start by picking a memorable experience from your past. Each experience you choose should be emotionally important or impacting, like a graduation, a wedding, a funeral, your first day at school, your first sexual encounter, your first big break as an actor, a memorable military experience, a memorable and meaningful relationship, a rejection, winning an award, falling in love, having a baby, losing someone you love, leaving someone, discovering a beautiful place, coming home after being away a long time, etc. . . . etc. . . . Once you choose a memorable and meaningful experience, begin to just visualize it at first, and then support it sensorially. Go through it and attempt to relive it, at first as a memory and then by slowly making it more vivid and real. If you supply the sensorial elements as you move through the experience, it will change from a memory into a more tangible reality. Asking questions about the sounds and odors indigenous to a special place will bring the reality directly into your ears and nose. Once you begin to feel, taste, smell, and hear the objects that comprise your memory, you will experience a "replay" of the original event.

As you take the trip, ask as many sensory questions as you want and respond to them directly with the sense that you query. Encourage the expression of your emotional responses. The more you express, the more you are open to feeling. If you pique unconscious responses, the thrust of the experience will carry you where it will. Allow yourself to go anywhere it takes you. Be careful not to comment on what is taking place emotionally, or you will short-circuit the connection to the unconscious. If that does occur, just reinvest in the sensorial process and pick up where you left off. After completing an entire exploration of a single experience, ask yourself to remember any other memorable event that preceded the one you just worked with or that might have followed it. The time frame could be days, weeks, months, or even as much as a year in either direction. The amazing thing about a choice hunt is that once you remember one experience in a certain time period, it leads you to two or three more, and those lead to others, creating a kind of pyramid effect. You may get involved in a choice hunt that lasts for an hour or more, as you jump from one experience to another. Approach the exercise as an adventure, and encourage yourself to go on an unpredictable journey.

Example:

In a lying down position and with eyes closed, choose a specific experience from your past. For the sake of the example, let's say that it was the first time you kissed a girl. After choosing that particular event, start by asking yourself questions about it:

> "Where was I? . . . What kind of place was it? Was there anyone else there? Who was the girl? What did she look like? . . . What did she have on? How was I dressed?" etc. . . . etc. . . .

As you ask these questions, begin to *visualize* being in that place. Encourage the experience to "screen" itself on the inside of your closed eyelids. As you get more involved in it, change the questioning process to sensory specifics, and ask the questions in the here and now, not retrospectively:

> "What is the color of her eyes? . . . (Respond with the visual sense.) How close am I standing to her? (Respond tactilely in proximity terms.) What does she smell like? (Respond with the olfactory sense.) How many odors do I smell?" (Respond in the nose.)

Go through the entire experience asking sensorial questions and responding with the specific sense involved. While on this track, you will begin to have many of the same feelings that you had at that time, even if it was twenty-five years ago or more. These emotional responses come from the storage room of your unconscious and help you to make a connection with it. As the experience becomes real and you begin to relive those old feelings of fear mixed with excitement, you cross a line into the unconscious; the richer the emotional response, the stronger the connection. Since it is your unconscious that has held those feelings and impulses for so many years, releasing the *same* sensations is an indication of your success in making that conscious-unconscious connection. After completing "the first kiss" experience, you might ask yourself what followed it with this particular girl. Did you kiss her a second time? When? Where? What happened before that experience? Were you turned down by other girls? If so, when? where? and by whom? This kind of investigation allows you to "piggyback" experiences—one leading to three or four others.

Another way to locate experiences is by identifying time frames: the first grade in school, the second grade, junior high, college, summers, winters, holidays, memorable Christmases, and so on. Besides being an enormous tool for reaching the unconscious, choice hunts are incredible emotional preparations for getting ready to act. The more you do them, the easier they get.

IMAGES

There are three approaches to this particular technique: (1) Images, (2) Fragmented Images, and (3) Fragmented-Image Visualization. The first is done premeditatedly and the other two impulsively.

Have you ever wondered, What ever happened to my Teddy Bear? my model airplane? that BB gun I grew up with? Where did these things go? Do they still exist? Does someone else have them? How did they disappear from my life? They were so incredibly important at one time! The places and people that comprised my existence—what happened to them all?

For three years, between the ages of twelve and fifteen, I was totally involved with the Boy Scouts. They were one of the most important things in my life. The basement of the Lutheran Church was our meeting place, and it became my second home. Whenever I entered that room, I felt a rush of warmth and good feelings. Even now, forty years later, when I think of that place and the objects and people in it, I feel a mixture of varied emotions. If you have lived for several decades, it almost seems as if you have had many different lives. When I recall periods of my life, it seems as if each one was more than a chapter in a book, more like a book in itself. Who was that person on that life path at twenty, full of ideas and commitments, following a specific direction, having relationships with people that were going to last a lifetime— or so he thought at the time? Where are all those people and what happened to those ideals and commitments? It all seems like someone else's life, not mine! Yet it was my life, and I lived it seriously. I realize that we grow and change and outgrow people; I know that we evolve and discover new things, that we change goals and directions. That's what life is all about! In each period of our lives, there are places, people, objects, and experiences, the memories of which become the substructure of our inner life—our unconscious! Our personalities are molded and faceted as a result of the collection of all these objects that have affected and sculpted us. That treasure is there to be discovered and used in a creative framework! All that we must do is find the ways to recall it, to pique it, to dig up the cornucopia of buried gold.

There are many reasons for going back to the various times in one's life. First, they contain the raw material that performances are made of. Secondly, when an actor uses a past experience to stimulate a desired emotional life, he is also making a connection with the unconscious. That connection, whether he is conscious of it or not, enriches the life he is experiencing and expressing on the stage, and that, as I have been saying in these two chapters, is the desired goal of the work. Instead of depending on chance or accidental ignition of unconscious inspiration, he must use the tools for consistently creating those "accidents"!

The approach I call *Images* is dealt with by collecting in your memory the lost and forgotten objects of your life. It isn't necessary for all the places and objects to have been forgotten; it is enough that they be out of your mind at the time. Sit down in a quiet place where there aren't any distractions, and begin to think about and remember places from your past. Start with a bedroom when you were younger. Search your memory for the objects in that room. As you begin to see them with your "inner eye," bring them into your present environment; attempt to see and re-create them outside of your mind. Ask sensorial questions, and allow yourself to "trip off" as a result of the way these objects affect you. You need not stay with that room for too long, particularly if, let's say, you are distracted by something sitting on a table there.

The memories of those objects with which you become involved will bring with them associations and thoughts of people that were related to them. For example, my first camera was a Falcon; it was an inexpensive plastic camera that used thirty-five-millimeter film. I have had many very expensive professional cameras since that one, but never one nearly as important! A couple of weeks ago I thought about that camera. I have no idea what precipitated that memory, but there it was on my mind. With the recollection came a flood of memories that were overwhelming: I saw the camera in my mind's eye and immediately thought of the store it was purchased in: Leo's Camera store on Roosevelt Road. I saw Leo, with his shiny bald head and his broad smile, instructing me on the use of the camera and on photography in general. I wanted to be a professional photographer for a number of years, and that camera was the first instrument that ignited that ambition. I remembered Morty, my friend. We "hung out" together for years, but I hadn't thought of him for a very long time. His face jumped into view, and I was filled with warmth at the sight of that little, round, fat face with the sparkle in the eyes. We used to go to the park and photograph "the great pictures of the future." We spent hours looking for that "special shot" and ended up photographing cute girls instead.

I also thought of my mother and father and of how they were in those days, and I cried because I missed my father. I remembered seeing him a whole block away, coming home from work, and laughed to myself at his unique walk: he seemed to list to the left, which made you think he might topple over at any moment—but he didn't! I saw Tony hitting balls in the school yard across the street from my house, and I thought of that school. I became angry; I could feel the hot liquids running through my body. I had suffered a lot of abuse and trauma at that damned school! There was Mrs. Lane, my teacher, who treated me terribly. She was so critical and judgmental I never felt I could do anything right. I used to get sick every morning before going to school, and the twenty-yard walk there became "the last mile" for me every day for several years. Then I thought of Chris, and Ralph, and Buddy, who made my life a nightmare with their prejudice and abuse of me. I wished in that moment that they were standing in front of me. I could have at that very instant destroyed all three of them! And then I thought of little Anthony, who died of a brain tumor at the age of nine, and I felt such a rush of grief over a death that had occurred forty-five years ago!

I also remembered sitting around the kitchen table with my father and mother and sister, listening to the evening radio shows. My mother would putter around the kitchen doing the dishes, stopping every so often to listen more intently to *Mr. Keane, Tracer of Lost Persons.* We would talk and laugh. I remembered my father's infectious laughter and began to chuckle and cry at the same time. I recalled that we had one of the first recording machines—a Federal. My brother had brought it home one day, and for years after that we all made records, singing and joking and "tumulting." What a wonderful time that was! I wished for it to be back! Then I thought that it was . . . I was re-creating it all over again, giving it life, and feeling the impact of all those things. In the space of a few minutes, I had run the gamut of emotions, and it had all started with a camera, a Falcon camera that I wish I still had!

After completing the journey, I felt as if I had really been on an emotional trip. I not only felt more vulnerable, affectable, and readier to act; I also felt as if I had opened a door into the unconscious. I was flooded with impulses and feelings, some of which I didn't even understand. The connection lasted for several hours and affected everything I did, thought, and felt during that period.

About a year ago I ran across an autograph book I had used at my grade-school graduation. A lot of my classmates had written little jingles in it, starting with "Roses are red, Violets are blue . . ." and so on. Another journey started. I remembered people I hadn't thought of in years, things they had said to me and I to them, the way they used to dress, and activities we had shared together. Again, the trip started with an object, an autograph book.

There are countless objects and places connected to the unconscious, and each of these can impel you to incredible experiences. Sometimes you may start with an object that you have had for a long time, holding it or looking at it and allowing it to stimulate whatever it will. At other times, just sit quietly and let your thoughts jump around the various times in your life, and see what you land on. As the various memories flood into your consciousness, allow each object to impel you where it will. Help your images by attempting to verify their reality through the use of Sense Memory. Images is an exercise you can practice daily, at any time. It will strengthen your relationship to the unconscious and at the same time be an applicable preparation for acting in a scene.

Fragmented Images

This technique is approached impulsively; as a matter of fact, it is the impulsiveness of the involvement that often yields the most important results. Like Images, this exercise uses places and objects to supply the impetus. Start it by arbitrarily suggesting things from your past. Very quickly suggest an object from a time and place in your life, and rapidly go on to another. Suggest the first thing that jumps into your head, and as soon as you have named the object, go on to the next. Allow yourself to be affected by each suggestion, but do not dwell on it. Keep the exercise going for as long as you are functioning with it, and then allow for the carryover.

Example:

Standing or sitting, start by focusing on a time period, for example high school:

"Parking lot . . . (Switch!) Car . . . blue Dodge . . . (Switch!) Cafeteria . . . noise . . . Ray Lindberg . . . milk-drinking contest . . . (Switch!) Parker-fifty-one pen . . . I love it . . . black and silver . . . lost it . . . Spanish teacher, what's her name? . . . Rosemary . . . beautiful . . . bell . . . change classes . . . The hangout across the street . . . olive burgers . . . play pool after school . . . The new building . . . like it . . . football games . . . sitting in the stands . . . cold . . . love it . . . check out the girls . . . Ruth . . . Cookie . . . wow! . . . Someone put a dead cat in her locker . . . awful . . . study hall . . . who studies? . . . Don't like school . . . the halls are depressing . . . Allan . . . he's crazy, but fun . . . cars . . . cars . . . Pontiac . . . mine . . . love it . . . Dates . . . want to be liked . . . Chemistry lab . . . mix strange stuff . . . Can't be serious . . . talking about sex . . . wondering about it . . . hair blond and wavy . . . pompadour . . ."

Again, continue the exercise for as long as you want, moving into different periods in your life. If you want to stop at any point and "trip off" on one of the objects, feel free to do that. Another variation of this exercise is to do it nonverbally, silently suggesting the stimuli and encouraging yourself to respond with sounds or gibberish. The value of this approach is that it will help you to express your emotional response to each suggestion if you haven't already been able to do that.

Fragmented-Image Visualization

This approach is very similar to the one above, and it works in the same way. The variation came about as a result of an experience in one of my classes. One evening, an actress was attempting to do Fragmented Images, but she was experiencing considerable difficulty with the exercise and was very frustrated by it. She stopped and said that her internal images were occurring faster than she could express words related to the objects and that that was creating a kind of short-circuiting effect. I told her to go with the images impulsively and forget about verbalizing anything. She did . . . and had a great deal of success with the exercise. I incorporated this discovery and created this variation in the Image area.

In this exercise you go from object to object in the same manner as with

Fragmented Images, only you do it silently, allowing all your images to crystallize as you switch from one to the other. As with any visualization process, it is preferable to support the inner visualizations with outer sense-memory work. It is my belief that visualization promotes intellectual involvements. As you visualize objects and quickly try to re-create them, the objects themselves will stimulate the recollection of others. Thus, as you become more deeply involved in the exercise, it will continue of its own momentum. Follow the path of your images and of the thoughts that they stimulate, no matter how far afield they seem to stray. As I mentioned in the section on dreams, the unconscious functions with its own kind of logic, which is very different from the way the conscious mind works. All three of these exercises yield excellent results.

MEMORY-LANE FIELD TRIPS AND EXPLORATIONS

There is an old bromide that states, "One man's junk is another man's treasure." It's true! There are thousands of antique shops, junk stores, thrift shops, swap meets, and the like all around us. What is responsible for the great success of such places and events? Why is it difficult to pass by a lawn or garage sale without stopping for a "look-see"? The fascination is universal. What are we looking for? What is it that we expect to find on that table filled with junk from times gone by? Possibly we don't know it, but we are looking for our past! We are trying to have the experience of déjà vu. How many times have you bought something at one of these places only to throw it in a drawer and forget about it? You look at the many objects on the table or in the display case, and one attracts your attention. You stare at it for a few moments and are not aware of what it is that attracted you to it. It is an old pocketknife, similar to thousands made in the same way and shape, with a cracked and yellowed stag-horn exterior and a tarnished, too-many-times-sharpened blade, and you have an impulse to buy it! Why? Do you need a pocketknife, and better yet, one that is as old and beat-up as that one? No! It isn't the knife; it's *your uncle*, who sat for hours whittling pieces of wood, which later turned into wonderful carved figures. You sat with him and discussed the world, your future, his philosophy of life, for many of your growing-up years. He had great affection for you, and you for him. He influenced much of the way you look at the world now. It was a good time in your life. The knife in that case is echoing the sounds and feelings of that time, and your unconscious responds to them. The impulse to hold it and have it comes from the feelings stored in your unconscious. The same holds true for negative responses: when you see or hear something and you have an immediate repulsion to it, that too relates to some experience in your life that has been piqued by the object.

Part of your instrumental and craft involvements should include explorations like these. As time allows, visit places like the ones mentioned above, smell the odors, listen to the sounds of an old toy, pick up objects and feel them. Allow yourself to be open to whatever happens. Know that your awareness of the impact of these objects on the unconscious will make you better able to use the experience in the creative process. Stand and hold something, and allow it to make you feel whatever it stimulates for you. Don't try to relate it to an incident or a specific time; just feel! The exploration is not limited to objects that you can hold in your hand; it extends to furniture, carpets, buildings, old records, and sounds of all kinds. Opening an old Prince Albert tobacco can might be the door to "the twilight zone"; old magazines piled high in a thrift shop could take you on a stroll down memory lane into the land of Oz! Besides creating a liaison between the two states of consciousness, this exercise puts you in touch with many wonderful choices that are just lying around for you to use in the next play or film you do!

THE ULTIMATE-CONSCIOUSNESS CHOICES

Identifying and cataloguing the choices that are connected to the unconscious is also part of the work. Often you stumble onto these choices while looking for ways to fulfill material. However, if you know that you are looking for gold, you go where the gold is to be found, and you are particularly sensitive to anything on the ground that glitters.

A very good way to identify a "hot" choice is to listen to the feelings you have when you think about it. If it scares you, if it makes you uneasy, or if it excites you in a fearful way, it is an indication that you have some deep life attached to it. Dreams can also suggest choice explorations; unfinished or unresolved feelings are a good area in which to look for choices; so are deep hurts. The choice I spoke of earlier—the time when my aunt was dying in the hospital and I thought I was in the presence of the Angel of Death—was certainly very well connected with the unconscious, for reasons related to my own terror of death and possibly feelings of helplessness and a deep belief in the supernatural. When looking for these blockbuster choices, start by identifying your own "availabilities": What are you terrified by? What makes you intensely insecure? Where is your rage locked up? What are your survival instincts, and what piques them?

For example, let us imagine that every day that you are going to look for *ultimate-consciousness* choices, you start with your fears: "What am I afraid of? I am afraid of total darkness! . . ." Find a place where you can be in total darkness, like a closet. Stay there for a while, and see what happens. If you feel strong responses that are not rational or logical, or if you begin to "trip off" as a result of being in that closet, then you will know that it is a possible choice to explore for stimulating an *ultimate-consciousness* response. "What else do I fear? I fear the ocean—not to look at but to be in, away from the shore, alone! It terrifies me!" You might sensorially attempt to create being in the ocean, alone and far from shore. If that doesn't work, go out on a boat and look at the ocean, and imagine being in it. In other words, try either to supply the stimulus that arouses your fears or to re-create it. "I'm afraid of high places; I fear falling." Sensorially supply the high place, and see what happens. Make a list of your discoveries, and use them in the future. The more work you do with the unconscious, the more "risable" you will become unconsciously.

Finding strong choices that pique responses from the unconscious depends on several things: being aware of the need to collect them, being conscious of the way things affect you, having the ability to identify an *ultimate-consciousness* choice when you come in contact with it, knowing where to look for it, and using your time wisely in the search. You might want to keep a journal, listing all kinds of choices and underlining the ones that are very strongly connected to the unconscious.

The *ultimate-consciousness* exercises are filled with choice possibilities. The choice hunt will most likely uncover many potential choices. Images and Fragmented Images will also yield a number of new ones. "I'm Five Years Old" is full of possibilities. Catalogue them for future exploration.

All of the techniques and involvements discussed in these first two chapters contribute to the relationship you will create between your conscious and your unconscious. If you do these exercises every day of your life, you will, without a doubt, be in control of the phenomenon of unconscious inspiration in your work. It is very important to allot time in your daily work schedule for exercises that deal with strengthening your connection with the unconscious. Many of the activities that you become involved with are natural to living. They include being more observant and aware and elevating your consciousness by using the techniques already discussed. Once you have experienced the incredible difference that occurs in your acting when it is supported by the unconscious, you will be dedicated to working with it from that moment on.

One of the most important prerequisites to accomplishing *ultimate consciousness* is trust! In every area of this craft you must learn to trust your impulses! You must have the courage to be irreverent to the material until you have found the blueprint that will fulfill it. You must trust your intuition even when it seems risky to do that! Taking chances, risking failure, exploring the unknown, getting out of the way of *ultimate-consciousness* inspiration when it occurs, being afraid and doing it anyway—these are some of the prerequisite abilities you must learn to possess.

3

ENSEMBLE

Ensemble is another overused and bandied-about word in relation to acting and theater. The dictionary defines ensemble acting as: *a system of theatrical presentation with an emphasis on an integration of all roles rather than on a star performance.* But is that all ensemble is really about?

For years, as a student of "The Method," I heard actors talk about accomplishing an ensemble state. Teachers would critique a scene and throw the word around as one spills popcorn at the movies! In my earlier acting years, even I used the word without a real understanding of its meaning. It is one of those impressive-sounding terms—like organic, moment to moment, or internal reality—which relate to an approach and which actors use when they want to sound as if they really know what they are talking about. In reality, ensemble is a phenomenon to be strived for; it is one of the highest forms of relating and acting! It is not something that can be accomplished just with time or experience; it has to be structured and created by a process, just like any other artistic achievement. There are prerequisite building blocks that must be overcome before the actor is prepared for consistently accomplishing ensemble. Everything in this way of work—all the techniques and exercises, all the preparations and craft approaches—lead to ensemble as one of the ultimate creative goals. The very foundation of the truth of this work is the accomplishment of BEING. From there one can reach truth, which in turn begets more truth and leads to impulsive, unpredictable expression, the major ingredient necessary to reach ensemble.

You know, it occurs to me that most people are interested in quick results. They look for the shortcuts and the quickie crash courses. They want to learn it all in a couple of weekends and then go out and become stars. The success of all of the miracle, "quick-fix" psychological or personality groups is that they promise a "cure" in one weekend and a few follow-up evenings! My wife constantly tells me that I "scare the hell out of people" by telling them that it takes a lifetime to become an artist and a master craftsman! "Who," she asks, "wants to work on something that he needs a lifetime to accomplish?" Well, there are a couple of misunderstandings here about the concept of mastering an approach and achieving art. To begin with, you are ready to act long before you attain full mastery of the approach and craft; it is a question of degree! Secondly, it all depends on what you want to accomplish: if you are not interested in becoming an artist and a master at what you do, if results are all that you are looking for, then this work is indeed not for you! But if you are a person who looks forward to the adventure of the journey, and not to just reaching the destination, then you are in the right place. Dedicating one's life to the joy and fulfillment of a voyage filled with adventurous exploration is indeed a way to have a life well spent! Ensemble is a result of much involvement in creating all the elements that lead to it—and that takes time and commitment!

WHAT IS ENSEMBLE?

Ensemble is reached in a relationship, on stage, when two or more actors are communicating on a moment-to-moment level, affecting each other and responding impulsively to the way they have been affected. The first actor expresses something to the other, and she responds in terms of the way she has been affected by him; he then organically and impulsively responds to her response to him, and so on, until they are both functioning authentically in relation to each other. Their behavior becomes dependent on each other in a sense. When this is accomplished, they both reach a place where their level of unpredictability is very high. The actors and the audience become involved in a *theatrical collaboration which accomplishes the goal of theater.*

If, as usual when actors act, each one is involved with what he is doing, what his next line is, where he has to be in the next moment, and keeping a running commentary on how he is doing, it is impossible to reach organic truth, much less an ensemble state. Ensemble depends on the actor's ability to surrender, to trust the moment and give in to the next impulse, even if it doesn't fulfill his concept of the character's behavior in that line or the next one.

There is a chronology to be followed here; it is like building a structure. First comes the foundation: relaxation, personal inventory, getting to a place where the actor is doing no more or less than what he feels—a BEING state. From that state—where the actor is expressing everything he feels moment to moment and allowing all the distractions to be included in his expression—he is ready to relate to another actor and to promote an *ensemble* relationship within the framework of the written scene. If he is dealing with the obligation of a piece of material, he must decide on a choice and an approach to that choice. Once he has done that, he can begin to work for that choice, allowing and encouraging all his impulses to be expressed. As the choice affects him

91

and influences his BEING state, he will hopefully begin to experience the emotional life of the character in the piece. As that occurs, the BEING state changes from the life the actor was experiencing before starting to work for the choice to the life that has been stimulated by that choice. It is still a BEING state: during all of it the actor *must* include all of his impulses, even the distractions; he must honor the truth of all his feelings. If all these elements are accomplished, he reaches an *irreverent* place, where he is *irreverent* to the idea and concept of the material. If he achieves BEING and is willing to be *irreverent,* he is ready to encourage an *ensemble* relationship on the stage.

Let us assume that the actor has accomplished all of the above and that he is ready to say his first line, or that he has, in fact, already been saying some of his lines. He is relating to the other actor, and she is responding to him with her lines. Whatever is going on emotionally for each of them is what is being expressed through those lines. She says her line to him, filled with the emotion that has been stimulated by her choice, the moment-to-moment reality, the environment, and him! He is affected by her in the moment, and whatever he is feeling in response to her is expressed in his next line. All that he is working for and experiencing is included in his response to her, but the way he responds *must* be a result of her effect on him. He must respond totally in relation to the way he has been affected by her. She in turn is affected by his response to what she has expressed to him and, in an unbroken chain, continues to respond to him, thereby creating a flowing ensemble relationship.

This, of course, is only part of what a total ensemble relationship is, the other important ingredient being the fulfillment of the relationship obligation of the material. It is of the utmost importance that the actors establish a connection with each other and become impulsively and organically dependent on each other while relating, but they must also create the life indicated by the material. Actually, their goal is to affect each other in the same way as the characters in the piece affect each other, and if they have the right choices, they can expect to be impelled in the same direction as the characters. If they are functioning organically and are being affected by their choices while at the same time responding authentically to each other, they should accomplish complete ensemble. Essentially, both actors have set up and created a circumstance that is parallel to the material. All of the impetus that would exist in "real" life exists on the stage; therefore, if neither of them interferes with reality, all they need to do is trust the moment and honor all their impulses.

If they continue to work for their choices, allowing everything that happens in each moment to become a part of the life on stage, they will function very much the way we do in life. If there is something as important at stake for them as for the characters, then they will be more involved and committed to that impetus than to the stage event. If you think for a moment and put all that I have said in the proper perspective, you will realize that this process of stimulating and responding to reality is far more "natural" than "acting"!

The obstacle that most actors encounter in their attempt to do this process is their concern with the conceptual fulfillment of the material! They might be rolling along quite acceptably, when all of a sudden they feel something that they immediately think is not right for the material, the character, or the relationship. At that juncture, what they usually do is short-circuit their reality and the ensemble relationship they have created and impose some other life in its place. This immediately separates them from the relationship they have established and throws them into a premeditative position where they begin to impose behavior that has nothing to do with the reality of the moment. Not only have they stopped relating in ensemble terms, but they have also compromised the authenticity of the emotional life they are expressing. They have ceased being real and begun to "service" the material from a logical, cerebral place, which means that they are no longer in a creative space but have moved into representation. They are presenting the life of the characters without experiencing it. If at the very moment of short-circuiting, their thought or comment that what they felt was not right for the material had been included as part of their expression in the scene, that split would not have occurred, and the behavior of the characters on the stage might indeed have been enhanced! If every actor in the world could understand and accept the idea that *he and the audience should discover his impulses at exactly the same moment*, all acting would be more electrifying! True ensemble depends on that kind of trust.

ENSEMBLE PREPARATIONS

With the knowledge that you do not begin the learning process with a concern for achieving ensemble, but that you must necessarily work on your instrument, eliminating obstacles before you use the techniques that promote the prerequisites for ensemble, you will understand in what order to proceed. All of the preparations in this section are used for other reasons also. All can be done by anyone, even a beginning actor. This simple word of caution is given so that an actor will not expect to reach a state of work or being that he has not properly prepared for through the use of other prerequisite involvements.

BEING WORKOUT

This exercise is a good one for getting ready to relate to another actor in any framework. It helps to involve you with another person selflessly! As you do this process, you lose any self-concern and self-consciousness that you may have started with. It is a rather simple exercise, which involves relating to the other actor moment to moment, on a here-and-now basis, in conversation. All the while that you are talking to the other actor, you must systematically acknowledge all the obstacles that are preventing you from being comfortable in the relationship. These can be a variety of things: tension, self-consciousness, fear, concern with how you look or with being on the stage, any obligation to do something or to be good, concern with the other actor, with what she thinks about you, attractions, repulsions, and so on. If you acknowledge these feelings out loud and to the other actor, the fears and concerns lessen considerably, and soon you become much more comfortable relating to her.

Example:

Two actors, sitting or standing face to face, begin talking, expressing what is going on in the moment:

HE: I feel funny standing here . . . I . . . don't know what to say.

SHE: Me too . . . I like the way you are looking at me! . . . I'm a little self-conscious.

HE: I feel very obligated to say something intelligent . . . I feel curious about you.

SHE: What do you want to know? . . . Asking that made me feel a little self-centered!

HE: I want to know who you are . . . I mean about your life . . . What do you do besides act? I feel stupid!

SHE: I don't know where to start to answer your questions . . . I wonder why you want to know about me . . . I feel a little suspicious of you!

HE: That hurts my feelings a little . . . but I understand! I mean, you're very pretty and you must get a lot of guys hitting on you.

SHE: I feel bad about having said that to you . . . and now I'm a little embarrassed! Yeah, I do get a lot of that, but what I was suspicious about wasn't related to that; I thought you were making conversation and that you weren't really interested in me!

HE: Well, that may be somewhat true . . . I am feeling very much on the spot, and I'm grabbing at anything that might get me off it!

SHE: I feel a little better . . . I'm not as self-conscious or obligated . . . I'm also more involved and interested in you. You're pretty honest about exposing your feelings.

HE: Thanks! . . . I feel a little better too. I'm still concerned with where to go from here. I wish I could just get comfortable saying nothing.

SHE: That's hard . . . Let's try that for a minute . . . O.K.?

HE: Sure!

(They might stand there for a few moments, looking at each other and becoming aware of what they feel in those silent moments.)

HE: That's worse! I felt much more self-conscious when I wasn't saying anything. Now that I've said that . . . I feel a little freer.

SHE: It's funny, I felt better not having to say anything! Now, I'm thinking of what's next.

HE: I'm attracted to you . . . Wow! That was a hard one! . . . I feel much better.

SHE: I knew that you were even before you said it . . . I'm flattered!

HE: I feel much better . . . more relaxed now . . . Really, I would like to know more about you.

SHE: Well, I'm twenty-four, I graduated from college . . . theater major . . . and I want to pursue an acting career.

HE: I have a similar story . . . only I'm twenty-seven! I don't feel like I have to make conversation anymore.

SHE: Me neither . . . I truly feel more in touch with what I feel, and I'm more related to you.

At any point where the two actors reach a comfortable place in the relationship and are responding to each other, they might carry the preparation into the words of a scene. At first, it would be wise to say the lines from their present reality, promoting the moment-to-moment relationship through the written words. As they accomplish that, they can sneak into working for their respective choices. It is very important that they do not interfere with the flow of reality while they are relating to each other. They should go to the choice without any interruption of that expression. If they both acknowledge all the obstacles during the preparation and include all of their impulses, they should have no trouble encouraging an ensemble state.

INTIMATE SHARING

When an actor chooses a preparation that will promote ensemble, he should have some idea of what he needs to confront, of what his obstacles are in the moment. The nature of any preparation is dependent on what the existing life is. Intimate Sharing is a very good way to encourage deeper feelings, and if that is a difficult area for an actor, then this is an excellent preparation for him to choose to create the foundation for ensemble. It may also be a good exercise to follow a Being Workout. The structure of this preparation is similar to that of any other two-person relationship workout: the two actors face each other and communicate verbally. If it is necessary to eliminate obstacles to begin with, that is where they should start. Beginning with meaningful exchanges, they should share intimate feelings that they have about things in their lives.

Example:

SHE: I feel . . . sad these days!

HE: Why?

SHE: I split up with my boyfriend about a month ago, and I'm really sad and depressed about it.

HE: I went through a divorce about a year ago, and I'm not over it yet! . . . I have a couple of kids, and I really miss them! . . . If I could get some work and make some money, I could take them somewhere.

SHE: I have never been married! I guess that's a mixed blessing. I wish I could get excited about anything . . . I'm just always so wiped out!

HE: What about your career?

SHE: What career? . . . I haven't gone out on anything in a couple of months! It's my fault! I sleep a lot — I guess to escape . . . I wish something good would happen in my life!

HE: It will, you'll see! I'm worried that I won't ever make it in this business. I love to act . . . God, how I love it . . . Nothing makes me feel the way acting does! I would still be married if I had been willing to give it up!

SHE: You mean your wife divorced you because you were an actor?

HE: Well, she didn't see any future in it . . . She wanted a more stable and comfortable life!

SHE: But didn't she know how unhappy it would have made you to give it up?

HE: Listen, I don't want you to think that she was a bad person. Actually, she was very sensitive; I still love her! . . . But she just wanted a different kind of life, that's all.

SHE: I guess I understand because I love acting too . . . My boyfriend was an actor, and he felt that his career was more important than mine. He was also very possessive!

They can go on sharing for as long as time allows. The goal of the exercise is for them to get involved with each other, to experience a deeper emotional exchange, and to begin to respond to each other on a moment-to-moment basis. Because they are sharing affecting things, it should take very little time for them to become more involved with their subject and with each other than they are with any of the acting responsibilities. The deeper they get into personal experience, the fuller the results of the exercise. As their concern for each other grows, the involvement deepens; and as that occurs, they respond more impulsively and fully to each other—which is the foundation for a continuing ensemble relationship.

Besides needing to choose an ensemble preparation that relates to where they are in the moment, the actors should also select one that is related to the material they are approaching. If, for example, the obligations of the scene demand a larger and deeper emotional life, the proper ensemble preparation can be chosen to fulfill that responsibility as well. In other words, the preparation could not only help the actors lay the groundwork for the relationship, but also prepare them to deal with the emotional demands of the piece. Since the subject matter of an Intimate-Sharing workout can lie in any area, each actor can choose to discuss and expose things that will promote the kind of life needed to fulfill the material. If privacy is involved, each one must make a judgment as to what he or she will or will not share.

DOUBLE EXPOSURE

Similar in style and effect to Intimate Sharing, Double Exposure is an ensemble technique which elevates curiosity and involvement between two or more actors. The emphasis is on exposure, not just intimacy, which is why this exercise has a much broader range than Intimate Sharing. The actors can expose almost anything and jump around from subject to subject. In the familiar fashion of conversing face to face, they relate to each other by progressively exposing more and more personal and meaningful things about themselves. As in any part of this work, neither one is *ever* obliged to violate or expose anything that he or she considers *private!* As the exercise progresses, it is hoped that the actors will become not only involved with each other on a deeper and more meaningful level, but also impulsively responsive to each other on a dependency level.

Example:

SHE: I very rarely tell anybody anything about my personal life! . . . My parents have a lot of money . . . and they have used that as a weapon against me! . . . If I were going to enjoy the fruits of their wealth . . . I would have to do everything they wanted . . . go to the school of their choice . . . date the boys they approved of . . . and so on . . . Boy, do I resent them! . . . I don't think they know how much!

HE: Don't you ever discuss it with them? . . . I mean, have you ever flat out refused to do what they wanted you to?

SHE: No! I mean, yes . . . in subtle ways . . . I was very rebellious when I was younger, but now that I need their financial support so that I can pursue my career, I have to keep my mouth shut!

HE: I was in jail for six months when I was eighteen! . . . How about that? . . . You didn't know that you were involved with a convict, right?

SHE: Jail? . . . What did you do? I mean, was it really serious?

HE: Well, it was to me then! . . . I was arrested for possession of marijuana! . . . In those days it was against the law to have even one joint!

SHE: It must have been awful! . . . Was it?

HE: Everything that you hear about jail is true, and then some! I survived it by mentally leaving! . . . I would live in the future. I would fantasize about what my life was going to be like and pretend it already was. I moved through those six months just like a zombie. They thought I was a mental defective, so they left me alone.

SHE: That makes me sound like Mary Poppins! The worst thing that ever happened to me is a speeding ticket, which my father had fixed! I must say that I am more interested in you after hearing that story. I want to know more about you now.

HE: No, tell me more about you . . . Are you happy?

SHE: Happy? . . . I don't know . . . I suppose I am. I feel like I haven't done one important thing with my life . . . I was born, I went to school, I had a "normal" childhood . . . got good marks, was popular in school . . . made out in the backseat of several cars . . . went to college, and became the disappointment of my parents' life!

HE: You seem to have quite a connection to them . . . Do you still need their approval so much? . . . I mean you mention them in every other sentence.

SHE: I guess I want them to be proud of me! How about you? What was your relationship to your folks?

HE: I had a whole bunch of folks . . . My parents were divorced when I was very young . . . I lived with my mother and her boyfriend, and when that didn't work, I moved in with my father and his second wife . . . She didn't like me, so I moved to a foster home, did a bunch of those . . . but don't get to feeling sorry for me. I met and lived with some incredible people . . . I had an education you can't buy! Approval? . . . No, I never remember wanting approval as much as I wanted to be touched and held.

SHE: Wow! . . . That's incredible . . . You seem very well adjusted. Are you bitter? I mean, don't you feel cheated? . . . I would!

HE: I did feel angry for a while, and then one day I woke up and realized that my childhood and all of my growing-up years were rich with the experience of knowing many people, and while they didn't hold me and rock me on their knee . . . each one of those people gave me some kind of love in his or her own way . . . I still communicate with most of them!

SHE: You make me feel like I missed something. The best time of my life was when I went to camp . . . don't laugh at me, O.K.? I was away from home and made friends that have lasted until now. I did what I wanted, went where I wanted, and was who I really am. It was those summers that made me want to act! If not for that time, I don't think I would have ever discovered my own identity.

The exercise will find its own momentum and direction as it goes on. It is important that both actors stimulate curiosity about each other and question each other. After a time, they might start to explore their choices. Double Exposure is a good involvement exercise, and if used correctly, it will encourage ensemble.

WONDER, PERCEIVE, AND OBSERVE

This technique has been discussed in great detail in all of my other books. It is a great involvement exercise, and that has been the context in which it has been explored. Used as an ensemble preparation, it accomplishes a level of selfless involvement which is a mandatory first step in being able to relate to another actor. It is therefore a good exercise for opening the door to ensemble, and if the actor makes a slight adjustment to it and uses Selective Emphasis as an additional approach technique, it can turn into a very important ensemble preparation.

Starting the exercise in the conventional manner, both actors, again standing or sitting face to face, begin to perceive, observe, and wonder about each other. The observations are about what is obviously there to be seen and observed; perceiving demands deeper scrutiny; wondering is the expression of their curiosities about each other. The more interest and curiosity they have, the better the exercise will go. Once the actors have accomplished a level of selfless involvement with each other, they can add to the wondering part of the exercise things that will stimulate a greater dependence on each other's responses. In the conventional approach to this exercise, the actors are cautioned against asking questions that relate back to themselves, but in an ensemble preparation, that warning is removed, and the actors are encouraged to ask such questions; for example:

HE: What do you think of me? . . . Do you like me? . . . Do you think I'm a good actor?

She is encouraged to respond to those "wonderments" honestly, and if they are truly interested in each other's responses, they will create an ensemble basis in relating to each other. It is important to note here that the wonderments should not relate back to themselves in the early part of the exercise, but only when they are both well on their way to selfless involvement.

TELEPATHY

This is an involvement exercise, as well as an ensemble preparation, where two or more actors relate to each other nonverbally. They sit or stand together and communicate their feelings and impulses to each other without words, gestures, or any other kind of indicative behavior. It is an intense involvement, which demands a high level of concentration. As the exercise unfolds, both actors establish a communication of their feelings and desires. The energy involved in attempting to understand and perceive each other's impulses draws them to each other like a magnet to iron and creates a dependency and involvement that promotes the chain reaction leading to ensemble.

BLIND COMMUNICATION

This exercise involves communicating without sight. The actors close their eyes and hold hands, then start to communicate by touching and feeling, as well as through sounds. No words are to be used in the exercise; all impulses are to be translated through the body and the voice. As the exercise moves along, and because of the natural insecurity produced by the removal of the sense of sight, the actors become increasingly related and dependent on each other. Nothing is planned at the outset; they just allow whatever they feel to find its way to being expressed physically. It is amazing how much the body can express and communicate if we only allow it to.

IMAGINARY MONOLOGUES

This technique has many uses: besides being a choice approach, it is used in instrumental areas as well as as a wonderful ensemble preparation. Each actor in turn does an imaginary monologue, while the other listens and responds. The content of the imaginary monologue is extremely important to the success of the preparation. If the actors get involved and are affected by the choices inherent in their respective monologues, they will be impelled to respond properly. It is also important that the actor who is listening allow himself to be affected by what is being said, even though he knows that the one doing the imaginary monologue is speaking to someone else. As the exercise proceeds, both actors become involved in an emotional dynamic that promotes the ensemble relationship. If the "listening" actor responds in a way in which the imaginary person might not or would not respond, it should be included by the other as unusual behavior and acknowledged as such.

Example:

HE: (Doing the imaginary monologue) You were always there with money, but you were never there for me in any other way!

SHE: (Responding to *his* imaginary monologue) That's not true! I am always prepared to listen to any problem you have!

(Her response is inconsistent with what he remembers of the relationship; to him what she says is blatantly untrue.)

HE: How can you say that? . . . Are you just plain lying, or is that how you remember it?

By dealing with her response in an accepting and inclusive manner, he promotes the reality while at the same time involving her on a deeper level.

When the first actor has gone as far with his imaginary monologue as he can or wishes to go, the other one can begin hers. The process is the same for both of them. At a certain point, that point of "truth" when they both know it is time to move on, they should begin working more specifically for their choices in the scene.

The purpose of using Imaginary Monologues as an ensemble preparation is the same as that of any of the other exercises: to involve the actors with each other on a meaningful level and to promote an impulsive responsiveness to each other in every moment. The more involved they become, the more there is at stake for each of them; and the greater the reality, the greater the success of the preparation.

IMAGINARY DIALOGUES

This exercise is very much like Imaginary Monologues, only this time both actors are talking to their imaginary choices at the same time. The exercise is designed to achieve the same result, except that it supplies impetus for both actors at the same time. It is slightly more complex than Imaginary Monologues in that the actors might be operating at cross purposes. *He* might be speaking to his mother, for example, and *she* to her lover, and that could create quite a number of complications in the dialogue. The first step in deciding to use Imaginary Dialogues, therefore, is to pick choices that are not so diametrically opposed. Furthermore, each actor must avoid being impelled along his or her own track and excluding the other one. They must listen intently to each other. In the third place, they must also respond to each other's monologues, including things that are antithetical to what their own choice might express. All in all, if used properly, this technique is probably one of the better ensemble preparations. In both of the above exercises, the actors will have a greater degree of success if they choose to take everything that is being said personally. (She is saying those things to *me!*)

Example:
(Both actors have decided to use people with whom they were romantically involved at one time.)

HE: (Speaking to the actress, but really relating to his ex-girlfriend) You know, I still think about you! . . . I wish it had worked with us!

SHE: (Speaking to the actor, but relating to her ex-boyfriend) It might have worked . . . I tried, but you split!

HE: Wait a minute, it wasn't me who left; it was you who took off!

SHE: How can you say that? Don't you remember how upset I was when you said you wanted your space and that I made you feel claustrophobic?

HE: I may have said that, but I didn't leave!

SHE: You mean you didn't physically leave . . . right? Well, what do you call it when you push someone out of your life? Sure, I walked out of your apartment, but you pushed me out!

HE: Well, maybe if you had more guts, you would have understood what I was going through, and you might have fought for the relationship.

The dialogue can continue along those lines; obviously, there are some contradictions, but the actors can mend the discrepancies if each one includes the other's reality into his or her own. It is also important that they consider the nature of the material they will be dealing with following the Imaginary-Dialogue preparation. Their respective choices should be selected with some parallel to the demands of the material. The above example would be appropriate if the scene that followed was about two people in a similar conflict.

BELIEVABILITY

This is possibly the most enjoyable technique of all. Every time I have the actors in my classes do a Believability workout for any reason, it takes me forever to get them to end the exercise. Not only is it a great deal of fun to do, it is one of the better imagination exercises, as well as an excellent ensemble preparation. As a choice approach, it is used to fulfill the obligations of material; as an instrumental exercise, it stretches the imagination and builds the actor's willingness to believe; and as an ensemble preparation, it creates a relationship between the actors that fulfills the demands of ensemble.

To do the exercise, the actors relate in conversational terms, mixing a little reality with a lot of untruth. They start with a framework of truth, things that have really occurred, and from that foundation, which they can both accept because it is factual, they embark on a journey of imagination, fantasy, and improvised theatrics. A Believability workout done for the purpose of stimulating ensemble should also be selected with a goal in mind: its nature and content should not only promote ensemble, it should also lead to the obligations of the upcoming scene.

Example:

Let us imagine that both actors have done all the exercises leading to the ensemble preparation and that they are now ready to select one of the techniques that will encourage ensemble. They know the obligations of the scene they are working on. It is a comedy involving an older man trying to pick up a young girl at the cosmetics counter of a drugstore in New York City. He finds her attractive, and she also thinks he's good looking. In this scene, he attempts to make conversation and to ask her out on a date. She is shy, but at the same time flattered by his attentions, and she coyly responds to his efforts. The subject of the believability that the actors have chosen to use as an ensemble preparation is based on the parallels in their own relationship. The basic resemblance here is that, like the characters, they find each other attractive, but none of the other elements in the scene correspond to realities in their lives.

It is important that the actor who starts the believability improvisation begin with the truth. Once the realities have been established, it is much easier to add the untrue elements into the relationship.

HE: Hi! . . . You know, I have been looking at you from across the class for a long time . . . Did you know that? I think you're beautiful!

SHE: Thank you . . . Yes, I've seen you staring at me.

HE: I have often wanted to tell you how attracted to you I am, but I have been afraid to open that door . . . for a lot of reasons.

SHE: Well, I'm flattered, and I don't know how to respond to you!

HE: I'm not trying to "hit" on you. I would just like to get to know you better.

SHE: You know, that sounds like a line!

HE: I guess it does, but I mean it!

SHE: Do you say this to all the girls you meet?

HE: No, just to the pretty ones.

SHE: (Enjoying the joke) Well, at least you're honest. Do you hang around places waiting for attractive women to appear?

HE: No, actually I've seen you a number of times before, and I'm embarrassed to admit that you have been the object of my fantasies for a while.

SHE: You are joking, aren't you?

HE: Well, yes and no; I have thought about you.

SHE: I don't know whether to take you seriously or not.

The improvisation can go on for as long as necessary to establish the ensemble connection. While both actors are using a base of truth, they are also

104

sprinkling the exercise liberally with imaginary things. There are a number of elements that service the responsibilities of the preparation in this case: first, as they get more involved and more personal with each other, they become increasingly interested in the attention they are receiving one from the other. This "vested interest" stimulates an even greater moment-to-moment involvement, which in turn creates an expectant dependency on each other, thus heightening the ensemble feeling of the preparation. Secondly, by using parallels to the material, the actors are also well on their way to fulfilling the responsibilities of the scene. Finally, the believability framework may allow them the freedom to express personal feelings that they have been reluctant to expose before. Believability is a very good technique since it offers so many possibilities while at the same time being enormous fun.

LOOKING FOR THINGS ABOUT THE OTHER PERSON YOU HAVE NEVER NOTICED BEFORE

This exercise is better accomplished if both actors remain silent. Its title says it all; the actors look for things in each other that they have never noticed before: color of the eyes, shapes, complexion, coloring, length of the hair or eyelashes, the emotional content of the eyes and the way it changes, the shape of the mouth, odors, mannerisms and other personality traits. The number of things that are available physically and behaviorally is staggering. This kind of involvement is extremely absorbing and will take both actors on a journey into each other. But it is the emotional responses to the various discoveries that create the elements of ensemble. As the actors explore each other and see things they were unaware of before, they stimulate responses that constantly affect and change their emotional point of view. It is those responses and changes that create the ensemble drama between them. We all have a natural curiosity about what other people think of us, and in such an exercise we particularly want to know about the various parts that the other actor is relating to. What is he looking at? we wonder; what does he see? Why is he so curious about my teeth? Do I have food stuck in them? . . . and so on. These responses stimulate other responses, and so on, until the entire involvement reaches an ensemble state.

ENSEMBLE WORKOUT

This exercise, unlike some of the others mentioned in this chapter, has specifically been designed to promote ensemble. It is a five-part exercise leading to the establishment of a relationship between two people on the stage. Facing each other, the two actors start by relating without words. Essentially, they stare at each other and communicate in the here and now.

After a short time relating this way, they are encouraged to add sounds to what they are doing. The sounds allow them to express vocally what they have hopefully established during the silent part of the exercise. By adding sounds, they are progressively creating reasons and opportunities to respond to each other. Once they do, the next step is to communicate in gibberish. This further adds to the depth of their impact on, and response to, each other. As they add each new part, they should not only become more involved, but more dependent on each other for impetus. After a time spent relating in gibberish, they then move on to words, continuing to express the same things they have been communicating in the previous parts of the exercise. In an interesting way, each part "piggybacks" the last one. By the time they are using words, the actors should indeed have established the beginnings of an ensemble relationship. The content of their communication can relate to any topic; usually it is established at the beginning of the workout and just continues to unfold as the exercise progresses. In the last part, each actor uses the memorized words of any monologue he knows. He moves from his own words into the words of a written monologue, continuing the ensemble relationship. Of course, the actors are totally irreverent to the material and are only using the written words to promote their own here-and-now realities. This last part of the Ensemble Workout is extremely important because of the inherent responsibility all actors feel toward the obligation of material and the logic of the words. If they are going to separate from their own organic truths, it will certainly be in this part of the exercise.

If, by chance, either actor begins to service the material, he should acknowledge what is happening and include that life while reinvesting in his real impulses. If he does this, he will get back on the track of his own truth. Upon completing all five parts of the approach, the actors may begin working for their respective choices, but they must be very careful not to make a separation between what has just been done and the beginning of the choice process. The latter should be a continuation of the preceding work, with no interruption.

This five-part ensemble preparation is designed to lead the actors to the edge of the creative process. If successful with it, they should be "instrumentally" in the right place to begin dealing with the material. If, for example, their first obligation is for relationship, they will already be halfway there as a result of the discipline of the preparation. Their choices—whatever they may be—should be approached as a continuation of the last part of the ensemble preparation. As both actors are relating through their respective monologues, they can begin to work for the choices that will service the material. If they are using a sensorial choice approach, they can sneak into the sensory questions and responses in between the lines of the monologue with which they are communicating. By doing this, they will both begin to experience the emotional life of the characters in the scene while still in the last part of the ensemble preparation. If they continue the process right into the written material, they can avoid any abrupt change between the exercise and the scene.

"YOU MAKE ME FEEL"

This is another very good ensemble exercise, which is approached in the same manner as all the others: both actors face and relate to each other in a sitting or standing position. They start with "You make me feel . . ." and respond to the moment-to-moment realities that evolve between them.

Example:

HE: You make me feel . . . self-conscious . . . the way you look at me . . .

SHE: That makes me feel responsible for you!

HE: You make me feel . . . angry . . . at that response! . . . I'm not asking you to be responsible for me!

SHE: Now I feel that I made you angry, and I'm sorry! I didn't mean it that way.

HE: That makes me feel better!

SHE: I feel better too . . . You make me feel . . . like something is expected. I'm not sure what I mean by that . . . but I feel an expectation from you.

HE: Now, that makes me feel . . . like you hit the ball back into my court! . . . I feel defensive! . . . You seem to push that button . . . There is a kind of accusation in your responses!

SHE: And that pisses me off! . . . . I'm just going with what's there for me, and you twist it into an attack!

HE: That makes me feel . . . misunderstood . . .

SHE: You make me feel like I'm victimizing you, and I don't like the feeling or the insinuation!

HE: You're making me feel like we are not communicating . . . just fighting . . . I don't want that . . . I'm sorry if I offended you . . . it wasn't intentional!

SHE: O.K. . . . . I guess I'm being a little sensitive too.

107

HE: That makes me feel a lot better . . . Now I feel that we can relate on a different level.

SHE: You make me feel . . . that I have the responsibility to carry the ball in this exercise! . . . Do you know that you are doing that?

HE: No, I don't! . . . You are making me very angry . . . Every time I try to be nice to you, you come back at me with some stupid accusation about how I'm trying to manipulate you!

SHE: That makes me feel like really taking off on you!

HE: So go ahead and take off! You don't frighten me at all! What is it with you? . . . Do you have a thing with men?

SHE: What an incredibly stupid generalization that is! No! I don't have a thing with men; actually, I get along with most men quite well! I just think that you want me to take the lead in this exercise and do it for you!

HE: That makes me feel like I don't want to relate to you at all! I just feel misunderstood by you . . . I'm hurt!

SHE: I feel ambivalent about that . . . On the one hand I don't want to hurt you, and on the other I think you're doing a victim thing again.

HE: Now I feel like this is a little funny . . . We keep going back and forth in the same areas . . . How do you feel about me in general?

SHE: Well, I don't know . . . I feel . . . a little hostile . . . but I also feel like I don't want to feel that way!

HE: So what can we do to change it?

SHE: There you go again . . . making it my responsibility . . . If you want to change things between us, do it!

HE: That makes me feel a lot better . . . I see what you are saying . . . Instead of doing something, I have been asking *you* to do it, right?

SHE: (Laughing) Yeah . . . that's it! . . . You got it . . . That's what you've been doing.

HE: O.K. . . . I understand! . . . I like your laugh; that makes me feel warm! . . . I like you.

SHE: I like you too . . . I feel good that we went through that. It cleared the air for me.

HE: I feel closer to you . . .

The purpose of this exercise is to pique responses in each other that come from reality and to promote those responses into an ongoing relationship that is affecting and involving. The entire process is aimed at creating an ensemble "dependency." If both actors are true to their responses, the exercise stimulates a dramatic involvement and an ensemble relationship. At first, it is very important to use the structure of the exercise—*You make me feel . . . That makes me feel . . . Now I feel . . .* etc. . . . —but after the actors are well into it, they can just respond to each other without the preface of *You make me feel*.

After the actors get into their choices, it is advisable that they continue the preparation silently under the lines. If they do that for a short period of time, it will help to promote what has already been established by the exercise, and it will also create a "bridge" between the exercise and the scene.

WORKING FOR A CHOICE
AND PROMOTING ENSEMBLE

Once the basis for ensemble relating has been established, the actors are ready to go on to the material and to carry that ensemble relationship into the scene. It is extremely important that they do not short-circuit what they have established when they start to work for their choices. On the other hand, they can adjust the particular ensemble preparation they choose so that it fits into the choice-approach process. If, for example, an actor is doing a "You-Make-Me-Feel" preparation and Evocative Words as a choice approach, he may intermingle the two as he works:

(To continue the preceding example)

SHE: Now I feel like we can go on from here . . . I think that you are very interesting on the stage.

HE: That makes me feel great . . . I also feel good about your work as an actress.

(At this point they could start working for their respective choices. They may continue the preparation out loud or remain silent while doing it.)

HE: (Starting his choice approach for the beginning of the scene, he relates to a specific person in his life silently, in an evocative-words inner monologue.) Helpless . . . hurt . . . she always does this . . . love her . . . doesn't respond . . . want her to act differently . . .

(Somewhere in this process he can include the prior preparation.)

HE: (Dealing with the actress on stage) Now I feel like she isn't listening to me . . . She seems different. (Going back to the evocative words) Beautiful . . . sexy . . . I love it when she smiles . . . wish she loved me . . . she always leaves . . . distracted . . . not involved . . . (He may again go back to the preparation, using the actress herself to promote the impact related to his personal choice.) You make me feel misunderstood and unseen . . . . I feel that you are the one who is manipulative, not me!

It is important to reiterate here, for the purpose of clarity, that the evocative words that the actor is using relate to another person in his life, not the actress he is working with. As he jumps back and forth between the preparation and the choice approach, he is hopefully intermingling the two people so that they, in a sense, become one. By going back and forth between the choice, the choice approach, and the actress, he can promote the desired emotional responses as well as retain the ensemble relationship. If he responds organically to the actress in the moment while at the same time being affected by his choice, the reality of the material becomes the reality on the stage. At the right time the actor can start the words of the scene, continuing to be involved with the choice approach and the ensemble preparation. At some point he will be able to drop the preparation and go with the dynamics of the relationship that has been created between him and the actress.

At the same time, the actress might be using a sensorial choice approach to promote the life *she* wants in the scene. Her choice might be a particular piece of music that brings up feelings of sadness and makes her wish for things that are lost (which is the obligated emotional life of the character in the play).

(Again returning to the previous example of the ensemble exercise)

SHE: Thank you . . . Your opinion . . . means something to me . . . You are making me feel positive . . .

HE: I feel very able to communicate with you . . . because I feel more accepted by you . . . How did we ever get off to such a negative start?

SHE: I don't know . . . Maybe we were tense . . .

(Somewhere in here she starts the sensorial process of creating that piece of music.)

"What do I hear? (Responding with the auditory sense) What is the first sound I detect? (Auditory response) Where is the sound coming from? With which ear do I hear it the most? What does it sound like? What is the very next sound? What kind of instrument does that sound like? . . . How many different instruments do I hear? . . . How do the various sounds mix? Can I separate them? What is the predominant sound? . . . Is there a melody I can hear? What does it sound like? . . ."

The questions can continue for some time, and she can also include the ensemble relationship by internally or externally responding to the actor the way she did in the prior preparation. As she creates the music and is affected by it, she will begin to feel what the character is feeling in the scene. Both actors should be very connected to each other at this point. As their emotional life evolves and parallels the content of the scene, the ensemble relationship will become the reality of the play. The actors, who started with their own here-and-now realities, will be experiencing different realities and responding to each other as they did in the preparation. If their choices are right for the material, and if they are successful in creating them, then the actual reality of the emotional life stimulated by those choices will fulfill the demands of the play while at the same time promoting ensemble.

If the actors are experienced with the work, they will be cognizant of the need to make choices that stimulate relationship. While he is working for another person, using Evocative Words, he is still relating to her in the ensemble framework that they established in the preparation. She is working to create a specific piece of music using Sense Memory as a choice approach, while also continuing to relate to him in the framework of the preparation.

It is extremely important that the ensemble preparation be chosen with a knowledge of how it will work in tandem with the choice the actor has decided on. If the preparation is intrusive on the choice approach, it will create an obstacle to ensemble. For example, if the actor's choice approach is a complex running inner monologue or an imaginary inner monologue, stopping to do the "You-Make-Me-Feel" preparation would interfere with the flow of these choice approaches. A better selection might be an ensemble preparation which is nonverbal and involves going with intuitive responses to the other actor on a moment-to-moment basis while doing the Inner-Monologue choice approach. This knowledge comes from practice and experience with the process.

While the actor is involved with establishing the ensemble and working for his choice, he should also be *irreverent* to the material for as long as it takes to stimulate the life it demands.

ENSEMBLE AND THE ULTIMATE CONSCIOUSNESS

The elements of this work fit together like the well-cut pieces of a picture puzzle. When everything is done "right," all the pieces fall together. The more experienced the actor is with the process, the easier it gets. Any interference or short-circuiting of the natural process of life, and the possibility of accomplishing truth, ensemble, and a response from the unconscious becomes remote.

If the actor:

· Eliminates instrumental obstacles
· Reaches a BEING state
· Stimulates selfless involvement with the other actor
· Works to create an *ensemble* relationship (using the aforementioned techniques)
· Creates an impelling choice through the use of a choice approach
· Is willing to be *irreverent*
· Selects choices with a knowledge of their ability to impact on the unconscious
· Is willing to allow, permit, accept, and express all impulses on a moment-to-moment basis

then there is indeed a chance to be real, accomplish an ensemble relationship, fulfill the material, and possibly cross the line into *ultimate consciousness.* In light of what has already been discussed in the previous chapters on consciousness and the unconscious, it becomes very clear that picking choices that will appeal to the unconscious is a matter of trial and error. Acquiring a vast repertoire of choices that have an impact on the unconscious depends on exploration and experimentation. When actors reach ensemble and supplement it with a trip into the *ultimate consciousness,* it is an experience that neither they nor the audience soon forget.

There are some things that the actors can do in the ensemble preparation to lay the groundwork for a possible journey through the unconscious while in a scene. Before starting an ensemble preparation, they can try any of the *ultimate-consciousness* exercises. If they use a primal moan, they can go from that into an ensemble preparation, carrying the residual emotions into it. Intimate Sharing can help them find the key to the unconscious, depending on what they choose to share with each other. In most of the ensemble techniques, you can selectively emphasize certain elements with an eye to reaching the unconscious: you can look for things in the other actor that remind you of important people in your life or choose what you wonder about in the wonderment part of that exercise; you can select to share things that are deeply rooted in your unconscious, when doing Intimate Sharing, or use the way the other actor affects you in the "You-Make-Me-Feel" preparation to pique unconscious responses. If every actor who stepped on a stage was equipped with a process as rich as this one, the experience of *ultimate consciousness* would become commonplace instead of happening only occasionally.

EXAMPLE OF TWO ACTORS
INVOLVED IN AN ENSEMBLE PROCESS

Using the approaches listed above, I would now like to draw up a specific "blueprint" of the steps involved in reaching ensemble and possibly piquing the *ultimate consciousness*.

Both actors should do the following exercises in the order given:

1. *Personal Inventory:* At the same time or separately, out loud or semi-audibly, they should repeatedly ask "How do I feel?" and respond to the question in the moment.

Example:

"How do I feel? . . . I feel some tension in my stomach . . . I feel anxious. How do I feel? . . . I don't know! . . . I feel congested . . . obligated to feel something. How do I feel? . . . I have tension in my neck and forehead. How do I feel? . . . I am aware of her standing over there . . . I am concerned with what she will hear and think! . . . How do I feel? . . ."

Doing Personal Inventory will help both actors find out where they are and what they need to do next. If there is no substantial tension problem, they needn't do a relaxation exercise. If tension seems to exist to the degree that it is an obstacle, the next involvement should definitely be relaxation.

2. *Relaxation exercise:* There are a number of good relaxation exercises that the actors can choose from if either or both of them decide to do so. Each one can select the one that has proven to work best for him. Relaxation techniques have already been described in great detail in all my other books. They include Rag Doll, Logey, Tense and Relax, and Weight and Gravity.

After completing the relaxation group, the actors are ready to explore any remaining obstacles or blocks.

3. *Dealing with the Demons:* This can be the third step if either of them feels that there are still some obstacles standing in the way of BEING. Dealing with the Demons is done by expressing moment to moment what is going on inside. Something like Personal Inventory, it differs slightly from that exercise in that the actor is encouraged to ventilate and express all feelings of obstacles, blocks, or anything else that might stand in the way of his being comfortable doing no more or less than what he feels. Exposing the "demons" helps to loosen their grip and to disperse them.

Example:

"The biggest demon I feel is the obligation to be good. I feel anxious about what I want to happen in this exercise. I feel a little competitive with her . . . I'm afraid that I won't be able to get down to my real feelings, and I'm not even sure what those feelings are! I feel some leftover tension in the back of my neck . . . I'm afraid to let go of this part of the exercise and go on to the next."

Dealing with the Demons should be done until the actors feel comfortable and in a BEING state. Provided that they are both in the same place and are ready to take the next step, they can move on to the involvement area.

4. *Selfless Involvement:* Here again there are many choices that will take them to their goal. They may elect to do a Two-Person Being Workout (although not totally selfless, it can get them progressively more involved with each other), or they may "wonder, perceive, and observe," silently "look for things they have never seen in the other person before," or do any exercise that will take them away from their concern with themselves. If both actors have been successful in becoming selflessly involved, they can approach the ensemble preparation.

5. *Ensemble Preparation:* If they are involved in doing a scene or a play and have choices in mind as the next step in this process, they would be wise to discuss the nature of the ensemble preparation so as to pick the right one to best approach their choices from. Another important consideration in choosing the ensemble preparation is to select one that will hopefully stimulate and pique the unconscious. It is the goal of the actor to reach an ensemble relationship while at the same time creating a foundation for communicating with the unconscious. As I stated earlier, certain ensemble preparations, if approached with selective emphasis, can do "double duty" insofar as they are aimed at deeper feelings. If, in an Intimate-Sharing preparation, the actor explores and exposes deep and meaningful things to his scene partner, the possibility of igniting unconscious impulses is much greater. If both actors are also aware of the specific choices and choice approaches that they are going to use following the ensemble preparation, they can then select one that will not intrude on the choice when carried into the approach process.

All of the ensemble preparations have been detailed in this chapter. If you are using this blueprint as an exercise and there isn't specific written material involved, you can use any of the preparations for the sake of the lesson or experiment; but again, if you are dealing with the obligations of material, make an appropriate choice.

The ensemble preparations are: Being Workouts; Intimate Sharing; Double Exposure; Wonder, Perceive, and Observe; Telepathy; Blind Communication; Imaginary Monologues; Imaginary Dialogues; Believability; Looking for Things about the Other Person You Have Never Noticed Before; The Ensemble Workout; and "You Make Me Feel."

The actors should get involved in the promotion of the ensemble preparation until they are both relating in ensemble terms. They will indeed feel when that happens: there will be no self-consciousness; they will be comfortably involved with each other, responding moment to moment with what they feel; and the relationship will work like a finely oiled and engineered piece of machinery. One impulse will be stimulated by another, and the degree of unpredictability will be at its highest. Both actors will discover each new moment as it occurs. It is at this peak of relating that they might sneak into their respective choices.

6. *Working for the Choice:* The ensemble preparation should overlap into the beginning of the choice-approach process.

Example:

Let us say that the actors have been doing an Intimate-Sharing ensemble preparation and that their choices are other people in their lives. The choice approach they have both decided to use is Imaginary Monologues, talking to each other as if they were the other people. Remember that the two actors at this point have an ensemble relationship; they have accomplished all the prerequisite exercises and techniques and are functioning on a high level of relationship. They are sharing intimate truths about themselves, and each of them is being affected emotionally by what he is exposing, as well as by what the other person is telling him.

HE: (Intimate Sharing) I sometimes get so depressed I stay in bed all day . . . and then something good happens and I get elated . . . My mood swings are incredible! . . . I spend a lot of time despondent about my life . . . I'm thirty years old and I feel like a failure!

SHE: I know how you feel! . . . I'm not so despondent as I am lonely. I feel like I'm sacrificing my life for a career . . . But I really don't want a family . . . not now . . . I feel ambivalent about that . . . I feel like I should want what my mother wanted . . . or better yet, what I think she wants me to want! Do you feel lonely?

HE: Sure I do! . . . I want to be with someone . . . but I can't afford it. I mean in more ways than one . . . I can't afford the time it takes to cultivate a relationship.

(Somewhere in the midst of this sharing, either actor can begin the Imaginary Monologue to the person he or she is talking to.)

HE: (Continuing) I mean how can you work for a living, study acting, go on interviews, socialize with the right people, and still find time for a relationship? (At this point he starts his Imaginary Monologue to the person in his life, doing it as a continuation of the Intimate Sharing, in an unbroken line.) You could never accept that; you always gave me a hard time about not spending enough time with you . . .

SHE: (Starting her Imaginary Monologue and including his in terms of the way she is affected by what he is saying) What about you? Every time you wanted me to be there, it was always on your schedule . . . I have a life too!

HE: Sure, I know that! . . . But you always seemed to make it harder than necessary . . . It was as if you wanted to create that conflict! (At this juncture the actor might return to the Intimate Sharing.) It's true, she would always wait for the right opportunity to make me feel like a shit! I bent over backwards for that relationship. (Again returning to the Imaginary Monologue) And don't say that you didn't, because you know you did! . . . Remember that time we were supposed to go skiing at Mammoth and my agent told me to hang around town . . . because he was waiting to hear about an important interview? Well, you know how you treated me . . . I went and blew that opportunity!

SHE: (Picking up her response to what he just said and relating it to her own reality and person) So you want to compare injustices, do you? You drove me out of my mind with your jealousy and possessiveness! "Who are you rehearsing with? . . . Where are you meeting him? . . . Where were you last night? . . ." (At this point she might return to the Intimate Sharing with the actor.) He really drove me nuts . . . I used to think that I was lying to him when I was telling the truth . . . I was miserable in that relationship . . . Now I'm lonely, and I don't know which is worse . . . (Back to the Imaginary Monologue) You were really something, you know . . . Do you remember that time you had me followed by one of your friends? I'm glad you're not in my life anymore, but I still miss you sometimes.

Both actors can go on for a while with this process, eventually eliminating the Intimate Sharing and just doing the Imaginary Monologues. When they both feel that the relationship and the emotional life have reached a parallel to the scene obligation, they can begin to say the lines. As they start the scene, their imaginary monologues become silent, and they continue to do them as running inner monologues, under and between the lines of the scene, all the while encouraging an organic response to each other. The life expressed in and through the words of the play must come entirely from the way they affect each other and from the impact of their respective choices. If they are irreverent to their concept of the material in this process, that should be encouraged and accepted. It is from this kind of irreverence that true ensemble is spawned and nurtured, not to mention the unpredictable brilliance that can evolve from this kind of creative license. If their choices are meaningful enough, either actor may succeed in sinking a shaft into the mine of the unconscious, bringing about an *ultimate-consciousness* experience. In that case, if they are indeed involved in ensemble, the other actor will also be catapulted by the force of that unconscious energy!

The six steps involved in attaining ensemble are good for any two-person relationship framework. Naturally, it is easier to accomplish the desired goal if both actors are trained the same way and share a common philosophy about acting. But if an actor encounters another with whom he does not share a common process and who is not willing to go along with the approaches, the process-oriented actor will have to do his best to use that process. Most of the techniques can be done silently and unobtrusively, and if the actor is experienced with the work, he can seduce the other into ensemble without the latter's knowledge that this is happening.

Once an actor has experienced the results of the process leading to ensemble, he will never again be able to settle for anything less. Ensemble relationships happen at times by accident, because many of the elements that stimulate ensemble exist or occur between two actors in a scene. All of you have either had such experiences or at least seen this happen; however, it is quite another story to possess the knowledge and techniques necessary to consistently build such a relationship on stage! It truly constitutes the difference between a journeyman actor and an artist. All the elements of this work fit together, first because the process is natural to life, and secondly because it has been structured that way. If you do your homework, if you commit to the process, if you make it a way of life as well as a way of working, then you will acquire the knowledge and practical ability to do the work and reach BEING, *ensemble,* and *ultimate consciousness.*

4

JOURNALS
AND
CHARTS

A journal is another tool for the actor. It serves many purposes and can be invaluable for future reference. It is a kind of diary where the actor records his daily activities, as well as his feelings about significant people and events. He thus chronicles a myriad of stimuli and breaks down the component parts of his experiences into choices that can be used in his work. His observations and perceptions are set down on paper so that he may later refer to them to stimulate ideas and elements that can be used to create characters on the stage. Everything of significance that he sees, feels, thinks, and observes is written down each day.

Besides being a complete record of the activities and events of his life, a journal acts as a blueprint of the actor's daily work process. Becoming an artist is largely dependent on a lot of hard work, on a daily schedule that involves the instrument in a variety of exercises and disciplines designed to eliminate instrumental obstacles and take the actor forward on the road to instrumental freedom and BEING. This schedule also includes craft exercises and explorations, which are part of the circle of the work. An intelligent actor budgets his time so as to balance the hours spent on instrumental techniques with equal time to strengthen his craft process. A daily journal helps him to record and keep track of everything he has been doing over a period of time. Being able to look back over a month, let's say, and to follow its chronology, can be very valuable in pushing him forward on the journey. If there is a lot of repetition and covering of the same ground, that will become evident to him when he reviews his journal. In short, journalizing is a very important process for every actor. The *how* is equally important.

THE ACTOR'S DAILY JOURNAL
GENERAL GUIDELINES

Start with being practical about the actual notebook that you will use as your journal. It should be thick enough to contain a year of daily journalizing. Nothing is more exasperating than having eighteen books to thumb through to find the desired entry. The notebook you decide on should also be sturdy, since it will take a lot of abuse. I personally like a larger-size book, since it allows one to have freedom of space rather than having to cramp sentences into margins that are later impossible to decipher. Eight and a half by eleven — typing-paper size — is very good. Carry your journal with you everywhere you go since you will want to make entries at various times, as things happen or occur to you. Carry it around as you would your wallet or house keys. A lot of the writers I know use tape recorders, which they keep at their sides even while driving. In the jacket pocket of most playwrights you will always find a little pad or notebook filled with bits of information, thoughts, and observations that they may later use in their work.

There aren't any requirements as to the style in which you write; that will develop as you become more practiced. Avoid rambling! Be specific about everything you write. At some future time, you may look at a paragraph and wonder what you had in mind when you made that entry, but when you write something down, do so for a reason.

There are other important guidelines to follow:

1. *Be descriptive:* Detail places and objects; describe colors, shapes, sounds, and ambience. If you are recording an encounter between two people that you are observing, describe not only their behavior but the way they are dressed, their responses to each other, and any extraneous involvements.

2. *Record your feelings:* Note your responses and the specifics of how you feel about everything you describe — your emotional point of view about it. Not only is it important to report what you feel; it is also invaluable for future reference. It will allow you to remember and possibly use stimuli that you might not have thought of otherwise, and it will enable you to chart your growth and the changes in you by letting you see the evolution in your emotional attitudes over a period of time.

3. *Encourage yourself to report your observations and perceptions* — what you see, how you feel about it, and what you perceive beneath the

obvious. Again, this activity will allow you to elevate your perceptions, develop your intuition, and stimulate a deeper involvement with external stimuli. By including those perceptions in your journal, you are making sure that they will be available to you in your future craft work.

4. *Relate to everything in sensorial terms:* When describing objects and people, do so *sensorially,* even though it is very difficult to describe anything that way. How do you record an odor on paper? What can you say about the feeling of an object or the texture of a piece of material? What special words do you use to describe a sound? It is really difficult, if not impossible. What I mean, then, is that you suggest the sensory elements that may pique real sensorial responses when you reread your journal. "I sipped my iced tea, and the combination of that special tea smell, mixed with the overwhelming odor of lemon, excited my taste buds." Just by recording the description in sensorial terms, you have ensured that it will appeal to your senses as you reread it. You will know what "that special tea smell" means! It will go directly to your olfactory sense. If what you recorded is interpreted by your senses when you reread it, it will push those sensory buttons and be a usable tool in your acting. You may also describe sensorial responses in comparative terms: "It sounded like a high-pitched flute"; "It reminded me of the taste of walnuts"; "The texture was like a fine grade of sandpaper," etc.

5. *Make special note of possible impacting areas:* As you journalize, you will run into many experiences that push important buttons: stimuli that touch the unconscious; people who, for one reason or another, remind you of others in your life; or simply the recognition that something you record will make a good choice for a scene at some future time. Put an asterisk alongside such discoveries. Remember that all parts of the work fit into each other and that a journal can be used as a recording tool to elevate your consciousness, as well as to chronicle the elements that are keys to the unconscious.

6. *Record your feelings about acting:* As you grow and evolve, it will become very clear to you how earlier insecurities and worries about your work have vanished with practice and time. It is very important to you as an actor to be able to track that growth by having it on paper. In addition to building your self-esteem, doing this will help you to trace in specific terms exactly what you did to overcome obstacles in your life and your work. That knowledge will enable you to use similar techniques to overthrow obstacles you may be dealing with in the present, thus ensuring your continuous growth. Include everything you think is necessary. Don't feel limited in time or space; just be

careful not to indulge in editorial. Remember that you are an actor and not a writer!

THE ENTRIES

Begin each entry with the date, month, year, and exact time of day. You may start with how you feel or with what you want to say. You may make numerous entries in any one day, so don't feel obligated to ramble on for long paragraphs just to fill up paper. An entry might be as short as a single line: "I feel very tired today . . . I am not looking forward to the day!" If you feel like it, you may list some of the reasons you feel tired and don't anticipate the day positively. You may say, "I drank too much last night, and I feel bad about that! Why do I do it when I know how rotten I will feel on the next day?" or "I am not looking forward to another day of the same thing!" or you can just leave it with the single sentence you started with. Since you will most likely make a number of entries each day, make sure that each one is preceded by the time. You might also want to add the location; for example, "9:10 A.M., sitting at the table in the patio of my apartment."

Avoid becoming preoccupied with making entries. Keeping a journal is a way to record important thoughts, feelings, and experiences. It is a supplemental tool to your work, not the work itself. Over the years, I have known actors who became so involved in journalizing that they would literally panic if they forgot their notebook at home. Another trap to avoid is to let what you put down on that paper take the place of experiencing the feelings you are writing about. Don't record everything! Be selective! As you gain experience in journalizing, you will be able to make decisions about what to make note of and what not to.

Once you have memorized the six steps in keeping a journal, it will be very simple to make your entries with an eye to including those various elements. Start by asking yourself what you want to say. Why do you want to put it on paper? How are you going to describe it? Reread all entries to make sure that you included everything you wanted to say. There will be times when you will have to record an experience after it happens. Since it would be unwise to interrupt a heated discussion, for example, to make entries into your journal, you will have to recall the incident at a later time. Note the time of entry as well as the time when the incident occurred. Trust your memory. Remember: *almost nothing is sacred!* So don't worry about remembering or recording every detail. It is almost certain that you will recall enough to make the entry very important to you.

Another way of keeping a journal is to use audio tape. This presents an advantage in that you can record your voice with all of its emotion and feelings about what you are entering. When using tape, keep the same format: list the date, time, etc. . . . and do that for each entry. Listening to tapes you recorded years earlier can be very important in identifying your emotional states, the level of emotional and vocal connection you had at the time, and the nuances of your responses to the content of each entry. The drawback of audio tape, however, is that you always seem to need batteries at very inconvenient times and that, for some strange reason, you are always out of tape . . . and where did that tape you recorded last week disappear to? Somehow it seems much simpler to hold on to a pen or pencil and to know where you laid your notebook down.

THE JOURNAL—AN EXAMPLE

"Sunday, February 9, 1986–10:15 A.M.

It's raining! I'm looking out the window, feeling depressed. Sitting on the sofa in my favorite, beat-up terry-cloth bathrobe, feeling sorry for myself! I don't know why I get so depressed when it rains, but I do! Objectively, it's beautiful out there. I can smell the rain even through the closed windows. I smell the rain on the cement sidewalk below and the odor of the trees outside the window. I'm having my morning coffee, and that is always a good feeling! I love the taste of that first cup in the morning. It makes me feel secure . . . Now, I couldn't explain that one to save my life! I feel at odds with everything this morning. Why don't I just settle in and enjoy the day?

Sunday, February 9, 1986–12:30 P.M.

I'm dressed—ta da! Feel a little better, but I just realized that it isn't just the rain that depresses me . . . it's Sunday! I have always been depressed on Sundays. It started when I was a kid in grade school. Sunday meant that the next day was Monday and back to school . . . My freedom was over for another week! You know, I would know it was Sunday even if I came out of a coma! There is something about it that you can almost taste! I can look out the window and know that it's Sunday—not Saturday, but Sunday. What is that? I guess it is the lack of traffic . . . the quiet . . . and maybe some of the sounds. Anyway, I feel at a loss. I can't make my usual business calls. I can't be busy, so I guess I'll have to relax and try to enjoy having time off! I could have scheduled a rehearsal today! . . . Why is it that I feel so incomplete if I'm not working on something?

Sunday, February 9, 1986–7:00 P.M.

Wasn't a bad day after all. Once I got myself together and out of the apartment, I felt much better. About four o'clock this afternoon, I got a telephone call from my mother. It wasn't what she spoke about that upset me; it was the sound in her voice. She sounded really depressed . . . down! She's been very alone since Dad died, and I guess she's having a hard time with it. I felt helpless. I didn't want to call attention to how she sounded, but at the same time it affected our entire conversation. She always tells me how worried she is about me, and she thinks I should think of doing something instead of acting. That doesn't help my morale any! . . . The rest of the day and early evening were fine. Dinner was nice. I like Larry! He's always up, or he works at being up. It's really interesting how many people there are in the world who think you shouldn't be an actor! . . . Not Larry, he's always encouraging. I guess that's one of the things I like about him. You know, where you eat is very important to the enjoyment of a meal . . . I made a mental note of that at dinner tonight . . . I liked the restaurant we ate at . . . I mean, the linen napkins and tablecloth . . . The lighting was comfortable, and I liked the color of the walls. I will definitely go back there again. It's still early, so I think I'll work on my monologue for class. I just got a shot of creeping insecurity when I said that about working on the monologue . . . When, dear God, will I be able to do what I love and not be so scared?"

The three sample entries above are simple expressions of what the actor was feeling and experiencing. There is nothing profound in any of them. They are, however, filled with rich material that he can look back on and use in his work. They contain a number of things: his feelings about the day of the week and his insight about where all of that started, his relationship to the weather and how it affected him, the sensorial descriptions that made each experience richer, and a blueprint for the future. The actor could use any part of those entries as a springboard for re-creating that entire Sunday morning. He could explore his relationship to his robe and the responses that could be stimulated by re-creating it at some future time, when it might be a perfect choice for a scene, or his reaction to the morning coffee and what it meant (here there is a possibility that the coffee is connected to many other important morning experiences—which might possibly connect with some unconscious life, even though the actor wasn't aware of it when he made this particular entry). In the first entry, there is a reference about feeling at odds with everything, and if he wanted to pursue that feeling, I am confident that he could identify the component stimuli which created it. In his second entry, he talks about feeling at a loss because he "wasn't doing anything." I am sure that means in the pursuit of his career. If that appears repeatedly in his journal, it would indicate that there is a problem here that he should deal with: one, he is over-identified with his work, and two, he needs to develop other interests. There is some insight into the problem with the statement that he feels incomplete when he isn't working. His third entry is filled with a variety of thoughts, feelings, and insights. He includes some sensorial description of the restaurant and also alludes slightly to his relationship to his mother. His insecurity about acting is evident in the last part, but it seems that he is aware of the problem and accepts its existence.

Not every entry in your journal will qualify for the Pulitzer Prize, and some of the things you commit to paper might even seem a little innocuous when you reread them, but it is important to establish a consistency. There will also be days when you won't feel like making any entries. That's all right, don't! It is your life that you use to create from, and, in a sense, this journal is a record of that life. Doesn't it sound logical that it isn't possible to remember all the details of your everyday life? The journal records and holds them for you to use and enjoy anytime.

"Monday, February 10, 1986–8:05 morning

Got up feeling good, positive . . . I like Mondays . . . It feels like a new beginning. Looks like a nice day. I love white billowy clouds that look like you can walk on them. I feel anxious about all the things I have to do today, and at the same time it's exciting. I have to go to "Unemployment." I hate that place! Why do I feel like a panhandler when I go collect my weekly check? I actually get a nervous stomach, shit! I paid that money in; it's mine, isn't it? I guess that I don't really feel it is mine . . . Actually, I feel like a loser every time I walk through those doors and get into that line! Just the smell of that place sets me off. I guess that's all I have to say to you, dear journal! I feel like there's more, but I don't know what it is, so I'll talk to you later.

Monday, February 10, 1986–2:38 P.M.

Damn it! I have one of those periodic interviews at the Department of Employment next week: 'Where have you been looking for work? . . . I realize that, as an actor, you can only do so much, but have you been doing all that you can? . . . You know, we can revoke your privileges anytime if we feel that you are not doing your part in securing employment!' God, how I hate that patronizing attitude . . . I can see the denigrating look on that bitch's face right now! Well, anyway, I got my money today with a minimal amount of aggravation. But it was as I expected it would be: the moment I went through those double glass doors I got that office odor right in the face . . . It smells like a combination of floor wax, paper, perspiration, and the way money smells. I like observing the people and trying to figure out what each of them is like. What a sterile place! Why don't they get a decorator? . . . I guess they don't want to make you look forward to returning!

I had a great rehearsal today with Sandra! Really felt like I used the time well. She seemed very ready to work also . . . I hate her apartment though. I get depressed there. Hey, maybe that's why the scene worked so well today! I realized that the most depressing thing about her place is how dark it is in there . . . I need light . . . preferably sunlight.

I'm still upset about my periodic appointment at Unemployment next week . . . It's going to ruin my whole week! I hate that bitch!!!! Mrs. McFee . . . She delights in the torture. I can see her expression at this very moment: she screws up her face and narrows those beady rat eyes of hers and fires her next question at you the same way a snake thrusts its tongue out. I have to be polite because that bitch has my life in her hands. I hate the phony smile I give her. I hate being phony ever! I know who she reminds me of . . . Oh, my God, it just came to me this minute . . . She reminds me of my fifth-grade teacher, Mrs. Bloom . . . who, I truly hope, is still dead and being eaten up by the worms! That woman made school and my life a living nightmare . . . People like that should never be allowed to teach! I could never be right, for being wrong! Whenever she said something to me and I would obediently respond, 'Yes, Mrs. Bloom,' she would tell me not to be so agreeable! . . . Whenever she put her face right up to mine I could smell the fat on her body, and it nauseated me! I used to think that one day she would come so close to my face that I would, with lightning speed, bite her nose off! Hey, both those bitches are great choices! Mrs. McFee doesn't look anything like Mrs. Bloom, but there is a resemblance in their personas and in the underlying bitterness and unhappiness they feel in regard to their own lives. The repressed anger is the same, and the rhythm of their speech is pretty close. Mrs. McFee doesn't have a fat body odor; she reeks with the smell of Woolworth perfume.

I still have the rest of the day left, so I'd better get busy.

Tuesday, February 11, 1986–Afternoon

I went on an audition for *Hunter* today. I really related to that line from . . . oh what is the name of that play, the one where he is drunk, doing this bitter monologue about his twenty years in show business and the awful commercial interview he went on the other day? . . . Well, anyway, he has a line, 'Acting . . . what a tacky business!' That's exactly how I felt this afternoon, sitting in that office, looking the part over—it was a single sheet of paper with three innocuous lines with no explanation about who the character is, what he wants, what he is doing. I guess I am happy that I got out on an interview though . . . Yeah, whom am I kidding? I'm ecstatic! Why do I still get so nervous? After ten years of studying acting, five years as a professional, I get tense for three lousy lines! . . . It's not the part that makes me tense; it's how much the whole damn thing means to me . . . I know I'm a good actor. I just want to work so much that I get uptight whenever I get out there. I have to do something about that . . . I use the work . . . I do my preparations . . . and I still have some tension. I hope I get the job. I need it! That guy I read with was a real mannequin. He looked at my chin all the way through the reading! . . . I mean, I know he isn't an actor . . . or at least I hope he isn't! That office was the size of a toilet in a nineteen-thirties gas station. Can you imagine spending eight hours in a room you can't spread out your arms in? I think he was more nervous than I was. Oh, dear Lord God, I want to be a star!"

All your entries should express the things that are prevalent in your life at the time. Some of those entries will cover most of the six steps involved in journalizing, but don't be concerned if you don't fulfill all of those requirements every time. They are just guidelines to help you fill your contributions with rich material that you can use as an actor.

"Friday, February 14, 1986–10:42 A.M.

Slept late today . . . Had some horrendous dreams. Woke up with the after-effects of that. I only remember fragments of those dreams. One of them was about being lost in this place that seemed very familiar. I knew where I was but didn't know where *it* was. That sounds strange! I mean, I knew the house I was in . . . but the house itself seemed to be in a place that I had never seen before. It made me feel disoriented and insecure . . . I woke up with that feeling. The walls of the room I was in looked as if they were made of dough. When I sat in a chair, it collapsed and enveloped me . . . What the hell does all that mean? All the colors were muted . . . drab grays and browns . . . There weren't any bright colors anywhere! The pictures on the walls were a combination of some of the things I have had hanging in all the different houses and apartments I've ever lived in. I remember one part of the dream where I wanted to leave, but I didn't know where I was, so I couldn't leave . . . I felt trapped . . . As I remember that part, I get that trapped feeling again. Wow! What a dream! I know enough about dreams to understand some of what it means. I guess that the house is the place where I live now, and the fact that I was lost or didn't know where it was is symbolic of my insecurities about not knowing where I am in my life right now or where I'm headed. The drab colors probably mean that I'm a little depressed and not excited about anything. And the walls made of dough? . . . That's simple! I have the feeling that there isn't anything solid in my life. Well, I think that's pretty good interpreting for a guy with a minor in psychology.

I'm sitting here in my 'Peanuts' robe, and I don't want to get dressed or do anything. I've been really discouraged lately. Every time I sit down to do some acting work, I wonder what it's all for. Hey! I am really down. I wish I could do something that would lift me up a little. I do things that get me involved and feeling good: I work on my craft, I'm doing a lot of scene work in class, I get out there every day and hustle for work, I have some good friends, I'm healthy—at least physically . . . ha, ha, that's a joke . . . I must keep reminding myself that I am doing exactly what I want to do with my life! How many people can say that?

I just reread this whole entry, and I sound like a promo for a course in positive thinking. Why don't I just let myself alone and be depressed? What's wrong with that? There's a lot I can get from that dream—and look at the impact of it already!"

From all these different entries, you can see that a journal may contain a wide variety of moods, feelings, thoughts, and experiences. Since you are the only one who will ever read your journal, you can regard it as a personal record of your life. Say whatever you want; ask questions; fling challenges at yourself and the world. In just a few months, your journal will be rich with material that will give you insight into yourself and help you grow as a person and as an actor. Your entries will open doors to the understanding of behavior—yours and others'. Your journal will become a rich reservoir of choices for your scene work as well as for your professional life. The patterns that you identify will help you to pinpoint your problems and, in many cases, to solve them. Having a journal allows you to see yourself with an objectivity that a mirror doesn't supply. It affords you the opportunity to read about yourself as if you were reading someone else's life story.

JOURNAL LOGS

A journal log is somewhat different from a personal journal and more like a ship's log. It is a record of your work on the craft, on scenes and monologues, and just like the daily journal, it is invaluable. It is approached in a similar fashion: you keep track of the time, day, and date, as well as of the name of the project that you are involved with, and write a day-to-day report of your approaches to the fulfillment of the piece. All comments and difficulties are included as well as successes and breakthroughs. Your daily exercise work can also be included in your journal log if you like. It will help you to create a direction in your work. There are a number of reasons why you should use a journal log:

1. It provides a complete record of each approach you use.
2. It documents the successes and failures of each process.
3. It helps you to trace your progress with the work.
4. It becomes a blueprint for repeating the scene at a later time.
5. It can be used to keep a record of your daily exercises.

Every actor will develop his own technique for keeping journals. It is important that you don't get wrapped up in becoming a writer. A journal is a report, a record of activities and experiences, and should state the feelings and thoughts of the actor as he or she records each experience.

THE JOURNAL LOG—AN EXAMPLE

"Sunday, March 1st, 1987

Started rehearsal today on *The Woolgatherer* with Joyce. We met at the workshop and read through the scene; then we discussed our feelings about it. She was a little concerned with the elements of her character, and I felt very much the same way. One of the reasons I chose the scene in the first place was that I thought it would be a stretch for me. She felt that her character was shy, introverted, and had some pretty complex psychological problems, whereas she herself is outgoing and gregarious, with not too complicated a psyche. My character definitely has a lower state of consciousness than I and is much more the 'animal' than I am. The scene we chose to do was the one in her apartment where he tries to seduce her. After reading through it and discussing our fears about it, we attempted to identify some of the obligations. I said that his driving force was to sleep with her and that my obligation would be the impetus for that. Joyce was unsure where to start. She acknowledged the importance of the character elements but also felt that her character was lonely and fascinated by my character. It was a question of whether her behavior was predominantly impelled by her nature or whether it was possible to deal with the other obligations before addressing the character elements.

I suggested that we start with our own realities and explore the parallels there. Knowing that I was very different from my character in a variety of ways, I didn't obligate myself to the fulfillment of any of the elements in the scene. All I want to do at first is establish the beginnings of a relationship between us and attempt to find any similarities or parallels that might be used as a foundation to build on.

We started to relate to each other with an emphasis on getting selflessly involved. I had only known Joyce slightly in class and knew very little about her life. We related on a moment-to-moment level, encouraging our curiosities about each other. We shared our perceptions and after a time talked about some of the similarities between us and our characters. Joyce felt shy and slightly intimidated by me, and I told her that I found her attractive. We also discussed the importance of dealing with the place. Her character lives in a dingy apartment with all the windows boarded up. My character refers to the place a couple of times, and it is an important statement in the play. We both acknowledged that the workshop was pretty seedy and realized that there weren't any windows there at all. Possibly, we could use the available environment to create from. We spent a couple of hours dealing with our own realities and decided to call it a day.

Monday, March 2, 1987–Evening

After dinner I reread the scene. I guess I was looking for new clues about the character. I feel a little anxious about this scene because I don't identify with him. He is very basic, uneducated, crude, and judgmental, and he seems to live for the satisfaction of his appetites. He is somewhat perceptive about her and does come up with some insights, but they seem to have a defensive or self-serving purpose. Our rehearsal today established the beginnings of a relationship, but while I find Joyce attractive, I would not at this point make any attempts to seduce her, and certainly not in the same manner as the character does. I think that finding our own realities is important in establishing a relationship and creating the elements of ensemble, but it seems that the place to start is with the dissimilarities, the character elements.

Tuesday, March 3, 1987–Afternoon

Started our second rehearsal on *Woolgatherer* with a relaxation workout followed by a Personal Inventory. I discovered a few demons, so I did a little 'dealing with the demons,' expressing all my anxieties about the play, the rehearsal, and my confusions about where to go from there. Joyce did some preparations too, and then we began to relate to each other. She said that she felt that one of our obstacles was that we were too polite to each other, that there was definitely conflict in the scene, and that we should start to deal with it right at the beginning! I agreed with her, and we decided to explore each other for impetus in conflict areas. I checked out my BEING state and acknowledged that I wasn't doing any more than what I felt, so I started to look for things in Joyce that I could be critical about. We started to relate with some selective emphasis about things we found irritating in each other. At first, it was arbitrary, a little contrived, and we acknowledged that we were reaching for things. Then I hooked into something real . . . I told her that I hated her pompous criticisms in class and that I thought they were patronizing. She was visibly hurt by that, and we were on track. I thought that she would get defensive and retaliate, but she seemed to retreat into a shell. She got less and less audible, and for a time I was concerned about the damage I might be doing. I backed off a little, and she stopped and informed me that she was using a certain adjustment and that I should not be concerned with her well-being, and, for God's sake, to do my work and not to worry about her . . . I was both embarrassed and angry at the way she talked to me, and I used that to reinvest in the scene preparation. We continued exploring this tack for about fifteen minutes, and I decided that the only value of this technique was that it broke the ice between us. We agreed that while it helped to open up some conflict areas, what we were doing wasn't servicing the impelling elements in the scene. He gets angry at her and begins to attack her because she rejects his advances. I decided to explore the sexual attraction and the need to seduce her. She decided to look for the things in me that were both fascinating and frightening, and we related verbally only when we were impelled to. I started to emphasize the things in her that turned me on. I related to her mouth, her breasts, her slim waist, and wondered what it would be like to kiss her and feel parts of her body. I did some sensory speculation about making love to her and had some success in creating an attraction and a desire for her. At this point it was pretty cerebral, though, and while I had sexual feelings towards her, I didn't feel impelled to satisfy them. It seemed that I was successful within a scene framework, but as for the reality I was still at the drawing board. We discussed it and decided to explore some of the character elements. I felt that I was too 'civilized' to feel or relate to a woman the way the character does and that I would have to find a way in which to pique my baser energies and appetites. I asked myself a lot of questions, like what kind of animal I might explore, what the component parts of this character were that I could find parallels for, what sub-personality I possessed that was like him, and whether I knew anyone like him. At this point I felt overloaded, so we broke for the day."

Later on in this book I will get into the rehearsal process in depth, but as you can already see, rehearsing is an incredible exploration. By recording everything you do in your journal log, you avoid going over the same ground twice. It also helps you to establish a chronology of process. When I was keeping a journal and logging all my scenes, I discovered that it was also a way to ventilate my fears and anxieties. Instead of incubating them throughout the entire rehearsal process, I was able to put them on paper and alleviate them somewhat. As you work on material, you discover that each scene brings with it unique obligations and responsibilities, and while you have a specific process for preparing and fulfilling material, you must also deal with who you are and what obstacles are keeping you from the realities of the material.

"Wednesday, March 4, 1987–Morning

We couldn't get the workshop space, so we are in my apartment . . . Can't make too much noise; feel restricted. Last night I explored getting a sense of a few animals. I tried a lion and a mandrill and rejected both of them. Neither animal stimulated that sensual or sexual desire. I felt predatory. The mandrill did, however, supply a feeling of baseness and mental slowness. I realized that, as emotional as I am, I really spend a lot of time in my head. Cliff, the character, is much more impulsive and basic. He only figures things out when necessary, and while he is basically intelligent, he certainly has not developed his intellect to my level. Today I decided to explore a gorilla. Besides the fact that I do gorillas well, I thought that it might open some doors. It did stimulate an animal quality. It piqued an aggressive part of me, and I was able to relate to

Joyce with more aggressive expression; but instead of stimulating sexuality, it made me feel playful, aggressively playful. I wanted to push her around a little. It worked well for her though: she felt fascinated by me and my animal behavior and at the same time wary about what I was going to do next. She told me that when I was exploring the gorilla she felt very fragile. We broke for lunch and talked all the way through it about what our characters wanted out of life. What did Rosie want? Why did she collect a closetful of sweaters? What drove Cliff? Was getting laid the spice of his life? We got into a discussion of what we wanted and how sex was always lurking about somewhere! A person who loves what he does and is involved with life on a very conscious level puts sex in a kind of perspective, while people who struggle to exist and barely survive often have a very different relationship to sex and sexual appetites. We decided that it might be a smoke screen for Cliff, that he might want something much deeper, but that he was afraid of commitment and/or rejection.

After lunch we did some 'reentry' preparations. I expressed feeling closer to Joyce and freer with her now. We did an 'I Want, I Need' exercise. Both of us talked about our own personal life and moment-to-moment needs. She expressed a need to be seen and accepted by people, particularly by me at the moment. She also said that she was interested in having a friendship with me and that she found me interesting and somewhat confusing. I expressed that I also wanted to be accepted by her and that I wanted her to be impressed with me. I found in our needs some possible parallels to our respective characters. I wondered what Cliff did to impress Rosie, what I did, if anything, to impress Joyce, and how I could incorporate that reality into the scene. Cliff has a very good sense of humor, and it manifests itself in the way he pokes fun at Rosie. I personally could identify with that obligation since I have almost made a career out of teasing people I care for. This was our fourth rehearsal, and I was beginning to feel some of the connections with the material. There was a lot left to be done, but I felt I was on the track. We spent the rest of the afternoon exploring needs and desires and finding parallels to the material. We hadn't even thought of doing any of the lines yet. Neither of us wanted to fall prey to any logic or concept at this point, and since we had both agreed to take as much time as necessary to do the scene, neither of us felt rushed.

Thursday, March 5, 1987–Afternoon

Last night I searched my memory for a time when I had felt angry at a woman for rejecting me . . . I couldn't remember! I had felt irritated and led on by a few females in my life, but nothing that ever made me behave viciously. Cliff comes to Rose's apartment to make love to her, and when that doesn't happen, he gets angry and abusive. I asked myself what would make me behave like that. Have I ever been so disappointed that I lashed out at someone?

I decided to do an Imaginary Monologue. I chose my ex-wife to talk to and told Joyce that I wanted her to allow me to affect her if I did. I talked to Joyce as if she were my ex-wife, selectively emphasizing all the dissatisfactions in the relationship. I accused her of using sex as a weapon, given as a reward when I was 'good' and withheld as a punishment when I was "bad"! It didn't work! I felt too much hurt and grief, and Joyce couldn't relate to it. I was very frustrated in today's rehearsal. I felt blocked! I did a 'Vesuvius,' expressing all of my frustrations, and asked Joyce to do some of the lines near the end of the scene, just before Cliff leaves. I carried my frustration into the lines, and it felt right—only for the wrong reasons! My frustrations were temporary, while his are not.

I needed to take an inventory of what I had already done in the rehearsals and of where we were in relation to the obligations that we had already identified. I felt good about the relationship between Joyce and me. We were more comfortable with each other and able to risk more with the work. I had stimulated an attraction and had impulses toward her in that area. She felt much more interested, and, while generally not as intimidated by me as she had been in the beginning, she felt more attracted to me and intimidated by that. I felt that we were more able to relate to each other in conflict areas than we had been in the first rehearsals. We could even identify some of the real contrasts between us as people. Cliff and Rose are very different, and while Joyce and I are not quite so dissimilar, we really come from very different backgrounds. She is a WASP, and I am Jewish. Her values and her upbringing are antithetical to mine. We are going to explore that soon. The animals I tried failed to produce the right elements for the character, even though all three had a significant impact on my behavior. It seems to me that I feel a gap specifically in the character elements. I must break down the component parts of the character and find a viable approach technique for bridging that gap.

We spent the rest of this rehearsal telling each other about our lives and our upbringing. We really are very different people. Besides our religious backgrounds, the priorities we grew up with were very different also. There was a whole sense of propriety in Joyce's life that didn't exist in mine. The do's and dont's in her life were very restrictive. She confided to me that she had been a virgin until she was twenty-two. I asked her what had changed in the way she looked at life. She said that acting had altered her view on most things and that she felt liberated as a result of studying acting. I asked her if she was more like Rose before her liberation, and she responded with 'Definitely!' I identified an attraction to non-ethnic-type women and remembered a time in my life when I was almost obsessed with the conquest of the pedestaled porcelain-skinned WASPs I used to go to high school with. We both agreed that this seemed to be a very rich parallel to the material and decided to look for a way to explore it.

Friday, March 6, 1987–Morning

I hate morning rehearsals! It was the only time we could get the space. Last night I came up with a choice and an approach technique for exploring our antithetical personality elements, and I shared them with Joyce. I really feel that in order to go back to a time and place where our priorities were very different from what they are now, we would have to do an affective-memory exploration. I told her that I knew it was complex and time-consuming, but that I thought it was worth it. I further explained that I had a perfect experience in mind. It involved my first love relationship in high school, with a girl also named Joyce. The event I wanted to use was the last time I had seen her. We had had a terrible argument, and I had said things to her that I regret to this day! She was not only a WASP, but the daughter of a Protestant minister. I adored her, wanted her, and was obsessed with her sexually, but she never let me make love to her. Joyce thought for a while and also came up with what she thought was a good possibility. We both started to sensorially create the environments of our respective experiences and progressively supplied more and more of the necessary elements. I worked for over an hour, completely losing track of time. I started to endow this Joyce with the features of the other Joyce and slowly began to have strange throwback feelings of deprivation and rejection. I was hot with desire for her! I literally could not keep my hands away from her. The actress responded quite violently . . . in fact, she slapped me, which added to my rage. I was really into it! I started paraphrasing the lines of the scene, and she responded more like Rose than I would have imagined. Then we started to say the lines exactly as written, and I felt the gnawing reality produced by my Affective-Memory choice approach: I felt connected with Joyce—both of them—and I really experienced an ensemble feeling between us.

When we finished the exercise, we both felt like we were flying. We danced around the room and hugged each other! It was wonderful! We discussed in retrospect what we remembered of what had happened and decided that Affective Memory in these choice areas was worth further exploration in relation to the fulfillment of the scene responsibilities. The only negative I experienced in the whole process was that I was still too "refined" for the character and that I would have to look for a choice that would parallel those more basic character elements.

Monday, March 9, 1987–Afternoon

Took the weekend off, but couldn't stop thinking about the scene. I feel a little overwhelmed by the whole thing! I realized over the weekend that there is so much yet to do. I know that a scene is a work in progress and that you build it like a house, one brick at a time, but it seems endless!

I made a list of things that I have to do in future rehearsals, and I feel a little better about everything. I want to create a place that will make me feel as Cliff feels in Rose's apartment. I need to find a handle to the character, just in the area of the differences between us. I want to establish a relationship with Joyce that more closely parallels the one in the play. I feel that the emotional obligations will fall into place if I create the choices that impel my needs and find the obstacles to fulfilling those needs.

I started today's rehearsal with the customary instrumental preparations and asked Joyce if she knew any two people in the world who were like Cliff and Rose. She said she would have to think about that one, and she did. I was stymied. I couldn't think of a single person, except actors I had seen in films. I thought of Brando in *Streetcar* and felt that that was much too stylized a character. Joyce offered a few suggestions, but they didn't strike the right chord for me. All of a sudden I thought of a perfect possibility. There is a guy I have known for a number of years. His name is Sam. He hangs out at an actors' coffee shop, and we have a casual relationship . . . but he is perfect! He's from New Jersey . . . not well educated. He even drove a truck for a living, like Cliff. He's crude and has a vulgar kind of consciousness about women. He is also intelligent and charming, and I have seen him flirt with women quite successfully. He can be bitingly sarcastic and is a perfect choice to explore. Using the Externals choice approach, I started working specifically to get a sense of Sam. I created his rhythms, mannerisms, worked for his leading and secondary centers, and even attempted to get his speech patterns. After about half an hour of exploration, relating to Joyce with my own words, I began to experience some of the feelings and impulses that had been eluding me since our first rehearsal. I felt much more in touch with the animal energy and less sensitive or concerned with Joyce's feelings. I looked at her as if she were a juicy piece of meat (sexually speaking), and I had impulses to put her down. I actually enjoyed the contrast in our relationship. I felt better off than her, and I enjoyed being sarcastic. I refined the process and began to subtilize Sam's rhythms, mannerisms, and tempo, and I felt more and more like Cliff!

Whatever I did with getting a sense of another person seemed to work great for Joyce. The more I felt piqued by the sense of Sam, the more she retreated behind her wall. She seemed interested, but frightened of me; I hurt her feelings and made her angry, and in a strange way I was getting off on it. I realized, however, that working for Sam wasn't enough. I also needed what had been stimulated by the Affective-Memory exploration. But how could I combine the two choice approaches? I instinctively know that the Affective-Memory choice and getting a sense of Sam pique some very deep and important unconscious life, and I want somehow to combine the two.

Tuesday, March 10, 1987–Late afternoon

I had a strange dream last night about Joyce! It was sexual, but also sadistic! I can't remember all the details, but I felt very excited sexually. She was crying and begging me not to hurt her—but I wasn't hurting her; I was laughing at her. This is a good sign! Obviously those choices I have been experimenting with are reaching the unconscious. I tried the affective-memory exploration again, but this time I worked to establish a sense of Sam first. It was really strange; it was as if that whole experience with my girl back in high school had happened to someone else! I didn't have as much success in this rehearsal as the first time I had tried the choice. I had a great thought though: Joyce, my high-school girlfriend, lived with her father and mother in an apartment that was above a linoleum shop in a poor part of Chicago's Near North side. It was an awful place, and I always felt uncomfortable when I picked her up to go on a date. I decided to make an adjustment in my Affective-Memory approach and, instead of using my car as the place where the original experience took place, to use the living room of her apartment. Instead of re-creating the experience as a total affective-memory experience, I also resolved to endow Joyce the actress with the features of Joyce my high-school girlfriend, in terms of the way she looked then, the way she was dressed the last time I saw her, the sound of her voice, and the odors in that awful room, and to see where it would lead. In addition to that, I decided to also work for a sense of Sam.

We worked for three hours and had the best rehearsal yet! My choices and approaches were dynamic! By using the specific choices I had selected in conjunction with each other, I was able to address three of the obligations in the scene:

1. The time and place
2. The relationship
3. The various emotional obligations and transitions

Because of the specific nature of my choices, I feel that a lot of the life I experienced in the rehearsal had some unconscious support."

Keeping a journal log is a very good way to establish a continuity from one rehearsal to another. Each actor will record his work and his impressions in a different way, and each will be at a different level of craft. I chose to create the above example, using two actors with some experience in the work, so that the reader could better understand the journal-log process without having to deal with, or understand, the specific creative process. The example only covers the beginning rehearsals. A journal log should trace the process from the first rehearsal to the last. All exercises and techniques should be listed, accompanied by a specific report on the results of each involvement. Describing the failures is an important prerequisite for growth. We learn from failing! We also discover where a specific choice will lead, and that is invaluable for future scene work.

ANOTHER KIND OF JOURNAL

I often suggest that an actor keep a journal to help in the process of unlocking past experiences. Sometimes, while working with actors in my class, I discover that certain of them are completely out of touch with their childhood. They cannot recall anything before the age of ten. For one reason or another they found it necessary to block out their earlier memories. I ask such actors to do an "I'm-Five-Years-Old-and-I . . ." exercise (see chapter 2) and to stay with each age until they run out of impressions, at which time I move them along to the next age, and so on. The exercise has been incredibly helpful in opening those closed doors, so I designed an activity that can be done essentially in the same manner, but in the framework of a journal. Using a tablet or notebook, the actor starts with "I'm five years old and I . . ." and fills in the blank as he would in the verbal exercise. I ask him to do this daily and to feel free to start with any age. I also advise him to leave many blank sheets of paper between the various ages so that he can return to any of them if he so desires.

You may find a place in each day's work schedule to include this kind of journalizing. As a verbal exercise, it not only opens doors into your past, but also establishes a connection with the unconscious. If you are already in touch with your life as a child, it may not be necessary or important to keep such a journal; however, if you can afford the time, it is also a great way to acquire new choices for your work in scenes.

THE "I'M-FIVE-YEARS-OLD" JOURNAL

(It isn't necessary to date this kind of journal.)

"I'm five years old, and I . . . am sitting on my daddy's lap . . . He's bouncing me up and down . . . He blows up his cheeks with air, and I push the air out . . . I'm five years old, and I . . . am sitting at the table with all my brothers and sisters, and everybody is talking loud . . .

"I'm five years old, and I . . . feel alone with all these people around . . . I do things to get attention . . . but I don't get attention! I'm five years old, and I have a lot of toys . . . Everybody gets me toys . . . My father loves me, but my mother doesn't . . . I'm five years old, and I play in the backyard with the girl downstairs . . . She's Italian . . . Her name is Ida, same as my sister's. I'm five years old, and I live on the third floor . . . I don't like living up here . . . I like playing on the landing in the hallway . . . Danny and me . . . we play there all the time."

(This may comprise a single entry in the journal. It is important to allow many blank pages so that you can continue at another time.)

"I'm six years old, and I . . . start school . . . I'm in the first grade . . . I hate school . . . The teacher is so mean . . . I liked kindergarten much better . . . She doesn't let us play . . . We just do the abc's . . . I already know them . . . My sisters taught me! . . . I'm six years old, and all the other kids have young mothers who take them to school . . . My mother is old and it embarrasses me . . . I asked my older sister to take me to school . . . I didn't tell my mother why . . . She would be hurt . . . I like it when they bring the milk in class . . . I like chocolate milk . . . but my mom says it isn't good for me and to get white milk . . . I get chocolate anyway . . . I like it! . . . I want to be a milk boy and get the milk from the school kitchen . . . but the teacher says it is heavy, and she chooses the bigger boys . . . At home I drink coffee sometimes, and none of the other kids do . . . I have much older brothers and sisters, and that's why I can do a lot of things that they can't do."

Once you have established the journal and have been through the ages up to fourteen or fifteen, you can return and add a journal entry at any age.

Keeping a journal might at times feel like a task, and you may resist sitting down to make an entry, but after you have established a routine it will be like brushing your teeth every day. After a few short months of journal keeping, you will be able to look back over your entries, and you will be thrilled and amazed at how much you will gain from reading them.

CHARTS

A chart is to the actor what a building blueprint is to a contractor. It traces the step-by-step process by which he creates a role. It is a tool. Most actors are vague and confused about their process, if indeed they have one to begin with, but whatever you do to create the realities of a character in a play, you should have a clear day-to-day record of it. It keeps you focused and clear about what you have already done and about the next step you are going to take. If the actor has a process with which he has some degree of mastery, a chart is like a navigational map that traces his journey from the first leg right to his destination. As with all the techniques, there is a right way to do this. Once you learn the rules, you may take some liberties with any approach to make it your own, but first you must commit to doing it the way it is taught to you. There are essentially two kinds of charts: the obligation-choice-and-choice-approach chart and the continuity chart. Both are very important to the actor.

THE OBLIGATION-CHOICE-
AND-CHOICE-APPROACH CHART

As its title indicates, this chart is designed to create a visual map of your process of work in each scene of a play or film. The process I have created, which has its roots in the Stanislavsky system, is divided into three craft areas. Once the actor is instrumentally ready to approach the material and work with the craft, he has specific responsibilities and techniques to use in relation to that material. The three major categories of craft are:

A. **The Obligations,** the responsibilities of the material, what the actor must fulfill. There are seven main obligations that exist in material:
   1. *The time-and-place obligation* means that the actor must create the sense of a place which will stimulate in him emotional impulses which are similar to what the character in the piece feels about the place he is in. He must also deal with the time of day or year.
   2. *The relationship obligation* is the actor's obligation to create, through his process, the realities of his character's relationship to the other characters in the play.
   3. *The emotional obligation* is the actor's responsibility to create, through the use of his craft, a reality that parallels what the character feels in each scene of the play.
   4. *The character obligation* is the responsibility of the actor to stimulate physical, emotional, intellectual, and psychological parallels between himself and the character in the piece.
   5. *The historic obligation* relates to accomplishing the fulfillment of attitudes, customs, mores, and specific behaviors that are indigenous to a particular time in history.
   6. *The thematic obligation* relates to the statement of the play and the actor's obligation, through his behavior, to promote that statement.
   7. *The subtextual obligation* is the responsibility to the fabric of the play—the ambience, the feeling underlying all the relationships and behaviors of the characters. It relates to the essence, the quality of the piece. Each actor in a play must structure his work so that he contributes to that subtextual element.
B. **The Choices:** This part of the craft involves the objects the actor uses to stimulate the fulfillment of any or all of the seven main obligations. A choice can be almost anything: a person, a place, a piece of music, a photograph, a letter, odors of any kind, the weather—in short, a person, place, or thing. An actor uses a choice to stimulate a desired feeling, attitude, response, behavior, or relationship. The right choice will fulfill all of the main obligations.

C. **The Choice Approaches:** A choice approach is the pragmatic process through which the actor creates the choice. For example, suppose the actor is working with the time-and-place obligation. He chooses a place (the choice) and decides to use Sense Memory as his choice approach. By using the Sense-Memory process, he will create the place. At this very moment there are twenty-five choice approaches to fit every circumstance of material. At the completion of *Irreverent Acting,* my third book, there were only twenty-two, but since then three more have been added to the list (see chapter 6).

(For a much more detailed exploration and description of the three major parts of craft, refer to *Irreverent Acting.*)

When the actor is ready to identify the obligations in a scene and to begin the process of working to fulfill the responsibilities of the material, it is time to start work on the chart. It is a rare occurrence when all seven main obligations exist in a single piece of material. If, for example, the play or film is modern, there will be no need to deal with a historic obligation; and if there is no definable thematic statement in the framework of your character, that eliminates the thematic responsibility. So whatever the actor identifies as the obligations of his piece, he will choose to deal with them one at a time and in a logical chronology.

Usually, the first step is to begin with the place. It is important for the actor to create an environment. Doing this will stimulate the behavior and the emotional point of view of the character and take the actor off the stage and into the environment of the play. There are times when another obligation must be dealt with first, and in that case the actor should start his chart and his explorational journey with that specific obligation.

Structuring the chart is simple. You can use a notebook, the left-hand page of your script, or a collection of single sheets of paper. Draw two lines down the length of the paper, creating three separate columns. The left-hand column is for *obligations,* the middle column for *choices,* and the right-hand column for *choice approaches.* List your first obligation near the top of the left-hand column, and move to the center column to write down your first possible choice. After making that decision, list the choice approach near the top of the right-hand column. So at the beginning of the rehearsal journey you will only have a single entry in each column. As you explore the various choices and approaches, you will either draw a line through a particular choice and/or approach or underline it as the one you intend to use for the piece. If you are approaching two obligations in the same scene, you must of course list them under the scene number and work for each choice, one at a time.

Besides the indication of what each column is, there must be an identification of the act and scene number in each section of the chart. The obligation-choice-and-choice-approach chart is a working document that the actor uses as he explores the craftual possibilities for fulfilling the material. If he uses the empty left-hand page of his script, the chart will always be available with the material. This will enable him to have his "blueprint" next to the scene it applies to.

For example, let us say the obligation the actor decides to start with is the time and place. The script describes the place as the front yard of an old farm house where the character grew up as a boy. It is dilapidated and badly in need of repair. It is midmorning and the character has driven many miles to return to the scene of his youth. As he stands looking at the gaping hole where the front door used to be, he nostalgically recalls memories of his early life. The actor playing the part was brought up in a large urban area, and the closest he ever came to a farm was a picture in a magazine. Our actor identifies the impact of the farm on the character in the play and must make a choice which will stimulate similar thoughts and impulses for him. He decides to create the backyard of a house he lived in for about ten years as a young boy. He picks that choice because he recalls many of the same growing-up experiences as the character in the play.

In the left-hand column, under "Obligations," he writes "Act I Scene I" and lists his obligation: "Time and Place." He also writes an abbreviated description taken from the script. Directly across, in the middle column, he lists his "Choice": the backyard of the house on Monitor Avenue in Chicago. This is the personal place that the actor has decided to create in order to stimulate an inner organic life similar to that of the character. In the right-hand column, under "Choice Approaches," he will list the specific process he decides to use to create the choice, the backyard in Chicago. In this example, he decides to use Sense Memory.

OBLIGATIONS	CHOICES	CHOICE APPROACHES
Act I Scene I		
Time and Place:		
Farm house where he grew up; midmorning	Backyard at house on Monitor Ave. Chicago	Sense Memory

That is the way the chart would look at this point. In this instance there would also be an *emotional* obligation, since the place has such an impact on the character.

Emotional:		
Nostalgic, sad, a feeling of another and better time	Same as above, adding specific objects, like a dog, trees that I planted, etc.	Sense Memory, adding Evocative Words

The chart is constructed one obligation, one choice, and one approach at a time. As the actor creates each choice and decides on its effectiveness, he will either underline it, verifying it as permanent, as shown below:

Act I Scene I

Time and Place:

Farm house where he grew up; midmorning	<u>Backyard at house on Monitor Ave. Chicago</u>	<u>Sense Memory</u>

or, if the actor decides to scrap it for whatever reason, he will draw a line through it, being careful not to obliterate the writing since today's discard may be tomorrow's treasure, and immediately under it he will write another possibility:

Act I Scene I

Time and Place:

Farm house where he grew up; midmorning	~~Backyard at house on Monitor Ave. Chicago~~	~~Sense Memory~~
	Boy-Scout camp . . . in the woods	Sensory Suggestion and Inner Monologue

As he changes the place he must make an adjustment with his choices related to the emotional obligation of Act I Scene I.

Emotional:

Nostalgic, sad, a feeling of another and better time	~~Same as above, adding specific objects, like a dog, trees that I planted, etc.~~	~~Sense Memory, adding Evocative Words~~
	Specific people present at that time in that place	Imaginary Monologues to those people

There might be additional obligations in Act I Scene I, or that may be the extent of the responsibilities in that scene. If it is, the actor now has documentation of what he did in the rehearsals and of what worked and what didn't! He can also move into the next scene with the confidence that he will remember exactly what he did and where to return to in the next rehearsal. It is important to note here that it might be advantageous to him if he wrote a few comments about why he discarded one choice for another, how that first choice affected him, and why it seemed wrong for the material. By doing this, he creates a built-in reference of his specific experiences with a particular choice, which will enable him to make decisions about using it in the future under other circumstances.

In Scene 2 of the play, an old boyhood friend, seeing our hero, comes over to talk to him. He has visibly aged and appears much older than the main character.

OBLIGATIONS	CHOICES	CHOICE APPROACHES
Act I Scene 2		
Relationship:		
Boyhood friend. Character is somewhat shocked and saddened by the ravages of time and his friend's level of consciousness (he attempts to cover it).	My cousin, with whom I grew up (perfect parallel)	Sensory Endowment (the actor has slight resemblance to cousin)

In this example the actor chose a cousin for whom he has very similar feelings. Recently, on a trip home, he visited his cousin only to discover him old and sickly, his consciousness almost the same as it was twenty years ago. He had the same values and priorities and a total lack of knowledge about how to preserve his health. The choice in this case addresses the relationship responsibility of both who this person is to the character and of how he feels about him, so it really fills the bill. After exploring it in rehearsal, the actor decides to use it and underlines it.

My cousin with whom I grew up	Sensory Endowment

In the next scene, the actor confronts the character obligation. The character is very rich.

Act I Scene 3

Character:

Secure and benevolent with a mature sense of life. Feels well-off.	A certain combination of clothing, a specific jacket, a very expensive wristwatch	Objects That Come into Contact with the Body

After attempting to work for the above choices, the actor decides that they don't stimulate the benevolence or maturity, only the sense of being well-off and a little pomposity.

Character:

| Secure and benevolent with a mature sense of life. Feels well-off. | ~~A certain combination of clothing, a specific jacket, a very expensive wristwatch~~ | ~~Objects That Come into Contact with the Body~~ |
| | The feeling after one glass of a particular wine, and my son | Sense Memory Imaginary Monologue to my son (approached through inner-monologue technique) |

After trying the alternate choices and approaches, the actor feels much more on the track of the character-element obligation. He decides that the sensorial response to the wine makes him feel mellow and secure, while working to relate to his son makes him feel loving, benevolent, and mature. It also stimulates an affection for the other character in the play.

| The feeling after one glass of a particular wine, and my son | Sense Memory Imaginary Monologue to my son (approached through inner-monologue technique) |

The chart should be constructed with an eye to keeping it simple, legible, and clear.

This is the way the composite chart should look to the actor after he has decided which of the choices to use in each scene:

OBLIGATIONS	CHOICES	CHOICE APPROACHES
Act I Scene I		
Time and Place:		
Farm house where he grew up; midmorning	~~Backyard at house on Monitor Ave. Chicago~~	~~Sense Memory~~
	Boy-Scout camp . . . in the woods	Sensory Suggestion and Inner Monologue
Emotional:		
Nostalgic, sad, a feeling of another and better time	~~Same as above, adding specific objects like a dog, trees that I planted, etc.~~	~~Sense Memory, adding Evocative Words~~
	Specific people present at that time in that place	Imaginary Monologues to those people

Act I Scene 2

Relationship:

Boyhood friend. Character is somewhat shocked and saddened by the ravages of time and his friend's level of consciousness (he attempts to cover it).	My cousin, with whom I grew up (perfect parallel)	Sensory Endowment (the actor has slight resemblance to cousin)

Act I Scene 3

Character:

Secure and benevolent with a mature sense of life. Feels well-off.	A certain combination of clothing, a specific jacket, a very expensive wristwatch	Objects That Come into Contact with the Body
	The feeling after one glass of a particular wine, and my son	Sense Memory Imaginary Monologue to my son (approached through inner-monologue technique)

An actor may have many choices listed and rejected in the choice column. The important thing is not to construct a chart but to fulfill the material! Just be sure that you can read what you enter on the chart. If the actor finds it necessary to move things around—if, for example, he decides that he must work with the character obligation before the time and place—he might just transpose the obligations on the same sheet by drawing arrows indicating the order in which he will approach them. Another option the actor has is to make a four-column chart, using the fourth column for remarks.

OBLIGATIONS	CHOICES	CHOICE APPROACHES	REMARKS
Time and Place: Farm house	Backyard, Chicago	Sense Memory	Didn't work! Too many bad memories. Had a lot of conflict with the neighborhood kids.

The advantage of a fourth column is that you can keep the chart from getting cluttered. The disadvantage is that it seriously cuts down on the amount of space you have in each column.

N.B. If you have too many obligations in one scene, it would be wise to number them:

Act I Scene I

1. *Time and Place:*
   Farm house
2. *Emotional:*
   Nostalgic, sad
3. *Relationship:*
   Boyhood friend
4. *Character:*
   Secure, benevolent

THE CONTINUITY CHART

This chart traces the action of a piece of material from the first line through to the end of the play. If he structures it properly, the actor can tell at a glance what happened just before the scene he is about to do and what will happen immediately afterwards. It might sound strange and a little redundant to structure a chart when all you have to do is refer to the script! Well, if only it were that simple! But if every time an actor was called on to do a scene in a film, he had to run to the script, feverishly pore over the pages to find the right scene and then read the one preceding it, that would be very laborious and wouldn't always tell him clearly what he wanted to know.

There are a number of reasons for keeping a continuity chart: it helps the actor to structure the *flow* of the material. He can draw a through line of the action and emotional life of his character in the script. What happens in one scene affects the emotional life of the following scene. Knowing what the character is feeling and doing from one scene to another, the actor can always do the "right" preparation before any particular scene. By being aware of the evolution of his character's emotional life and behavior, he will also be able to make choices that promote that evolution. How many times have you seen a film where the character's behavior doesn't seem to make any sense? He doesn't seem to change from scene to scene or to learn anything from earlier experiences. Since films are shot out of sequence, two connecting scenes may be shot weeks apart. Once I saw a film where the best friend of the leading character was killed in one scene, but in the very next scene, in a different location, that character was relating to someone with no trace of any feeling for his friend who had just died! If that actor had had a continuity chart, he couldn't possibly have disregarded the death of his best friend! The choices an actor makes in relation to the responsibility of any scene must definitely be influenced by what preceded that scene. If in one scene the character has been experiencing grief over the loss of a parent, and in the following scene he is talking to his son about the boy's future, the actor would either need a preparation to carry the grief into that second scene, or he would have to allow for it in the choices he used.

The chart gives an actor a complete overview of how his character changes, evolves, and relates to the other characters. It signals the need for adjustments in his choices to accommodate aging and the transitions from act to act. It allows him to approach his role as a whole and integral part of a larger piece rather than as a kind of piecemeal reality. An actor can be quite good in each scene in which he appears but lack cohesiveness as a real person in the overall picture.

Creating a Continuity Chart

This chart too can be kept in a separate notebook or on the blank pages of a script. Starting with the first scene and detailing briefly the action and behavior in each scene, the actor describes the entire play or screenplay as if he were doing a synopsis of it.

Scene 1:

Joe (my character) comes home from Vietnam. He is happy to be home, but he is disoriented, sullen. He tries to relate openly and with affection to his family, his girl, but it is obvious that there is inner turmoil.

Scene 2:

Joe, alone in his old room, looking at his things, awards, etc., breaks down, sobs on the bed, uncontrollably.

Scenes 3 through 7:

Are a variety of scenes between Joe's parents and his brother. He isn't in any of those scenes. However, he is discussed. They are all concerned with how he appears. His brother assures them that in a short time he will be O.K. His father thinks it might be a good idea if Joe had some therapy.

Scene 8:

Joe is at the dinner table. Everyone seems happy and cheerful. Joe is trying to get involved in the lighter spirit of things, but we can see it is an effort. His brother, his mother and father, and his girlfriend are obviously pushing it in an attempt to lift his spirits. He knows what they are doing and is fighting resentment about it.

Scenes 9 through 12:

Are a montage of people talking, laughing, joking, eating, passing plates around the table. We see Joe hanging back and his tension building.

Scene 13:

Joe gets up to leave the table, and his mother questions why he is excusing himself. He attempts a lame excuse, and his brother and girlfriend try to get him to stay. He explodes, telling them that he can't see life as a party. Too many guys are lying out there dead, and "all you people act as if it never happened!" He storms out of the room.

Scene 14:

They all sit silently at the table, very disturbed about Joe. His mother starts to clear the table and begins to cry.

Scene 15:

Joe reenters, sees his mother crying. He is feeling bad, sorry about the scene he caused and inept at expressing his complex and conglomerated feelings. He goes to his mother and holds her. He tries to say something, and the only thing he can manage to express is, "I'm sorry!" Fade out.

Scene 16:

Joe, in a Veterans Administration Counseling Office. From the dialogue it seems that he has been here for some time, maybe an hour. He is frustrated with the doctor, who is doing most of the talking. Joe attempts to interject something every once in a while, and it is obvious that the doctor is somewhat patronizing toward him. The doctor finally asks him what he is feeling, and Joe begins to stammer, unable to express his feelings. He feels helpless, frustrated, and alone. He tells the doctor that nobody seems to know or care about what went on over there! The doctor offers him a prescription for tranquilizers. Joe gets angry at him and tells him that the solution to his problem is not to become a zombie! He storms out of the office.

Scenes 17 through 31:

Are a montage (no dialogue) of Joe walking through the city streets looking at people doing their thing. We see him stop and look in shop windows, see children playing. *He seems to be searching for something.* As the scenes progress, he becomes more and more frenetic; his pace quickens; his movements are fragmented.

Scenes 32, 33, 34:

Joe is back at his high-school football field, looking at the stands, and he intermittently hears the roar of an excited crowd. We see him for the first time as he might have been before Vietnam. He looks at the field and we can see that he is in another time. He looks ten years younger and has a slight glint of happiness in his eyes.

Scene 35:

Joe walking mid-field. Suddenly, we hear a truck backfire. Joe hits the ground and is back in the war. We see him in a jungle setting with explosions all around. He is filled with the anguish that men get in combat.

Scene 36:

Joe crawls right into the body of one of his buddies who is obviously dead, open eyes staring skyward and seeing nothing. Joe goes wild. He embraces his friend, sobbing, jumps up, and starts shooting his rifle in all directions.

Scenes 37 and 38:

We see a man standing in the bleachers, his point of view on Joe. Long view of Joe in civilian clothes behaving as if he were in combat. The man calls to him.

Scene 39:

Joe, hearing the man's voice, stops, looks around, sees the man, and is brought back to the present. Somewhat disoriented, he looks around and is back on the football field.

Scene 40:

The man approaching Joe on the field.

Scene 41:

Joe recognizes his high-school football coach. They walk toward each other.

Scene 42:

We see them (long view) embrace and talk, although we can't hear what they are saying. Joe seems emotional and excited.

Scene 43:

The coach's office. Joe and the coach talking. Joe's spirits are higher, and for the first time we see a spark of hope in his behavior.

Scene 44:

On Joe talking about how hard the adjustment has been! He tells the coach how guilty he feels to be alive when most of his buddies have been killed. He's angry at the people around him for their apathetic attitude about the war.

Scene 45:

The coach tries to explain the separation of the people from the war: how they weren't involved and how it wasn't real to them; it was like a late-night movie on T.V. He obviously cares for Joe.

Scene 46:

Joe in his bedroom late at night. We see a .45-Caliber automatic pistol on the bedside table. Joe is smoking, distraught. He utters a sound like a wounded animal. He picks up the gun and looks at it.

Scene 47:

Holding the gun close to his temple. We see his struggle. He can't do it and throws the gun on the bed. Lays his head into the pillow and begins to sob.

Scenes 48 through 56:

A series of cuts in a group-therapy session. There is a leader and about ten or twelve Vietnam vets talking. We hear each of them relate his feelings about being back home. There seems to be a common theme among them.

Scene 57:

We see Joe sitting in the circle, listening. He seems involved and relaxed, almost as if he felt at home here.

Scene 58:

The group leader, a therapist, talks about dealing with the problem of facing society again and letting go of the war and about how they must all deal with the ignorance of the people who weren't in the conflict.

Scene 59:

Close on Joe. He raises his hand and is acknowledged. He talks about the overwhelming feelings of guilt, related not only to his dead buddies, but to what they did over there. He is angry and is also making a plea for help.

Scenes 60 through 65:

A series of shots on the men in the group offering their opinions and feelings. There seems to be a similar energy among all of them.

Scene 66:

Joe's mother and his girlfriend having coffee in the kitchen of Joe's house. His girlfriend, Meg, talks about her fears for Joe and her insecurities about having any future with him. Joe's mother urges her to be patient with him and asks her if she loves him.

Scenes 67 and 68:

We see Joe and Meg in bed together. It is obvious that they have just experienced an unsuccessful attempt at making love. Joe (close-up), tortured, unable to talk to Meg, tries to say something but can't. Meg puts her hand on his head and tells him that it doesn't mean anything and that it's like recovering from an auto accident; it takes time.

Scene 69:

Interior of a church. We see Joe, Meg, and Joe's father and mother in the third row of benches listening to the minister. Joe is listening but not involved.

Scene 70:

The minister, talking about the will of God, tells the congregation that God gave man free will to do what he must do and that because man does not have the wisdom of God, he makes mistakes and creates evil on the earth. He talks about why there is disease and war and about the seemingly senseless destruction of innocent people. He tells his flock that this is man's will, not God's.

Scene 71:

Joe starting to become interested in what the minister is saying. We see a flicker of discovery in his eyes.

Scenes 72 through 80:

A series of shots of Joe in a military cemetery. We see the endless rows of crosses dating back to the First World War. Joe walks among them, stopping occasionally to look at the inscriptions. We see him close up. He is moved by what he sees.

Scene 81:

Joe's point of view on a grave marker too new to have a permanent headstone yet.

Scene 82:

Close-up on marker: the name: Harry Gilford, corporal U.S. Army, killed March 5, 1966; the place: Vietnam.

Scene 83:

Close-up on Joe, who obviously knew this man. Talks to him. Tells him how sorry he is it all happened this way and that he would bring him back if he could. He tells Harry that the only thing he can do for him is to go on with his own life and that by doing that he is making some sense of what his survival is all about. He also tells him that as long as he lives, Harry will be alive in his memories and thoughts and that, if it had been the other way around, he hopes that Harry would have done the same for him.

In this hypothetical continuity chart, I have tried to create a structure where everything is described from the point of view of a single character. The chart includes the action in each scene, as well as the character's emotional life and relationships. It briefly draws a picture of the character as he moves from scene to scene, thus tracing his evolution throughout the entire script. By reading the chart, the actor can see what emotional state the character has just experienced in the preceding scene and what will follow in the next one. Since the chart also explains what has taken place in the scenes where his character does not appear, the actor can make the necessary adjustments to allow for those intervals. In short, an actor can see at a glance what his preparative responsibilities are and can follow the through line of the material with a logical continuity of behavior and emotional life.

Included in a continuity chart are:

1. The scene numbers
2. A brief description of the action of the scene (what takes place)
3. A list of the other characters in each scene and of your character's relationship to them
4. A brief but specific description of the feelings, actions, and emotions of your character and of how they change or are affected
5. In the scenes where your character does not appear, a report of anything that the others say about him.

In conjunction with an obligation-choice-and-choice-approach chart, a continuity chart enables an actor to always know where he is and what he must do to fulfill the responsibilities of the material. If you create the two types of charts for every role that you do on the stage or in front of a camera, you will always have a specific outline of your responsibilities in each scene. You needn't have the lead in a film or a play in order to create a chart. Even if you only have a couple of scenes, the charts will prove invaluable to you.

5

CHARACTERIZATION

So much has been said and written about characterization! The word itself has taken on many meanings and interpretations and has even become synonymous with acting. Actually, characterization is the actor's involvement in creating the life of a character in a play or film. The *character obligation* is one of the seven main obligations of material.

I think that the entire concept of characterization has been distorted! The popular concept misleads the actor into wearing the cloak of another person, becoming "someone else." Most actors are taught to separate themselves from the character they are playing. From the beginning they relate on the level of "the character does this, the character is that; he feels . . ." instead of starting with a unity between themselves and that character.

A character in a piece of material is a person, male or female. If a playwright based a character on you and your life, and if the words and actions of the play further described you—your psychological makeup, your personality, and so on—then *you* would be the character in that play that some actor somewhere would be attempting to create. The character is a person; you are a person! There are similarities and dissimilarities between you, but the basic reality is that if you are going to "play" that character, then you *are* that character. An actor must never create a gap between himself and the character he is about to play. When he does that, it separates him from his willingness to believe that what is happening to the character is actually happening to *him!*

For generations, the popular concept and the belief in the theater has been that "the actor becomes the character." This is taken to mean that the actor assumes or acquires the behavior, idiosyncrasies, thoughts, and impulses of a particular character in a play. But I believe that the reverse is true: *the character becomes you!* If, for example, the character is a person very much like you physically, intellectually, and emotionally, then you don't have to do anything in relation to the character obligation except be who you are and express your feelings and impulses through the lines of the play.

Even a brilliant playwright can only write so many words to create and describe a character; for no matter how many words he does use, he will fall short of being able to totally describe a multidimensional human being. You are already a living, breathing, multidimensional person with many facets, colors, complexities, and so on. So if you absorb the character into yourself, then that character in that piece will take on the reality and the unique individuality of who you are. After identifying the specific components of a particular character, you can use your craft to pique those same aspects of personality in yourself, encouraging them to rise to the surface and become the predominant behavioral traits of the character. In addition, all the other complex elements that make you multidimensional and an unpredictable, interesting human being will also become part of that character. In short, when you absorb the character into your person, all that you are in terms of your unique way of relating to the world, your impulses, thoughts, and responses, will be included in everything he does. It is thus that an actor makes a unique and personal statement through every part he plays. Twelve actors could play the same role, and it would be different and unique each time.

In order to fulfill his responsibility to the playwright, an actor must identify the elements of a specific character and be true to the author's intention. It is important to note here that even though you include your personal impulses in every part you play, you must never violate the playwright's depiction of the character. However, you must ask yourself the question: is it not possible for this character in this situation to respond as I did in that scene? If the answer is yes, then I believe you are within the perimeters of acceptability.

WHAT IS CHARACTER?

It is the manifestation of the human condition and of human behavior. It is what a person is, physically, emotionally, intellectually, and psychologically; how he relates, walks, talks, thinks, and expresses himself; the type of person he is; what his specific idiosyncratic behavior might be. In a play, a character is a specific kind of person.

FINDING THE CLUES TO THE CHARACTER

When an actor picks up a script to read it, there are several specific things he should look for to find out who the character is:

1. What the author says about the character, his description of the character
2. What the other characters in the play say to or about the character
3. What the character says about himself

4. The actions and interactions of the character, his activities, involvements and idiosyncratic behavior—what he does!

The information gathered from these sources enables the actor to put together a picture of the character. Not all playwrights describe their characters. Many of them allow the play and the activities and behavior of the character to reveal who he or she is. However, if it is a fairly well-written piece of material, there will be plenty of information that you can use to build that character in you.

WHAT THE AUTHOR SAYS ABOUT THE CHARACTER

At the opening of *A Streetcar Named Desire,* by Tennessee Williams, there is a brief description of Blanche as she enters:

> "Her appearance is incongruous to this setting. She is daintily dressed in a white suit with a fluffy bodice, necklace and earrings of pearl, white gloves and hat, looking as if she were arriving at a summer tea or cocktail party in the garden district. She is about five years older than Stella. Her delicate beauty must avoid a strong light. There is something about her uncertain manner, as well as her white clothes, that suggests a moth."

The description is brief, but rich in information. We know that Blanche is delicate and aging, and Williams tells us that she is "uncertain" in her manner. His suggestion of a moth is an incredible clue for the actress. It gives her a feeling for the essence of Blanche.

Naturally, as the action of the play unfolds, the facets of Blanche's very complex character become obvious. However, the author's initial description is a good place for the actress to start her exploration of the character. She might begin by getting a sense of a moth through the use of the Externals Choice approach. Of course, there will be times when an actor will start with the author's description but later discard it or replace it with more impelling alternatives.

At the beginning of *Death of a Salesman* by Arthur Miller, there are brief descriptions of Willy Loman and of his wife Linda, which create an almost palpable fabric of the man and the woman:

> "From the right, Willy Loman, the Salesman, enters, carrying two large sample cases. The flute plays on. He hears it but is not aware of it. He is past sixty years of age, dressed quietly. Even as he crosses the stage to the doorway of the house, his exhaustion is apparent. He unlocks the door, comes into the kitchen, and thankfully lets his burden down, feeling the

soreness of his palms. A word-sigh escapes his lips—it might be 'Oh, boy, oh, boy.'"

Miller's talent with words allows him to paint a picture of Willy as a stooped man who is overworked and overburdened with life. We know his age and his emotional state and get a sense of his life.

Immediately after this description of Willy, Miller talks about his wife, Linda:

"Most often jovial, she has developed an iron repression of her exceptions to Willy's behavior—she more than loves him, she admires him, as though his mercurial nature, his temper, his massive dreams and little cruelties, served her only as sharp reminders of the turbulent longings within him, longings which she shares but lacks the temperament to utter and follow to their end."

In addition to telling us what kind of person Linda is, this passage also gives us more information about Willy and about the relationship between the two. A few pages later, Miller draws a brief character sketch of Biff and Happy:

"Biff is two years older than his brother Happy, well built, but in these days bears a worn air and seems less self-assured. He has succeeded less, and his dreams are stronger and less acceptable than Happy's. Happy is tall, powerfully made. Sexuality is like a visible color on him, or a scent that many women have discovered. He, like his brother, is lost, but in a different way, for he has never allowed himself to turn his face toward defeat and is thus more confused and hard-skinned, although seemingly more content."

In *Beyond Therapy*, Christopher Durang thus describes the character Bruce:

"He claims he is bisexual; and it is absolutely essential that he truly be that, absolutely 50-50. He should be attracted to women and to men; he should not be a homosexual who is kidding himself and trying to pretend to be heterosexual ... He should truly find Prudence attractive; he should truly want to be married with children in Connecticut, and he should truly find Bob and the gas man attractive and emotionally appealing as well. As Bruce says 'We have to accept contradictions in ourselves'; that is a wise statement on some level, yet in Bruce's life his blithe acceptance of his duality is clearly creating chaos. He wants things to work out and with a kind of blind optimism he just somehow believes that if he keeps meaning well and trying to be nice to everyone it will all work out. He is not very logical, but he's very innocent. If ever he were to be knowing or calculating, the play would change and be nasty."

Prudence, in the same play, must:

"Simultaneously be more than commonly intelligent . . . and yet be sufficiently uncertain of herself and vulnerable that she lets herself get into a stupid relationship with a macho-fool psychiatrist, and entertains a rather unlikely liaison with Bruce because he touches certain buttons of hers . . ."

Each of the above descriptions contain pieces of a jigsaw puzzle that will come together and finally draw a clear picture for the actor who is trying to create one of these characters. At this point he is collecting knowledge of the component parts of the character. If he goes to the next area of exploration, he can gather more information that will help him to sculpt himself into that character. Once he has accumulated all the information that the material will yield, he will be able, through a craft process, to build the realities of the character by absorbing these different elements into his own personality structure and surrounding them with the impulses, responses, thoughts, and dimensions that he already possesses as a person, thereby breathing life into the inert group of words that are meant to draw the image of a human being in a play. Later on in this chapter, I will show you how to use the craft to create the organic behavior of a character through your own instrument.

WHAT THE OTHER CHARACTERS SAY TO OR ABOUT THE CHARACTER

The dialogue in any piece of material supplies further information about, and clues to, the character. Pay close attention to what each of the other characters in a piece says about the one in question, how they relate directly to him, and what they do that supplies further clues to the type of person he is.

To illustrate, let us return to the example of *Beyond Therapy*. In the scene between Bruce and Prudence at the beginning of the play, Bruce tells Prudence that she's afraid of life, and she doesn't deny it. She, in turn, accuses Bruce of being insane, strange, and gay. So, in addition to what the author has told us about these two, they themselves go on to fill in the blanks with their dialogue.

The bedroom scene between Biff and Happy near the beginning of *Death of a Salesman* also gives us clues to the characters:

BIFF: (Talking to Happy) I bet you forgot how bashful you used to be. Especially with girls.

HAPPY: Oh, I still am, Biff.

BIFF: Oh, go on.

HAPPY: I just control it, that's all. I think I got less bashful and you got more so. What happened, Biff? Where's the old humor, the old confidence? . . . What's the matter?

Just a few lines of dialogue between the brothers, and an actor researching the character of Biff already knows enough about the contrast between how Biff used to be and how he is now. As the scene progresses, there is a lot more that we find out about the two brothers.

About midway through the play, Linda talks to Biff and Happy about Willy:

"He drives seven hundred miles, and when he gets there no one knows him any more, no one welcomes him. And what goes through a man's mind, driving seven hundred miles home without having earned a cent? Why shouldn't he talk to himself? Why? When he has to go to Charley and borrow fifty dollars a week and pretend to me that it's his pay? How long can that go on? How long? . . . And you tell me he has no character?"

Here we experience one character talking about another to still others in the play. This reveals additional facets of Willy Loman's character, as well as letting us know how Linda feels about him. All through most well-written plays, there is a wealth of material that, like a collection of millions of human cells, gives birth to the reality of the character.

It is not enough that an actor read a play or screenplay. He must know what to look for and also how to interpret and use what he discovers. For instance, what the other characters say to or about his character is an indication of what he is like, but from their own personal point of view. Remember that each character in a piece of material has his own prejudices and subjectivities. If, however, there is a through line or a pattern in the way a specific character is observed by the others, then the actor knows that there is some objective truth in what they say.

WHAT THE CHARACTER SAYS ABOUT HIMSELF

There are hundreds of examples of characters in plays who introspectively or retrospectively express things about their lives in endless monologues. Almost every piece of dramatic literature has at least one of those self-exposing monologues. It is in their content that the actor can gather further information, which will help him to construct the component parts of the character.

In the bedroom scene between Biff and Happy mentioned above, Biff has a fairly long monologue in response to Happy's question as to whether he is content out there on the farm. He starts with, "Hap, I've had twenty or thirty different kinds of jobs since I left home before the war . . ." and goes on to expose some very important things about himself: his confusion, his insecurities, and his conflict about pursuing "the American dream." He alludes to the fact that he has been a drifter and a day worker, ambling around the country looking for himself. He also exposes a value system which is entirely different from the one Willy shoved down their throats. In this passage, we learn a great deal about Biff and later on find out why these conflicts exist and where they started.

In the play 'night, Mother, by Marsha Norman, the character of Jessie has a wonderful monologue where she attempts to communicate the reason why she has decided to kill herself. It starts with "I am what became of your child . . ." and goes on to dramatically expose a life filled with disappointment and failure. The one line near the end of the monologue almost sums up her entire feeling about her life. She talks about herself as "Somebody I waited for who never came. And never will."

Near the end of Eugene O'Neill's Long Day's Journey into Night, Tyrone has a long, self-justifying monologue about what his life was like when he was younger. He is talking to his son Edmund and in his own manner rationalizing his miserliness. The monologue is very exposing. He talks about learning the value of a dollar and about his fear of the "poorhouse." He tells Edmund the importance of owning property and exposes his fear of losing everything. He goes on to contrast his life with all the advantages that Edmund has had. The line, "You said you realized what I'd been up against as a boy. The hell you do!" is the thrust of the monologue.

It is in all the things that a character says, as well as in what the author says, that the actor must seek the blueprint to the character. He must also read between the lines. For example, Tyrone is justifying his penuriousness to Edmund in a very righteous way, but his stinginess is actually a result of his feelings of insecurity and is neither righteous nor attractive. The actor approaching the role would need to find a subjective way to stimulate the kind of insecurity that would lead to the same type of rationale.

THE ACTIONS AND INTERACTIONS
OF THE CHARACTER

This is perhaps the most important way to find out who and what a character is. It deals with what he does: his actions, his mannerisms, and the way he interacts with the other characters. Through this, the actor can really understand the inner impulses of the character, although there are exceptions to that also; for example, Iago in Shakespeare's *Othello* says certain things, but his actions are quite antithetical to his words. He poses as a friend, speaks with compassion and support, while his actions prove him to be Othello's enemy. When an actor identifies such contradictions in a character, he must explore the character's actions to find out what impels him to behave in such a way. At the bottom of these actions he will discover the impetus that will give him the necessary information about the character.

In addition to *actions and interactions,* the personal behavior of the character—that is to say his habits, idiosyncrasies, and mannerisms—further affords glimpses into his individual fabric. A twitch, a stammer or some other speech difficulty, a fetish, the habit he may have of stroking his beard—all that a character says and does supplies clues to his structure and the kind of person he is.

Some Examples

Cyrano de Bergerac exposes his character in everything he does. He is a romantic and shows that throughout the play. He is also an expert swordsman and a poet.

Nora, in Ibsen's *A Doll's House,* finally stands up for herself and takes action; she leaves Torvald. It was "the door slam heard around the world," a statement made for all women, the first example of a woman standing up for herself.

Electra hangs around her mother while all the time plotting her death and waiting for her brother to do the deed.

Tom in *The Glass Menagerie* writes poetry on almost anything, including the lids of shoe boxes at the warehouse where he works.

Rex in *Lunchtime* spends his entire time attempting to seduce Mavis. All of his actions are centered around coming on to her.

In *Death of a Salesman* Biff avoids the women in the restaurant and won't relate to them.

The character Al in *In the Boom Boom Room* beats up Chrissy. He is violent and abuses her.

Blanche in *"Streetcar"* puts a shade over the light in her room and throughout the entire play avoids strong and direct light.

Billy Budd is hung in the play by the same name because he cannot defend himself on account of a stammer and an inability to communicate.

The character of Captain Queeg in *The Caine Mutiny Court Martial* has a habit of fondling ball bearings—which later proves to be the manifestation of a psychological problem.

You have all seen characters in films who keep repeating the same activities or actions throughout: physical types who are always lifting weights or squeezing handballs to strengthen their arms; self-involved, egocentric characters who are always priming and looking in the mirror; psycho types who play with a switchblade knife from scene to scene, and so on.

Each of the four areas of investigation yields fragments and colors that help an actor "piece together" the character. These clues constitute the armature on which he can build the character. Furnished with enough pieces, he can then go to himself and begin working with his craft.

THE FOUR PARTS OF CHARACTER

Once an actor has accumulated all the information about a character, he then makes it even clearer for himself by breaking it down into four separate areas. He does this, not only to get a better understanding of the character, but also to clarify his own work in terms of the craft approach he will use.

The four areas are the *physical,* the *emotional,* the *intellectual,* and the *psychological.* In order to clearly discern what the specific characteristics in each area are, the actor may want to chart the information he has gathered. However, in this case, a chart is drawn purely for convenience and clarity and is not a necessity.

Let us start with the *physical* characteristics, using as an example the character of Happy in *Death of a Salesman.* He is described as "tall, powerfully made. Sexuality is like a visible color on him, or a scent that many women have discovered." Thanks to this description, an actor can begin the process of creating those physical characteristics in relation to himself. The physical responsibility includes all of the character's movements, his demeanor, his actions, and his use of his body. Laura, in *Glass Menagerie,* walks with a noticeable limp. She wears a brace on her leg and is self-conscious about her handicap. In *A Streetcar Named Desire,* Stanley is described as being "of medium height, about five feet eight or nine, and strongly, compactly built. Animal joy in his being is implicit in all his movements and attitudes." Maggie, in *Cat on a Hot Tin Roof,* is "A pretty young woman with anxious lines in her face. . . . (Her) voice is both rapid and drawling. In her long speeches she has the vocal tricks of a priest delivering a liturgical chant, the lines are almost sung, always continuing a little beyond her breath so she has to gasp for another." Martha, in Edward Albee's *Who's Afraid of Virginia Woolf,* is "a large, boisterous woman, fifty-two, looking somewhat younger. Ample, but not fleshy." In William Inge's *Loss of Roses,* Helen Baird is described as a "tired-looking woman who long ago gave up her youth and no longer strives to make herself sexually attractive" while Lila "is an extraordinarily beautiful woman of thirty-two, blond and voluptuous, still with the form and vitality of a girl." All of the authors' descriptions quoted in an earlier section of this chapter give us indications about the physical attributes of the characters.

The *emotional* area encompasses the way the character relates in an overall sense—his or her emotional fabric. For example, a character may be described as sullen and introverted, another referred to as volatile and hostile by nature. "She is almost always jovial"; "she is gregarious and outgoing"; "she speaks haltingly and seems unsure about everything"—these are all indications of the emotional nature of an individual. Whatever the psychological impetus for any manifestation of a person's emotional fabric might be, it is indeed that fabric that is revealed whenever he expresses himself.

The *intellectual* area refers to how intelligent or unintelligent the character is and how he uses or doesn't use that intelligence. It also relates to his education, his intellectual station in life, his use of language, and his ability to communicate from the specific level of his intelligence. The killers in the play *Rope* and in the novel and film *Compulsion* were extremely intelligent, but psychotic. The gifted Cyrano de Bergerac expressed his intellect in the poetry he wrote and the words he spoke. The intellectual powers of the famous Sherlock Holmes are legendary and have become the symbol for deductive reasoning. Elementary, my dear reader!

A character's intellect is manifested in the way he relates to every other individual in the piece. An actor must investigate the character's intelligence if he wishes to fulfill all the elements of that character.

Another important component to consider is the *psychological* nature of a person in a piece of material—his essential psychological makeup. Would he or she be considered well-adjusted or disturbed? Does he display more than the normal amount of insecurities? Is she subject to paranoia? suspicious by nature? unstable? There have been a multitude of plays or films in which the main character was impelled to action by the overwhelming nature of his psychological state. Adolf Hitler is a prime example of a complex human being who has been dramatized countless numbers of times. An actor approaching this character would certainly have to deal with the man's paranoia, his deep-seated hatreds, and his megalomania! What are the component parts of this kind of psychological state? The man was, after all, quite intelligent!

The character of Danny in the play *Night Must Fall*, by Emlyn Williams, is an incredibly disturbed person, who goes around killing middle-aged women and saving their heads, which he carries around in a hatbox. During the course of the play it becomes obvious that he has felt abused by people, most particularly by older women who he feels have denigrated and humiliated him. Possibly, it started with his own mother. Here is yet another dramatic example of a leading character who is motivated to action by his psychological state.

A prime example of a character steeped in psychological problems and complexities is Hamlet. Here we have an individual with a very complex belief structure. Ernest Jones wrote a book exploring Hamlet's obvious Oedipus complex. His compelling need for revenge, his religious beliefs, which keep him from killing Claudius at prayer, and his paranoia in relation to Rosencrantz and Guildenstern create quite an interesting psychological structure for the actor to deal with.

CHARTING A CHARACTER IN THESE AREAS

Let us use a hypothetical character:

PHYSICAL	EMOTIONAL	INTELLECTUAL	PSYCHOLOGICAL
Young, tall, and attractive. Nice relationship to, and acceptance of, his body	His ambition tends to make him hyper. He expresses himself at very high emotional R.P.M.'s	Better than average, but pushes his expression in this area beyond his endowments.	Feels like he is not enough; lives in the shadow of a very successful father whom he could never please.

The characterization chart is a very good way to start. It identifies the actor's responsibility to the character obligation and allows him to build that character in relation to his own instrument. To make things a little easier, the actor can include characterization into the obligation-choice-and-choice-approach chart. The emotional character obligation constitutes the foundation of that character's emotional fabric, but as the emotional obligations vary from scene to scene, all of the choices that the actor uses to fulfill those individual scene obligations will have to affect the character's emotional structure listed at the top of the chart.

CHARACTERS IN KNOWN MATERIAL

For the sake of real clarity and understanding of the concepts of characterization, I am going to identify the component parts of two characters in well-known plays, using all four areas to do so.

Let us start with the character of George in Who's Afraid of Virginia Woolf, by Edward Albee:

Physically: George is middle-aged and not in trim condition. He drinks too much and does not exercise. His lack of success and happiness probably expresses itself in his posture and physical essence.

Emotionally: George has not given in to Martha, but he certainly has no illusions about attaining great success at this time in his life. He is resigned and sarcastic and probably spends time being depressed.

Intellectually: He is very intelligent and has a great deal of knowledge. He teaches at a college and is quite articulate, as the play informs us. His intellect affords him a very good understanding of language, and he is very verbal.

Psychologically: George is very complicated. This is perhaps the most important area for the actor to explore. His motives for staying in a horrible marriage with Martha and subjecting himself to her abuse, and what he gets out of it, are directly related to his disease. His self-esteem level is very low. He is probably quite identified with his "victim energy," although at times he appears to be the victimizer! He seems to need what Martha dumps on him. In some strange and twisted way I think he loves her. Together they seem to travel back and forth from a father-daughter to a mother-son relationship, somehow supplying each other's needs and piquing each other's insecurities. He is indeed very insecure, and I imagine that his insecurity reaches well into the sexual area. He seems to enjoy the agony of his ambivalence about throwing Martha into the arms of other men. For an actor approaching this role, this is a psychological challenge of the highest order.

Another example might be Snakeskin in *Orpheus Descending* by Tennessee Williams:

Physically: He is very attractive in an animal way. He is extremely sensual, and having traded on his sexuality all his life, he has developed physical qualities and movements that are very provocative. Even his jacket and his nickname are made of a sensual "skin."

Emotionally: He is conservative in his expression. There is an economy of emotional expression about him, almost as if being emotional were more than he wanted to give anyone; but this may also be a protective mechanism. He seems to have compensated for his lack of emotionality by being verbally graphic when he talks to Lady and Carol.

Psychologically: He too is very complex. Since he has spent his whole life "at a party," using his body to get what he needed, his self-esteem is or has been pretty low. He's a loner, who presently supports himself by singing and playing a guitar or by doing odd jobs when that is not available. He doesn't seem to trust people, so it would appear that he has been hurt in the past. From some of the things he says to Lady, and his sympathy for her pain, it is fairly obvious that he has been hurt and has learned to protect himself. He fears responsibilities but doesn't want to waste the rest of his life as he has the first part of it. On some very deep level, in the nucleus of his being, I think Snakeskin is a frightened child.

Understanding all of the facets of a character in a piece of material allows the actor to create the skeleton on which to hang the rest of the obligations. Once he understands his responsibility to any character, an actor can begin his process of work by isolating each area and finding the similarities between himself and that other person, then identifying the differences.

APPROACHING THE CREATION
OF THE CHARACTER ELEMENTS
WITH THE CHART

All right, now that you have some understanding of what character is and what its components are, *how* do you make these things real, using yourself to do so? What kind of process do you employ to stimulate physical expression or an emotional life that comes from an organic place and fulfills the character? *How* do you increase or decrease the level of your own intellect and pique psychological behavior which is essentially alien to your life?

Fulfilling character elements is approached in the same way as any of the other six main obligations of material, through the use of choices and choice approaches. First, you identify the similarities between you and the character in one of the four areas. For example, let us say that the character is well built and has a very strong frame and a good sense of his body. You are strong and well built, and while you are not as aware of yourself physically as the character is described to be, you could, with very little effort, mirror him physically. In this example the similarity is so great that all you might do would be to "selectively emphasize" being aware of your physical prowess.

Emotionally, the character turns out to be very good-natured, a true innocent easily brought to laughter. Let us say that in this area you are quite different from him. Your makeup is not to be good-natured—in fact, you are prone to moodiness; you are certainly not an innocent, and while you laugh occasionally, something has to be really funny to elicit laughter from you. Not only are you dissimilar but antithetical to each other! In this case, you might look for where the innocent child lives in your being, starting with the exploration of a time in your life when you can remember being good-natured and innocent. Let us, for the sake of this example, assume that as a young boy you felt good about your life, trusted people, and had a kind of innocent naiveté. You could do an Affective-Memory exercise related to a specific time, place, and possibly even event, to discover the stimuli that made you feel that way. Once you identify these components, you might use them to discover people, objects, places, and behaviors that put you in touch with those qualities in you even today. If, for example, you are mellow, good-natured, and fun loving around certain of your friends and loved ones, you can sensorially endow the other actors in the play with the qualities of these people and, in addition to that, create humor in their behavior. You might also do a series of vulnerability exercises to lower your protective behavior, thereby making yourself more available to your own open good-naturedness.

As you proceed to deal with the intellectual responsibility, you discover that the character is natively as intelligent as you are but that he seems to think and express himself with less acuity. In other words, he appears to have a lower level of intelligence than you. In this specific instance, dealing with the emotional elements of the character might have an additional impact on the way you relate. If you feel more secure, good-natured, and innocent, you might also move, think, and talk more like the character. If this doesn't work, you could inhibit your mental acuity with various kinds of running inner monologues which would serve to create distractions and slow down the rapidity with which you "mind-mouth" connect and relate.

In the psychological area, you might elect to emphasize all the good things in your life, surrounding yourself with objects and with an environment that would stimulate a heightened sense of security and well-being to match the character obligation and counteract your own insecurity and distrust.

Overall, though I have given examples in all four areas, it is quite possible that by dealing with one choice, such as the affective-memory experience, you might indeed fulfill almost all of the character responsibilities.

The character obligation is one of the seven main obligations of material. When an actor auditions for a part in a play or a film, he is usually like the character physically. He is similar in type. In a reading, the people casting the role will also look for similarities in emotional structure and even possibly in intellect. Since it is very difficult to ascertain a person's psychology in a brief audition, it will come down to their getting a sense of the actor in this area. In other words, unless an actor is experimenting in a class or workshop or some other laboratory, he will most often be cast in parts where the character has attributes and endowments similar to his own.

For centuries actors have worn the cloak of certain characters and assumed characteristics that were imposed rather than created. It has been considered acceptable in the theater and in films, and even expected as part of the actor's talent, to be able to "do" many types of people. Only in the last sixty years or so has there been any real concern with reality! Stanislavsky came along and said that if a character in a play felt something—joy, grief, and so on—then the actor must find a way to experience the same emotion. Furthermore, if a character displayed certain physical or psychological attributes, the actor had a responsibility to create those as well. For all those actors who adopted "The System," or "The Method," it became a question of *how* to do that! Stanislavsky, and later Strasberg, supplied some organic approaches to acting and characterization, but there were serious gaps in their process. Not to be misunderstood, I must say that I think both these men made enormous contributions to the acting process and to the theater. Their genius provides the foundation for all the work that I do and have created. I mention all of this to underscore a very important truth, which is that if the actor does not have a specific process, a *how* to fulfill all the elements that a playwright has created in a character, he will necessarily fall short of being totally organic in the end.

So how exactly does one fulfill character? If you understand the three major parts of this craft, *obligation, choice,* and *choice approach,* you will be able to deal with all the elements of characterization. The first step, after reading the material and acquiring all the information you need, is to divide the elements into the four categories outlined above: the *physical,* the *emotional,* the *intellectual,* and the *psychological.* Once you have done that, start the characterization process by figuring out what the similarities and the differences are between you and the character. Beginning with what is distinctly similar, use your craft to bring to the surface those elements that are not immediately conscious or manifest in your behavior. Often, it is just a matter of consciously emphasizing qualities that will bring a certain facet of your character into play. Whatever you want to elevate or stimulate, do so through a specific choice and one of the available twenty-five choice approaches. Whether the element you are after is there, near the surface, or lies deeply buried in your being, the proper craft process will help stimulate or unearth it.

SOME SPECIFIC EXAMPLES USING THE CRAFT

Let us describe a hypothetical character:

1. *Physically:*	He has just started lifting weights. He is therefore extremely aware of his body and wants everyone else to notice it too. He carries a tape measure and is constantly checking for muscle development.

Let us imagine that the actor is fairly well built, that he has spent some time in the gym working out, but that he is not that concerned with his body or his muscles. He can, however, recall that "pumped-up" feeling, how good he felt and how physically aware he was after working with weights. It did indeed make him want to be looked at! So our imaginary actor decides to work to re-create that specific physical reality, and he does so through his craft process:

THE CHARACTER OBLIGATION:	Physical, as described above
THE CHOICE:	His own body, the sensation of blood in his muscles—particularly in the pectorals, biceps, and deltoids (that "pumped-up" state)
THE CHOICE APPROACH:	Sense Memory to re-create the specific sensations in the various parts of his upper body (the actor does this by asking the specific sensory questions and responding very specifically in the area of his body that the question is directed to)

2. Emotionally:	The character is brash and talks so loud that he can be heard ten feet away. He brags about himself and his accomplishments constantly. What saves him from being a complete boor is that he is charming and good-natured. It is evident that he wants to be liked by everyone.

In this particular case, the actor can see that the character's psychological problems are almost exclusively responsible for the nature of his emotional life and the way he relates to the world. Therefore, he decides to deal with the psychological area first.

3. Psychologically:	The character is very insecure. He grew up in a family that never acknowledged anything he did. He was constantly criticized, as far back as he can remember. He feels worthless on a deep level. He needs and wants love but fails to get it. More than anything, he needs approval.

The actor, who is himself fairly secure, does not identify with the character, since he is better adjusted by far. He therefore acknowledges the need to affect his level of confidence, heighten his need for acceptance and approval, and see where that will take him. He decides to try a couple of choices.

THE CHOICES:	A litany of specific insecurities, emphasizing the areas dealing with rejection, failure, and loneliness. In addition to this choice, the actor decides to look for a lack of interest, acceptance, and caring in the people around him (the other actors in the play).
THE CHOICE APPROACHES:	1. Inner Monologue, consisting of a litany of insecurities (done by talking to oneself through an Inner Monologue)
	2. Available Stimulus, using the real people around him, emphasizing anything that manifests itself—such as rejection, disapproval, and so on—and adding Believability as a second choice approach.

Example:

"I feel like I'm never going to get what I need! . . . I've been working to be recognized for years, and still nobody knows me. These people have their little cliques, and I'm not included! I'm getting older, and I have absolutely no security about my future. I feel like a failure. I spend most of my time alone . . . I don't have a steady girlfriend, and I have never done well with women. I feel unnoticed, and I wish I could do something that would attract people to me! My family thinks I'm a fool. They wanted me to go to Harvard and study law. I guess they have given up on me."

He can go on with this for as long as it takes to really stimulate the level of insecurity and need that is desired. When he gets to a place where he feels that he is experiencing some of the same impulses as the character, he may sneak into his second choice approach.

For his second choice approach, the actor starts by using the available stimulus, the people in the play. He selectively emphasizes (exaggerates) anything that they do or say which can be construed as a lack of acknowledgement or a rejection of him. When he has exhausted the realities, he might want to add Believability to his approach.

As explained before, Believability is the process of using some of the truth of what is happening and a lot of untruth or fantasy. After getting to whatever place the litany of insecurities has led him to, the actor would start the Believability process.

Example:

"They are all avoiding me. When I caught Joan's eyes, she quickly looked away. Every time I come into the theater, they stop talking, just as if they had been talking about me! They never invite me to lunch or dinner with them. None of them have ever said that my work was good. In fact, I feel their critical eyes on me all the time."

Very little of what the believability was made up of is true, but there is enough truth to hang the untruth on, and if the actor continues on this track, he will most likely stimulate the desired results.

Let us imagine that this actor is successful in dealing with the psychological elements of the obligation and that he stimulates most of the desired emotional life but fails to impel himself to be "charming and good-natured." Instead, he feels left out and insecure, and while he wants to gain acceptance, his impulse is to isolate himself rather than seek acceptance by being bombastic. He knows that the choices are right for the underpinnings of the character's behavior, but he needs an adjustment to impel himself to go after the other actors' acceptance. So he decides to work for a choice in the emotional area.

THE CHARACTER
OBLIGATIONS: To be brash, to brag about himself, and at the
(*Emotional*)   same time to be charming

In order to fulfill the obligations, the actor decides to emphasize his sexual attraction for the women in the play and to find things about the men that he admires and that make him want to be accepted by them.

THE CHOICE: The people in the play (Available Stimulus)

THE CHOICE
APPROACH: Available Stimulus, selectively emphasizing the
                     other actors' attractiveness by isolating features
                     and personality traits that will stimulate admira-
                     tion and attraction

When he combines all the choices and approaches listed in both the psychological and emotional areas, the actor finds that the combination intensifies his insecurities. At the same time, creating a need for what these people possess impels him to go after their acceptance and to solicit it by exaggerating his own attributes—which of course compensates for his feelings of inadequacy.

As a result of the other choices and approaches, the *intellectual* area essentially takes care of itself. Since the character is not as conscious as the actor, he seems less aware and intelligent. Preoccupied with his own insecurities and needs, the actor also becomes less aware, more self-involved, and thereby seems less conscious and intelligent.

In every case, whether or not the actor needs to deal with all four areas of the character obligation, once he identifies the specifics of his responsibilities, the process is essentially the same. He must ask himself what the responsibility is, what he must stimulate or pique in himself, and *how* to do it—or in other words what choice and choice approach will provide him with the impetus to behave in a particular way.

Let us now return to Snakeskin and, using the character elements defined above, supply the possible choices and approaches that an actor might use to fulfill the obligations in all four areas.

For the physical, the actor might start by doing sensuality exercises to elevate his own relationship to sexuality. He might even explore using an animal to create the physical sense of a snake skin. He might work to stimulate a heightened awareness of the differences between himself and the opposite sex, adding elements that would create greater sexual attraction.

For the emotional choices, since Snakeskin is not gregarious or emotionally expressive, the actor might use the things in the people around him that make him feel shy or mistrustful, anything that would represent a threat or a judgment on their part. He may also elect to work for other specific people in his life who intimidate him and elicit a certain emotional conservatism in him.

THE CHOICE
APPROACHES:
        1. Available Stimulus, using Selective Emphasis in areas that would stimulate shyness and distrust
        2. Endowments (the actor can sensorially work to create different people in his life in relation to the actors in the play)

To do Endowments, you ask sensory questions about the similarities and contrasts between the person you are working with and the one you are trying to create.

Example:

"What are the similarities in the shape of the face? (Respond with the visual sense.) What is the shape of the forehead? What is the difference in the shape of the forehead? (Always respond with the sense involved.) Where are the lines in the forehead? How are they different? How deep do they sink into the skin? What are the similarities in the shape of the eyes? How are they different? How much farther apart are her eyes than those of the person I am working with?"

The comparing and contrasting process may go on for a while, and then, when the actor is well into creating the imaginary person, he can begin to ask questions that will mold and sculpt that person's features on the actor he is working with.

Intellectually.   Snakeskin seems to know things. He also knows how to think. His intelligence is made manifest in his reasoning abilities and in his imaginative storytelling.

There isn't much difference intellectually between the actor and the character. Snakeskin has a normal intelligence, which is neither unusually high nor abnormally low. Since his emotional state is what it is, his intellect does not noticeably reveal itself.

Psychologically: He is a loner and seems to have trouble trusting people. There is some evidence of pain in his life. Here again, the psychological foundation of the character seems to be the impelling force behind his manifested behavior in the play.

Let us say in this instance that the actor is fairly well adjusted, married, and that he is doing what he wants to do with his life. He is not a loner and has no trouble trusting people as a rule. However, he has been somewhat hurt in his early life. When he was a preteen-ager, his parents were divorced and he was shuttled back and forth to a variety of foster homes. During this period, he suffered a great deal of trauma, feelings of being displaced, and a sense of rejection that remains with him on some level even today. He remembers that during that period of time he retreated into himself and displayed many of the same behavior patterns as the character.

THE CHOICE: A combination of several foster homes

THE CHOICE
APPROACH: Affective Memory, creating, one at a time, memorable fragmented experiences in each of these places

In addition to the potential impact of this choice, there is a distinct possibility that it could be an *ultimate-consciousness* kind of choice. If that proves to be true, it could fulfill many of the character obligations and at the same time create life from an unconscious source, making the experience a hundred times richer. The choices in each area would have to be approached one at a time and the chronology experimented with.

TAPED EXCERPTS OF ACTORS WORKING ON CHARACTERIZATION IN A WORKSHOP

The following excerpts were recorded in my class while we were working on character obligations. A variety of responsibilities and approaches have been included to give the reader an opportunity to share other actors' experiences with the process.

Excerpt I

MARK: (Describing a character from the play *In the Boom Boom Room,* by David Rabe) His name is Eric. He's thirty years old, intelligent, well-read. He is sexually and emotionally starved, very self-involved, not very considerate of other people . . . and he's very insecure. He's in therapy . . . conscious of the need for help.

ERIC: So how would you approach it?

MARK: I would start with my own sexual and emotional starvation.

ERIC: Let me ask you a question: How do you know that you are sexually and emotionally starved?

MARK: Well, from time to time I feel the impact of it!

ERIC: O.K. What are the ingredients of that? What makes you conscious, on a twenty-four-hour-a-day basis, of being starved?

MARK: I might run into someone that I am sexually attracted to and be reminded of my needs . . .

ERIC: What would you work for? . . . How would you approach it? Do you have anybody in your life?

MARK: No . . .

ERIC: Do you wake up with anybody?

MARK: No . . .

ERIC: What does your bedroom look like?

MARK: It's nice . . .

ERIC: Is there anybody else there besides you?

MARK: No . . . a cat . . .

ERIC: When you get into bed at night, you're alone?

MARK: Yeah . . .

ERIC: How do you feel about that?

MARK: I don't like it. I hate it!

ERIC: Are you aware of your romantic deprivation when you're alone?

MARK: Yes . . .

ERIC: Do you eat alone sometimes?

MARK: Yes, all the time!

ERIC: Yes . . . so the absence of the fulfillment is a place to start, isn't it? . . . How does the character's feeling of sexual and emotional starvation manifest itself in the play? . . . What are the ingredients that make him sexually and emotionally starved as written in the play?

MARK: He's very insecure with women . . . He finds one girl, and, totally, all his energies go right to her.

ERIC: How do you feel about yourself as a lover?

MARK: I'm good when I get it . . . Well, I have mixed feelings about that.

ERIC: Do you have any insecurities about performance?

MARK: Yes . . .

ERIC: What are they? . . . You don't have to tell us! Do you know what I'm saying? Suppose you got into that . . . into your insecurities about having someone, being able to fulfill somebody . . . performance . . . being impotent . . . all of that stuff, that would stimulate fear and insecurity which could be added to the fear of taking the risks to bring somebody into your life. Your insecurities on a one to one and your feelings of sexual deprivation would be intensely related to your fears of not being able to perform. A person who is impotent . . . or fears impotence . . . spends a lot of time thinking about sex. So, you see, that would be one approach . . . getting into your own fears and needs. The choice approach . . . could be a variety of choice approaches . . . You could work to create your sense of aloneness . . . at very important times of the day . . . in the morning, at night when you go to bed . . . and the absence of people. You could use all kinds of approaches to elevate your fears of not being a good lover, of being impotent, etc. . . . You could create people telling you things that have happened. So you could approach this from the psychological area.

The actor first identifies the character elements in all four areas, then the similarities, and then the dissimilarities between himself and the character. He then finds the impetus, the nucleus of what he wants to work for.

In the preceding excerpt, accepting the actor's impulse to start with the sexual and emotional starvation of the character as interpreted by him, I attempted to lead him into this area using his own realities. It seemed to me from Mark's description of the character that the impelling force in the character's life was his deprivation and the insecurity which caused it, making that a great place to start the exploration. Using his own parallel realities, the actor will be able to come from a place filled with the same frustrations and preoccupations. The approaches to the reality are many, and the selection is up to the actor himself.

I suggested to Mark that he work for his environment when he is alone, sensorially creating the absence of anyone. I further suggested that he get into his own fears and insecurities about adequacy and performance. He could accomplish this in a variety of ways, using:

1. Inner Monologues, taking a kind of inventory of his prior failures
2. Imaginary Monologues with specific people whom he is sexually intimidated by or has had experiences with
3. An Inner or Outer Monologue, listing his passions and needs for romantic and emotional fulfillment.

There were of course other character elements that were discussed, and if the area that Mark chose to explore did not cover those obligations, he would have to deal with them afterwards.

Excerpt II

SUSAN: (Describing Prudence in *Beyond Therapy*) O.K., the character is a woman, and she is intelligent and well educated. She's very vulnerable, she's a little bit afraid of life and of her emotions, she's someone who didn't like vanilla ice cream when she was a child, she's timid about things, she's having difficulty finding a relationship that she likes, she likes men, but she's a little bit afraid of them . . . do you want to know more? Is that enough?

ERIC: O.K., fine. How would you approach that in terms of making it a reality for you?

SUSAN: I would find, maybe, the differences first and . . .

ERIC: What about the similarities first?

SUSAN: The similarities . . . are just there. What do you have to do? . . .

ERIC: No . . . I . . . think that's a little cavalier . . . I think it's taking things for granted. "The similarities are there" is like saying "O.K." without really dealing with those similarities. How do you promote them? How do you get them to the surface?

SUSAN: I guess, in part . . .

ERIC: (Interrupting) Go over the first three or four descriptions.

SUSAN: O.K. . . . She's intelligent.

ERIC: All right, how does her intelligence manifest itself?

SUSAN: Partly through the lines of the play . . . She has humorous . . . intelligent responses to things that happen.

ERIC: So her intelligence manifests itself mostly in the interaction between her and the other characters? in her behavior?

SUSAN: Yes . . . she's vulnerable, and you see that also in her interactions with the other characters . . . in hesitation . . . things that she doesn't say . . . For instance, he says, "You're afraid of life, aren't you?" and she says, "Well . . ." and she doesn't go on with that; there's a real hesitation: How do I answer that? . . . She is afraid of life . . . and of her emotions . . . She has a sense of humor . . . and that also comes out in the lines . . . It comes out in sarcasm . . . and that is part of her intelligence.

ERIC: So . . . how would you approach that? . . . It's not even your first rehearsal! What are you going to do? . . . Do you want to break that down into four areas? . . . Describe the character intellectually.

SUSAN: All right . . . I didn't deal with the intelligence . . . I feel that I'm intelligent . . . she's intelligent . . . that's fine! . . . I did deal with vulnerability . . . and selectively emphasized insecurities and vulnerable areas in my own life.

ERIC: So . . . those were the ways you are like the character . . . See, if you are playing the character . . . you are the character! The audience sees you; they do not see the script . . . on the stage . . . they see you, *so you are the character,* right? So you decide how you are like that person and how you are unlike that person, and then what do you do? . . . You haven't said anything about the *how* yet!

SUSAN: Well, I said something about the how in terms of getting in touch with vulnerability.

ERIC: O.K. . . . Yes, you did . . . She's vulnerable . . . you're vulnerable.

SUSAN: Yes . . . and I selectively emphasized those things in an Inner Monologue . . . in a sharing monologue, in an Intimate Sharing with the other actor . . .

ERIC: Stuff that . . . would elevate your own vulnerability?

SUSAN: Yes . . . and my insecurities . . .

ERIC: O.K. . . . Go on, what else?

SUSAN: I think that's the only thing I've really dealt with.

ERIC: What about her insecurities? and her fear of life? That sounds to me like a very important psychological character element! Is she physically like you? . . . Could she be you?

SUSAN: Yes, she could be . . . but maybe not . . .

ERIC: Is your emotional fabric similar?

SUSAN: In some areas . . . but where it isn't is that I'm not nearly (so) afraid of risk and life as she is . . .

ERIC: O.K., so there is a separation there? . . .

SUSAN: Yes.

ERIC: I get the clear picture on the intellect, some of her psychology . . . in terms of being insecure, frightened of life . . . Physically, she could be you . . . so you don't have to do anything to . . . stimulate the physical difference, right? . . . O.K. So we accept that. Her intellect, her humor, her underlying insecurities, and her fear of life . . . what do you do to stimulate those things so that they become the fabric of who you are? Are you following this so far? We have to be "crystally" specific.

SUSAN: All right, let's pick what I didn't deal with then . . . the intelligence . . .

ERIC: Fine . . . How does her intelligence manifest itself on a level different from yours?

SUSAN: Well, she writes for a living . . . and I've done a little bit of writing . . . but I would never call myself a writer . . . and she's verbal—she speaks well . . .

ERIC: So how would you go about creating or elevating or ventilating or emphasizing that . . . verbosity . . . being verbal, articulate, etc. . . . . What kind of choice, what kind of choice approach would you use? . . . You know, sometimes all the character elements might be fulfilled simultaneously . . . meaning that you could work for one choice and get a sense of many of the elements of the character . . . You might not have to break them down one at a time; it all depends on your choice and choice approach. I mean, if you were working with a sub-personality and you could identify . . . Prudence . . . if you could identify a sub-personality which in reality is like Prudence, then if you did a facilitation (see p. 184) of yourself, you might stimulate the elevation of that sub-personality, and it could in one fell swoop create a lot of the character elements. But let's put that aside for the time being, because I'm not discussing sub-personalities yet . . . O.K., what would you do about being more articulate . . . more literary?

SUSAN: What comes to mind . . . is that I could use Evocative Words . . . in relation to a situation (personal realities)—or to my ego—where I feel I have been very articulate . . . I know what I could use . . . I could use my teaching, no?

ERIC: No . . .

SUSAN: Why not? . . .

ERIC: You're not dealing with the impetus . . . You see, I'm leading you into places where you can fall into traps . . . That's how you learn . . . I think . . . we develop . . . "lances and shields" for the most part to make up for, compensate for, our failings, to protect and defend ourselves. I think that the character element that you have to start with in relation to Prudence is her terror, her fear of life, and her insecurities . . . A lot of the other compensations would authentically evolve if you got into that . . . You see, when you are dealing with one character element, you find the impetus which stimulates and piques a lot of the other elements . . . Let's pursue that . . . Let's say I'm right—I could be wrong, but let's say I'm right—let's pursue it . . .

SUSAN: So we're back to insecurities again? . . .

ERIC: And her terror of life . . .

SUSAN: That's pretty much where I started . . . and what I did was that I selectively emphasized my own insecurities, particularly in relation to men, because that's what she's dealing with . . .

ERIC: How did you do that?

SUSAN: From my own personal reality . . . a sharing monologue with Mark (Mark is her scene partner) . . . some believability . . . a stream of consciousness . . . talking about things that make me feel insecure . . . a number of different things at different times.

ERIC: Did it work?

SUSAN: I had some success . . .

ERIC: You know, I saw your work . . . and your work had some nice authentic moments in it . . . It was organic on some levels . . . but I didn't experience what you're talking about . . . I didn't even feel a heightened level of insecurity about being on stage . . . I mean . . . you know . . . in terms of how deeply that runs in you—not that that's a good place to go, because it heightens the obstacles for you, but I think that the trap for you is that you don't go deep enough . . . This woman is terrified of life. You're talking about selectively emphasizing some of your insecurities . . . and I'm talking about getting to . . . *primal* insecurities! I think that's the key to stimulating a lot of those other character elements . . . So where do you go from there?

SUSAN: Primal moan?

ERIC: No . . . no . . . I think you really have to start with a litany of your insecurities . . . just to find out "where the bodies are buried." You know, on your own, dig deeply into your insecurities . . . like . . . I'll give you one . . . You're thirty-eight?

SUSAN: Thirty-nine.

ERIC: You're thirty-nine . . . Jack Benny's age . . . right? . . . You've never had a child, and I know from everything that you've said in class that you desperately want a child . . . Time is passing . . . You are real insecure about never having that dream fulfilled, right? You are also insecure about never meeting Mr. Right, you know, somebody that fulfills you on every level . . . You are also very insecure about the profession you have chosen . . . and whether there is ever going to be a real future for you as an actress . . . I'm selectively emphasizing . . . purposely avoiding all the good things in your life . . . getting down to where "If you can't stand the heat, you get out of the kitchen!" Where it really gets uncomfortable is where Prudence is! And that's where the compensational life comes in . . . That's why she answers the ad and meets this guy . . . *He might be, God, he might be!* See? Unless *you* have that impelling force, then you're just doing a scene, and you're here on stage because you're doing a scene. I think that's the important character element area to start with . . . You may have to do some embellishing . . . work in other areas also . . . but it must be as important to you as it is to Prudence . . . The reality must be the same . . . Out of your insecurities come the parallel realities and compensations. Anybody else want to say anything about this?

BOB: Yeah . . . once she "gets down to where the bodies are buried," how does she make sure that her redirectional behavior is what the character is about?

ERIC: She doesn't! . . . She doesn't make sure . . . You see, you want guarantees . . . you've got to go someplace else . . . In art there are no guarantees . . . Artists do not sit down in front of a canvas and say, "Today, this is going to be a masterpiece!" You explore! . . . She takes this into a laboratory, has rehearsals with the actor, and sees what unfolds . . . what evolves out of the choices . . . then she makes her adjustments . . . If her choices start to take her away from the material, she's going to have to go back to the drawing board to see what will take her to the fulfillment of the material. But you do not logically conceptualize the results you're after! You pick a choice and explore the choice and see what it will stimulate . . . You see, the whole thing is that *you don't want to know where it's going to take you!* That precludes any discoveries you're going to make . . . If she really gets into her insecurities, and she comes to this laboratory, and she starts working with Mark on the scene and he's really important to her, and that's a reality . . . then it's not, I'm doing a scene! . . . Something is at stake for Susan for real. Whether it peaks an *ultimate-consciousness* response or not, something is at stake for her because she has been rubbing her nose in her own life and in her own needs, and if she becomes verbally compensational or cerebral or intellectual, that might be the compensation that she creates to defend herself or impress him . . . I don't know . . . I don't know what comes first . . . but I do know that if there's a strong enough impetus, something will happen . . . if she doesn't tailor her behavior to fulfill her concepts.

Breaking down the character into the component parts already discussed allows the actor to approach it in smaller increments and makes it easier for him to create the different facets in relation to his own instrument. Often, one important choice will fulfill many of the character elements in all areas. In the example of Susan doing Prudence, dealing with her deep impelling insecurities and fears might help her establish the psychological foundation of the character, while simultaneously creating the intellectual manifestations of compensational life and stimulating Prudence's emotional life in the scene. If that happens, the actress, in a "grand slam," fulfills all the character elements with a single choice and a single choice approach.

CHOICE APPROACHES DESIGNED
TO DEAL WITH CHARACTERIZATION

Any one of the twenty-five choice approaches can be used to address and fulfill character element obligations. When dealing with a specific character responsibility, the proper choice and approach can make all the difference. There are, however, a few choice approaches that seem to lend themselves to the responsibility of characterization better than the others insofar as they yield more dimensional results. They are (1) *Externals*, (2) *Affective Memory*, and (3) *Sub-Personalities*.

There is a very good reason why these particular choice approaches work better: each one affects more facets of the actor's instrument. That is not to say that you would not achieve equally good results with any of the other choice approaches; it is just that when an actor uses *Externals* and works to get the sense of an animal, for example, it seems to affect him physically, emotionally, intellectually, and psychologically at the same time. The same is true for *Sub-Personalities*, and, most often, for *Affective Memory*.

THE EXTERNALS CHOICE APPROACH

This approach is number ten on the list of choice approaches. It comprises four separate categories: animals, people, inanimate objects, and insects. By using several approach techniques, the actor is able to create the sense of an animal, of a person, and so on, through his own instrument. This process, if done successfully, has a definite impact on his physical instrument. It piques emotions that are often not reachable through other techniques, and it even affects the intellectual and psychological parts of his being. For a complete and thorough explanation of this choice approach, refer to *Irreverent Acting*.

Besides what I have seen actors do with the Externals Choice approach, I myself have had enormous success with it, not exclusively in the laboratory, but on the professional stage and in feature films as well. Several times, the sense of a particular animal promoted the entire substructure of a character I was playing, and on each occasion using the approach fulfilled the entire character obligation.

If you thought for a moment, you would probably find a dozen roles in the theater and in films which could be approached by getting the sense of an animal. To use just two of the examples mentioned in this chapter: Blanche DuBois is described as having the essence of a moth. Suppose the actress used a moth to see where that might lead. Happy, in *Death of a Salesman*, could be approached by experimenting with a variety of animals, possibly a peacock or an eagle or maybe a mandrill. Almost any character could be explored through the use of Externals. Remember that there are three other categories besides animals: people, insects, and inanimate objects.

You work to create the sense of another person in much the same way as you do for an animal. The major difference is that, since you're already starting with a human being, you don't have to translate the behavior into human terms as you do with an animal. Another large difference is that animals excite the primitive in us; they shake the primal impulses loose and allow us to fulfill roles that we may not even be close to physically. Stanley in "*Streetcar*" is apelike. Blanche refers to him that way in the play. An actor playing him might have all the necessary talent but lack that animal quality. Working to get a sense of a gorilla might just do the trick for him. There have recently been films that required the actors to create the sense of an animal: *Quest for Fire, Clan of the Cave Bear, Iceman,* to name just a few.

The Externals Choice approach can be used to address any of the elements of characterization, even if the character is not animal-like. If, for example, one of the obligations is to be retarded, the actor could use certain animals that would significantly affect his behavior, his acuity, his intellect, and even his speech. Any emotional area can be approached by using an animal as the stimulus: shyness could be created by using any of a number of animals that might produce that organic state: a mouse, a rabbit, a squirrel, a wide variety of birds, and so on; a frenetic individual could be fulfilled through the use of a spider monkey; an ominous, stoic character with a dangerous essence could be approached by getting the sense of a coiling cobra or of a crocodile. The Externals area is very rich and has a tendency to hit all the character bases at one time. Of course it can be used to deal with the other six main obligations of material as well.

AFFECTIVE MEMORY

Here is another important tool for fulfilling character. A successful Affective-Memory workout can all at once send the actor back to another time in his life, where his sense of life, his physical makeup, and his psychological state were totally different from what they are now. At the same time it could sink a shaft into the unconscious, hopefully allowing for an *ultimate-consciousness* state.

In the space of a lifetime, we go through many changes. Certainly, we change physically; but we also undergo intellectual and psychological changes, as well as a multitude of personality evolutions. I have half-jokingly said that I felt as though I had lived several lifetimes in this one. I actually feel as if I have been several different people in this one life. When I was growing up at home with my mother and father and all my sisters and brothers, I was a particular kind of person. I had thoughts, impulses, feelings, dreams, and fears, which changed when I went out on my own. My second life was spent in the army. I was different then from the person I was at home with my parents. When I got married, that was again another life. When my children came into my life, again it changed, and so on until the present. Well, all of those "lives," complete with all of the feelings and personality elements involved, are available to me through the use of Affective Memory. If, for example, I were to play a character with a certain level of fear and insecurity, one who was not sure of himself and was tentative in his actions, I could go back to a time in my own life when I was like that. Since I am not like that now, I would have to dip into my unconscious where those feelings still live. Besides my emotional fabric, some of my belief structures have changed with the years, and while I may have entertained certain feelings and prejudices at one time in my life, that too underwent modification. An idealistic viewpoint may have been jaundiced by the way the world evolved, and if I wanted to get back to the kind of naive idealism I had as a youth, Affective Memory might be the very thing that would open that up to me. Again, the Affective-Memory approach is totally explored in *Irreverent Acting*. You may also refer to chapter 2 of this book for an example of the process.

SUB-PERSONALITIES

This approach seems much more complicated than it really is. The whole concept of sub-personalities is based on the theory that our personality has many parts and facets—which I believe to be the truth. The original idea of sub-personalities came from Carl G. Jung's theory of the archetypes. He gave those archetypes names to distinguish them from one another and to describe their function. Psychologically, the theory—and feeling—are that these sub-personalities can take us over and begin to run our lives. If we are controlled by a certain sub-part of ourselves, we manifest a specific kind of behavior, which dominates our lives, and we relate to other people through that sub-personality. The goal, psychologically speaking, is to function from a totally conscious state and to keep all of our sub-personalities in balance so that they may surface when we need them but never seize control of our lives. Essentially, this is a thumb-nail description of the theory. As actors, we needn't concern ourselves with the psychological aspects of this technique; all we need to do is understand how to use it creatively; and as a creative tool, it is simply wonderful! It can, when used successfully, supply dimensions of life and character that are colorful, rich, and unpredictable.

Each sub-personality seems to have a life of its own. Each is dimensional and has many facets. If the actor picks the right one to approach a particular character, he may all at once fulfill all parts of the character obligation. Each sub-personality has its own energy, and when the actor successfully facilitates its emergence, he *becomes that sub-personality*. For example, if the character is a very disturbed person, prone to outbursts of violence, the actor might call upon the "killer" sub-personality, who is violent and aggressive by nature, defensive and threatening. Each sub-person exists to be just what it is. The "pusher" in us has only one job, to continually push us to work, to accomplish, to complete things. That is his function. Getting familiar with all your potential sub-personalities will give you quite a repertoire of them that you can use to deal with characterization.

The Different Sub-Personalities

First, there are the basic archetypes: all of the child archetypes—the magical child, the vulnerable child, the frightened child, and so on—the inner critic, the pusher, the judge, the Satanic part, the killer, the messiah, the protector, the warrior, Aphrodite (the sexual one), the father and mother, the controller, and so on. (For a complete list, refer to *Irreverent Acting*.) In addition to the archetypes, there are the individual sub-personalities that each person might have, such as the lazy one, the beach bum, the coward, the clown, the rationalizer, etc. . . . There is no end to the kinds of sub-personalities that we each possess. The most important consideration is how to elicit a particular one, how to bring it up to the forefront of our consciousness.

There are a variety of techniques for doing that. The first is to have another person "facilitate" you, which means talk to the various parts of you to encourage them to "come out." There is a specific process involved, and the facilitator should have some experience with it. (There is a complete example of sub-personality facilitation in *Irreverent Acting*.) Since the actor usually does not carry around with him an experienced facilitator, he should look to other methods of appealing to particular sub-personalities.

Facilitation can be accomplished through a journal. Let us say, for example, that you are trying to reach your mischievous child. You would start by relating to that part of yourself in a written conversation.

Example:

ME: Hi! I would like to speak with the mischievous child . . . Are you there? . . . Can you hear me?

THE CHILD: (Responding) Who wants to know?

ME: Oh! . . . so you are there! . . . I would like to talk with you.

THE CHILD: Why?

ME: Well, I would like to get to know you . . . Maybe you could come out and play.

THE CHILD: I don't want to play . . . and I don't even know who you are. Come and get me . . .

As the journal conversation continues, you should get much deeper into the energy of the mischievous child. As that happens, you will be able to use that sub-personality to act from. If the character is influenced or controlled by a mischievous kind of energy and is, in fact, like that sub-personality in his or her personal relationships, the sub-personality might just fulfill all the character responsibilities.

Another approach for reaching a specific sub-personality is to work for choices that appeal to, and elicit, that particular energy. For example, there is the "Martin Luther" archetype, which is the moralist in all of us. Although we all have some of that energy, there are people who are totally controlled by it. If you were playing the role of a judgmental moralist and you wanted to get in touch with that part of you and call it to the surface, you might go to the things in life that stimulate moral judgment in you, making sure that you selectively emphasized these choices all around you. You might start the process by talking to yourself about things that "get your moral back up." You might do a litany on streetwalkers and prostitutes, if that happens to affect you that way, or selectively emphasize behaviors in the people around you that you find offensive to your moral sensibilities (e.g., smoking grass, snorting cocaine, etc. . . .)

Sub-personalities are a very complete way of approaching the demands of characterization. If you clearly identify a character as being motivated or controlled by a recognizable sub-personality, you could appeal to your own parallel sub and, if successful, excitingly fulfill all the parts of that character. Sub-personalities is the twenty-first choice approach, and, as is true of all the choice approaches, you must work with it in order to master it; but it is well worth the effort. If you make it part of your tool chest, you will have a tremendous device for approaching a wide variety of obligations in addition to characterization.

Some Characters Who Are
Identifiable Sub-Personality Choices

The preacher in *Rain* is definitely controlled by the Martin Luther archetype and is later taken over by a more lustful sub-personality. The character Marty in the film of the same name has a very low sense of self-worth. You might approach him by calling on the inner critic, who is always criticizing and diminishing you. *Dr. Jekyll and Mr. Hyde* is a clear-cut study of good and evil and would afford the actor an excellent opportunity to explore the "good" and benevolent sub-personality for the doctor while investigating the demonic subs for Mr. Hyde. Tartuffe is controlled by the hypocrite coupled with a lusting sexual energy. Characters like Medea are obviously controlled by the satanic sub-personality. Cyrano might be explored by using the archetypal hero, while Carol Cutrere in *Orpheus Descending* could definitely be linked to Aphrodite. Rose in *The Woolgatherer* and Chrissy in *In the Boom Boom Room* are both controlled by their victim energy.

There are endless numbers of characters in dramatic literature that you can identify as being ruled by an impelling sub-personality. While there are other energies and forces in operation in every case, it is still the primary sub-personality that motivates the character's behavior. If there are times during the play when the character changes and seems to become quite different from what he was before, the actor can discontinue working for the sub-personality he has been using and find another choice. It is entirely possible that a character in a piece may go back and forth between several sub-personalities; but whatever the elements in the four areas of character obligation are, you have a well of wonderful possibilities in this choice approach, as in many of the others.

THE CHARACTER BACKGROUND JOURNAL

All you know about a character is what the play itself tells you, and we have already been through how you find out about that. What about the life of the character before the play? What about his childhood, all of his experiences while growing up? Who were the people in his life? How was he influenced by those people? What was his relationship to his family that the play does not go into? How did he do in school? Who were his friends? At what age did he discover sex? What were the specific experiences that were crucial to the formation of his personality—the joys, sorrows, and traumas that the play never refers to? These are the realities of a real person who existed before Act I, Scene I. If an actor creates such a background in a journal, he will bring to the stage a multidimensional human being, while at the same time connecting his own life experiences to the life of the character. He will have memories and references to other people that will be carried onto the stage as a reality foundation for the character. If there are other people mentioned in the dialogue, and if the actor has already made those people real for himself by creating a full life leading up to the play, he will authentically respond to those imaginary characters from the reality of his own life. In addition to giving any character a full and rich background based on his life, the actor will make conscious connections with his unconscious life, which will seep into his behavior on stage.

Actually, there are often vast differences between the actor's life and the character's life. The actor, for example, may have come from a secure home with loving parents, while the character had a very different childhood. What the actor does in the creation of a character background journal is mix his own experience and background with that of the character wherever possible, and create imaginary circumstances where there are vast differences. It is like using a combination of reality and believability within the framework of a written scenario.

Creating the "prior life" of the character stimulates a visceral, organic, and authentic life. An actor brings his own life to the play when he has spent time creating this background. Everything that the character does or says has a foundation in what went before. In every line there is a reference to a prior reality or knowledge. Even if the connections are not obvious, they are there. When the actor sits down to create this journal, using information provided by the play and adding experiences from his own life, he comes face to face with understanding the components in the character's life that motivate and justify his behavior in the play. In addition to making those discoveries, he becomes clear about the kinds of choices he could use in order to fulfill the character elements. For example, if he is approaching a very insecure character, who cannot seem to satisfy his need to amass great wealth, and he can point to a specific time in his own life when that kind of insecurity might have started, he has a basis for a group of choices that may create the organic underpinnings of this character from his own reality. The fork in the road that separated him from the character could have occurred at any time, but if he starts with the creation of those early insecurities and continues to work for things that stimulate the same insecurities, he may very well achieve his goal.

Once you have read the play and are very familiar with the character in terms of what the author says, what the other characters say about him, and so on, and even before starting to deal with the character obligations, you might begin the character background journal, starting at birth and creating a life for the character right up to the time when the play begins. At all times you should be aware of the realities of the character's structure. Do not violate the truths that are the character's! If, for example, he comes from a broken home and you don't, you must not distort his background in order to match your own realities, particularly if it is something that could have contributed greatly to his personality. In the above example, you might selectively emphasize a parallel in your own life that may have made you feel as if you didn't have a solid family unit while growing up. Suppose your father worked all the time and was rarely at home, and instead of having a father to go to, you went to your brother. There would be a parallel there.

Even though you are writing this in a journal and there is a tendency to become a writer instead of an actor, the creation of a life for the character will give you a foundation that you can relate to throughout the entire run of the play. The background, however, must not just come from your imagination onto the paper and remain there; you must use the information every time you rehearse, recalling and relating to experiences that may be used as part of a choice to stimulate the behavior in a scene.

A good example here is the bedroom scene between Biff and Happy in *Death of a Salesman.* The two brothers talk about their earlier life and the experiences they shared while growing up. They reminisce about things they did. Creating a character background journal that includes the life you shared with your own brother and filling it with dozens of parallel experiences not only would make what the character talks about real for you, but it would become part of the choice and approach process for making this other actor your brother. If you used Endowments, you could create your brother in relation to the actor you are working with. Once you have constructed this background, the lines in the scene will actually relate to specific things that really happened in your life and will now take on a meaning that they wouldn't have had otherwise.

EXAMPLE OF A CHARACTER BACKGROUND JOURNAL

Always writing in the first person, with no separation between you and the character, selectively emphasize the parallels and similarities between you, even if they have to be somewhat stretched by using Believability.

"I was born in the Midwest. My mother and father were middle-class people brought up to believe in the work ethic. My mother was a housewife totally devoted to my father. She cooked and cleaned and ministered to his every need. She obviously loved and respected him a great deal. I am the younger of two boys. My brother is two years older than I am, although I have always felt like his older brother. For whatever reason, I was my father's favorite. He tried not to make the preference obvious but was never successful in hiding the fact that he favored me over my brother Phil. All through my childhood, I was more popular than Phil and always seemed to attract more people into my circle. My father had a small business that he worked at seven days a week. In all the years I knew him, I can only remember his taking one vacation, which only lasted for a long weekend. He constantly spoke to me about the importance of money and how you had to prepare yourself to earn a good living. I always dreamed of exotic things, of running off and bumming around the country, experiencing life in many environments. My father called me 'a dreaming fool' and assured me that I would grow out of 'such foolish notions'! I didn't! I always loved him and respected him for his honesty and his hard work, but as I grew older I became increasingly aware of his limitations. With this awareness I began to challenge him, his ideas and his life. We were in conflict almost all the time. He couldn't help but find fault with me and was constantly critical of my dreams and desires. I knew that he wanted the best for me, but to my challenge of his ideals he retaliated by criticizing me. We grew apart, and I stayed away from home more and more. My mother, seeing the hostility between us, took his side and became critical also. Phil was always there for me! We were brothers, friends, and confidants. We shared many of the same friends, men and women, and all through school were inseparable. As the relationship between our father and me deteriorated, Phil began to do more to please him! He worked at jobs after school, put his paycheck on the table at dinner, and talked the talk that he knew would please my father.

· "I could see what was happening, and I understood it. Phil had always felt like second best and never thought that he could compete, so he always did things for me. I'm sure that he wasn't even conscious of what he was doing in this situation. He so wanted my father's approval and acceptance that he took advantage of the conflict between us. I knew that if I confronted him with it he would be very hurt and would deny it, so I never mentioned it to him. The situation at home deteriorated, and I grew further away from my parents, while Phil seemed to do more and more to follow in my father's footsteps. I spent more time with my friends and in rebellion quit school! I spent a couple of years going from job to job, aimlessly looking for what I wanted to do with my life.

"I moved out of my parents' house and took a small apartment in a seedy building on the wrong side of town. Phil and I saw much less of each other but never loved each other any less. Occasionally we would have dinner together, for which he always insisted on paying! Sitting there across the table listening to him was like hearing my father tell me about what was important in life. Without knowing it, Phil desperately tried to impress me with his accomplishments in the business world, and little did he know how sorry I felt for him! It took days to get over the impact of just one dinner with my brother. I was sad for him. He had sold his soul for the love of his father, never knowing or exploring what might have really meant something to him."

In the preceding example of a character background journal, I used the character of Biff to create a background for. Knowing the elements and forces that sculpted his life and formed his personality, I paralleled some of the realities in my own life, took some liberties, selectively emphasized similarities, chose not to deal with dissimilarities, and structured a background life that was close enough to the reality of the character and contained elements of my own life as well: I was born in the Middle West; everything I said about my father and mother was true; I do have an older brother named Phil. I have always wanted other things in life beyond what most people settle for and question. I had a very close relationship with my brother for many years until he left for New York. There was some conflict between my father and me, but not nearly as impacting. He wanted me to be more practical, but instead of being critical he nagged me constantly about my future. There was a period in my life when I felt as if I were lost. I did drop out of school and went on the road as a driver for a traveling salesman. I wanted to see the country, so I took that job. I wandered around for almost two years not knowing what I was going to do with my life. There were enough basic similarities between Biff and me for me to construct the character background journal. Of course, one must be more descriptive when going into actual events and experiences. The journal can be quite elaborate, or it can be simple and deal with the important events in the character's life. As you do these journals, you will develop a sense for how much to say and how deeply to go.

It is what you do with the journal after you create it that really counts! First, it is important to get a real sense of the things you write about. While making your entries, attempt to sensorially re-experience parts of each event: see the people, hear the conversations, smell the odor of your mother's cooking, and so on. Continually refer to the journal before and during rehearsals. Assimilate the events and experiences of your character through the journal, mixing the recollection of your own memories with those of the character. Talk to the other actors about the life of your character before the play, as a preparation to starting the rehearsal process. Do imaginary monologues with the people from your past, and include them as secondary choices to create the character's life in the play. Think about the ingredients of your character background journal before you go to sleep at night, and encourage yourself to dream about it. When selecting the choices and choice approaches that you will use in the play, let the journal guide you to the kind of choices that are "root" choices, those that may be at the core of the character's personality. This will also help you establish communication with the unconscious. Writing a journal is not nearly enough! If you don't use what you have created, it becomes just an exercise in writing, which can be thrown into a drawer and forgotten.

A TAPED EXCERPT OF AN ACTRESS
CREATING A CHARACTER BACKGROUND JOURNAL

(Recorded in my workshop while exploring the ingredients of a journal)
The actress is working on a scene from *The Woolgatherer;* the character is Rose.

MEGAN: Are you thinking of mixing the real with the unreal at the same time?

ERIC: Yes.

MEGAN: I think that she grew up in a poor neighborhood . . . Her father was an alcoholic who never worked . . .

ERIC: Does the play tell you this?

MEGAN: Her father was an alcoholic . . . I get that from the play . . . and he beat her.

ERIC: That's all from the play?

MEGAN: I'm not clear on that . . . It was a choice that I made . . . I know that he was an alcoholic . . . and her mother worked very hard. She rarely saw her . . . She was a very insecure child in school . . . Nobody really liked her. They thought that she was really strange . . . so she ended up living a lot of her life in books . . . in a fantasy world, making things the way she wanted them to be in her fantasies so she could stand being in the real world.

ERIC: O.K., whom are we talking about?

MEGAN: The character . . . Rosie. Do you want me to talk about me?

ERIC: Well, where are you getting all of this? Are you making it up?

MEGAN: I'm combining elements of me and what I have assumed . . .

ERIC: Good! That's what I wanted to hear . . . Which of those elements that you talked about are you?

MEGAN: Burying myself in books, not feeling liked or accepted.

ERIC: So Rosie and you are alike in those respects . . . In a sense you've created this scenario, right? . . . But it could fit . . . Go on. What else comes from you?

MEGAN: She's very good in school . . . like I was . . . always reading . . . very smart, very curious, always going to the library finding out about obscure and unusual things.

ERIC: Why do you think she did that?

MEGAN: I think it was one place where she could succeed . . . where she could get approval . . . She got good grades. She's smart.

ERIC: Were you?

MEGAN: Yes . . . I was also very curious.

ERIC: She ran to books and to her imagination because of her unhappy child life? Her father was an alcoholic and beat her . . . Why did you run to books?

MEGAN: Because I didn't feel accepted . . . because I felt that there was a safe place where I could let my imagination run wild, and nobody would think I was strange.

ERIC: People thought you were strange?

MEGAN: Yeah!

ERIC: People thought Rosie was strange?

MEGAN: Yeah!

ERIC: O.K. Go on.

MEGAN: I don't think she ever completed high school . . .

ERIC: Did you?

MEGAN: I did, yes . . . Rosie did not complete high school. She . . . uh . . .

ERIC: What did you not complete?

MEGAN: Well, I didn't complete some courses . . . but I passed them.

ERIC: But you didn't complete them . . . Do you have any incomplete areas in your education?

MEGAN: Oh yes, I have a lot of gaps!

ERIC: A lot of gaps . . . Can you relate to that?

MEGAN: Uh huh.

ERIC: So there is a good parallel there . . . Continue building it . . . See what we're doing here? So in a sense a character background journal builds the reality and the glue between you and the character. The character becomes you because you are using your own realities to build this character in parallel to what is or could be her. Now, if the author doesn't supply this, and you do, who's to say you are not right? Go on.

MEGAN: I got kicked out of the house at seventeen and had to find a job . . . Got kicked out because "Daddy" was so threatening. There is a question as to whether Rosie was kicked out or she just left . . . to get away from her father . . .

ERIC: What is the parallel in your life?

MEGAN: I can't think of one right off . . . except that I am a very scared person. I'm frightened of physical threat . . .

ERIC: You are? And so is Rosie!

MEGAN: And so is Rosie . . .

ERIC: Have you always been that way?

MEGAN: Yes, and of men too . . . I was brought up not to hit . . . Hitting was not good . . . I have always feared it in other people . . . I think anything physical is frightening to Rosie, and that is straight out of my life . . . anything physical, whether it's sex or hitting . . . very threatening. Her job at the five-and-dime is just another one in a series of jobs that she's had and been fired from or left.

ERIC: She works at the five-and-dime?

MEGAN: She does.

ERIC: You know that from the play?

MEGAN: I know that from the play. She's had a lot of jobs . . .

ERIC: Have you?

MEGAN: Yes.

ERIC: Name some of them.

MEGAN: I've taken care of other people's kids, I've washed floors, I've been a photolithographer, a bank teller, I've been a waitress . . .

ERIC: Some of those jobs Rosie could have done!

MEGAN: Yeah.

ERIC: O.K. Go on.

MEGAN: If she were a waitress, she would forget things exactly like me! She would be so spacy she would forget to bring the customers what they wanted. I have done that!

ERIC: We're drawing parallels . . . so in writing a character chart or a character background journal, I would suggest that you do it in the "I" and the "me" and not in the "she," O.K.? Go on. There's more.

MEGAN: She . . . I mean I . . . I think she continued her education by going to museums and talking to people about all these interesting things that are in the world . . . I still frequented the library . . . so basically that's the continuity in her . . . I mean, in my life: the books and the knowledge and the seeking of knowledge in a very innocent way.

ERIC: Can you parallel that?

MEGAN: I used to be so hungry to know things that I used to talk to people on that level to get more information, to know more things — not about people specifically, but facts. She knows facts . . . but not about people.

ERIC: So that parallels your own life? . . . What about her sensitivity . . . when those birds are killed? She comes apart, and they need to sedate her . . . Do you feel that way about animals?

MEGAN: Not as deeply as she does . . . but I feel that way.

ERIC: You do? . . . You care for animals? . . . Do you identify with her sensitivity on any level?

MEGAN: Yes.

ERIC: How do you feel about men? Do you have a parallel there?

MEGAN: Selectively emphasized, I can feel . . . I have a good parallel there.

ERIC: Give us an example.

MEGAN: I was brought up and taught to believe that men would want nothing but my body!

ERIC: So you were brought up to believe that for real?

MEGAN: That was the way I was brought up . . . by a very protective mother!

ERIC: And Rosie was too . . . right?

MEGAN: Yes, a very protective mother and a father to support that.

ERIC: He was what you had to watch out for!

MEGAN: Right.

ERIC: But your father wasn't like that?

MEGAN: No, my father wasn't like that . . . so, you see, that's the selective emphasis.

ERIC: Have you known men like that?

MEGAN: I have known men like that all my life . . . I find that most men relate to me on a sexual level.

ERIC: How do you feel about that?

MEGAN: It makes me feel resentful and angry and cheap and frustrated. It makes me feel like a piece of meat.

ERIC: Uh huh! Rosie feel that way?

MEGAN: Uh huh . . . Oh, and there's another thing here that's a very important element: Rosie and I . . . especially the part of my life I'm going back to . . . I don't feel like I was attractive, and any man that was attracted to me was a shit . . . because how could they be attracted to me and be a good person when I wasn't attractive sexually.

ERIC: That seems like a perfect parallel!

MEGAN: That is a perfect parallel.

ERIC: O.K. If you were to write this up in a journal, a character background journal, how would you "practicalize" the realities of your life, in parallel to Rosie's, so that you could use them on the stage or in front of a camera? Because otherwise it's busy work, isn't it?

MEGAN: What do you mean "practicalize"?

ERIC: How do you make that a reality that will feed into your acting, on a conscious (and, hopefully, unconscious) level? How do you work on what you just shared with us to put you in touch with it, to bring it into your work? Because what you were just doing in your character background exercise or journal was selectively emphasizing things in your life to create a journal, a life for Rosie. You are many things that she is not, and she is many things that you are not, so how do you practicalize this in your work?

195

MEGAN: What I have been doing . . . is an in-depth "When I was sixteen, seventeen, and eighteen" to get me back to that time in my life when there were more parallels between us.

ERIC: So you are doing the "I'm-Five-Years-Old-and-I . . ." exercise, starting at sixteen, right? What else?

MEGAN: I have a few specific instances that seem to trigger a lot of the feelings that are in parallel.

ERIC: And how do you work with those instances?

MEGAN: Sensorially.

ERIC: Good! You can also do imaginary monologues, talking to various people from different times in your life; you can go back and create your bedroom and the house you lived in; you may also do an Outer or an Inner Monologue going over your entire history before you start to work for the choices in a scene. By doing that, you may very well pique responses from the unconscious that you will carry right into the scene itself. Do you see the value of a character background journal?

If Megan takes all of the information and all of the parallels that she mentioned in this exploration, she will be able to create a fairly complete life for the character. Using her own specific experiences allows her to always have something to refer to when the character talks about her life in the play. Selectively emphasizing the parallels creates a vulnerability to the areas that the character is functioning in throughout the play. While Megan is different from Rose in many respects, drawing and supplying specific parallels stimulates in her a similar sensitivity to the circumstances of the play. There are many activities and techniques that an actor can use in order to act and to fulfill material. Character background journals are one of the most important tools.

Many times, when dealing with material, it is necessary to confront the character obligation first, since all of the other obligations are so influenced by the kind of person the character is. Remember to start with yourself! You and the character must merge and become one. Identify the various parts of the obligation, the *physical*, the *emotional*, the *intellectual*, and the *psychological*. Identify the similarities and the differences between you and the character, and work for the kinds of choices that will bring you together. YOU DO NOT BECOME ANYONE ELSE! THE CHARACTER IN ESSENCE BE-COMES YOU! In a sense, you absorb him into your being. So if you deal with, and fulfill, all the character elements drawn by the playwright and add your dimensional personality to the existing responsibilities, then you will make the unique statement inherent in your own persona. The character is who the playwright says he is *and more!*

Many actors consider characterization to be the fulfillment of *style*, the behavior of a character in an Elizabethan play, his dress, manner, style of speaking, and so on. Others reach for "handles" which they consider their responsibility to the character, things like a limp or a funny little twitch. Actors love to do accents; they really get into hanging the entire life of the character on some elongated drawl! Madness is another wonderful trait that they love to characterize. Unfortunately, these "handles" or manifestations of behavior—physical or otherwise—are all too often adopted, imposed, worn like an overcoat without any creative involvement on the part of the actor in constructing them. There are a number of reasons why an actor grabs on to these assumed impositions: they provide an element of security for him; they are activities and involvements that require energy and a kind of commitment to "doing" something, and this gives him a sense of security and a feeling of being involved. Besides, the sad reality is that most actors have little meaningful training in any process that might teach them where these characteristics come from and how they are approached and created organically.

Everything a character does in a piece of material comes from somewhere. A behavior is always stimulated by some object or impetus, while *the act of assuming almost anything is a result-form of acting.* It is representational! Dealing with style and period depends on some research into that period. It involves understanding the customs, mores, morality, religion, dress, knowledge, concerns, superstitions, and motivating forces in that society. If an actor is well versed in these things, he will approach the style and behavior of a character in a period piece by creative means! For example, the way people moved, sat, stood, greeted each other was extremely influenced by the simple reality of their clothing. In Elizabethan times they wore stiff ruffs around their necks, which affected the mobility of their neck and head; the men had rapiers and daggers, which had to be accommodated before they sat in a chair; they wore tights, which affected their walk and other movements. So if an actor just related to the costume of a particular time in history, some of the realities of movement and behavior would evolve organically. Morality and other kinds of consciousness indigenous to a particular period should be approached by finding parallels and substitutions. To understand the kind of jealousy and vengeful emotions that resulted from being cuckolded by one's wife, even though our present consciousness would not even allow us to consider the kind of revenge that was commonplace in those times, we as actors could work for, and explore, choices that would pique primal impulses in similar areas if we used the right emphasis. The principles of that period may seem ridiculous to us at present, but we do have our own principles, some of which could take us to the threshold of murder. So it is a matter of using what creates a similar reality for us.

The key to any character exists in one or more of the four responsibilities of characterization. If an actor is to play a physically handicapped person, for example, and that handicap is at the root of the character's behavior, he must not just assume the handicap, he must *create* it! He can do that in a variety of ways: he may use the choice approach of Illnesses and Restrictions; he can fulfill the obligation through the Externals Choice approach, using an animal or the sense of another person; or there are several other options that he might consider. Of course, every actor should be trained in the use of language and proper stage diction and have the versatility to speak English like a variety of characters, from an English duke to someone born and raised in the Bronx. He should also have spent time mastering the rhythm and music of many accents and dialects..

When creating a character, the actor should work for many of the elements that make up the component parts of that specific personality. These elements influence the way the character moves, speaks, and relates to others. With a little encouragement, a Southern accent may evolve as the actor deals with the other personality traits in the character. For example, if he approaches the character by working to create the sense of another person whose rhythms, tempo, and manner of speaking are slower, more languid, he can stimulate the accent from that place, using his knowledge of that particular dialect. There are times when an actor will just have to produce a specific dialect mechanically; however, at those times it should be like the icing on the cake; it should be approached after all the other realities have been created, and not as the skeleton on which to hang all the behavior. All character manifestations should come from a real place. If only the actor would ask himself, What caused or stimulated that manifestation, and how can I create it for myself? he would avoid representational imposition, which leads to empty and predictable work.

6

THE
NEW CHOICE
APPROACHES

At the time when my last book, *Irreverent Acting*, was published, there were twenty-two choice approaches; but since then I have created three more. The value of having so many choice approaches is that it supplies the actor with a richer variety of tools with which to build his role. Whatever the choice an actor selects to address an obligation in a piece of material might be, the specific choice approach is very important to the creation of that choice. Often, what determines the success or failure of a specific choice is the choice approach that the actor selects. The choice may indeed be very impelling for the scene, but the choice approach may not fit into the structure of the material. Because every piece of material and every character is different, there are cases where a particular choice approach is not structured to fit into the tempo of a character's speech, or where the actor doesn't have time to explore an object sensorially, or where one single choice approach does not create the dimensions of reality required in the scene. That is why there are now twenty-five options!

23. SHARING MONOLOGUES

We had been using this approach in my class for a couple of years before I realized that it had not been accounted for as a choice approach. Actors would get on the stage and begin preparing to do a scene or a monologue by "sharing" experiences. They would talk about incidents and events designed to stimulate the desired life. Afterwards, as is my custom, I would ask them what they had worked for, and most of the time they would say that they were doing a preparation that involved talking about a specific experience that made them feel the way they wanted to feel. After many such instances, I started calling what they were doing a "sharing monologue," never thinking of it as a new choice approach but only as a preparation for starting the work process. Then one evening in class, I asked an actor if he had continued to use the "sharing monologue" after the scene had begun, and he said, "Yes, as an inner monologue throughout the scene." At that point I realized that we had been using a separate and specific choice approach for quite some time without calling it such. You might be asking yourself, So what? If you're using it, what difference does it make if you give it a name or not? Well, it would matter less if the process remained in my own workshop, but since there are a lot of other actors around the world who use this work, they should be made aware of these new tools.

The Sharing Monologue is done by talking about an experience or event in your life. It can be the sharing of almost anything that is happening. It may include a report on how your life is going or on how you feel that day. It can be spoken to one or more people, as many as a full audience. It doesn't mean just rambling on without goal or direction. Usually an actor will choose to "share" something in a rehearsal or in class before doing a scene in order to stimulate the impulses that he wants to experience at the beginning of the scene.

Example:

"I have been feeling depressed lately . . . Nothing is going well for me . . . and I don't mean just today or yesterday either . . . It's been this way for a while now! . . . I mean over a year! . . . I keep thinking that things are going to change . . . but they don't! . . . Last New Year's eve I said that this year would certainly be different . . . Well, we're almost four months into it and nothing has changed! . . . I mean everything is rotten . . . I haven't had an acting job in . . . I don't remember how long . . . The last interview I had was three months ago . . . and that wasn't anything . . . I'm under a lot of financial pressure, and I hate waking up in the morning . . . My romantic life is nonexistent . . . and I feel very lonely . . . I know it's going to get better . . . but . . . frankly . . . I don't know if I can hang around and wait for it! I feel . . . like I don't know where to go to get help . . . Maybe I'm doing this to myself, but I really don't think so . . . I spend a lot of time sleeping . . . and watching television . . . I feel a little hopeless . . ."

Obviously this example comes from someone who is very despondent at this moment; or it could come from an actor attempting to selectively emphasize only the depressing elements in his life in order to promote a state of depression that would fulfill the emotional obligation of the monologue or scene he is about to do. In either instance, the above Sharing Monologue can be done out loud or as a silent Inner Monologue. There are a number of characters in dramatic literature that this particular choice would work for: Jessie in 'night, Mother, Biff in Death of a Salesman, Chrissy in In the Boom Boom Room, the actress in Talking With . . . , the main character in The Goddess, Alexandra DeLago in Sweet Bird of Youth, and many others. Of course, a Sharing Monologue can have any content: it can be full of joy and passion, or it may be a collection of confusions. The content can be as varied as there are actors to use the approach, but the structure remains the same.

Example of a Sharing Monologue Using an Experience:

"I will never forget the day my son was born . . . It's been twenty-five years, but I can remember that day as if it were yesterday . . . I waited in the fathers' waiting room for my wife to have him . . . and I felt a combination of anxiety and excitement! . . . It seemed forever before the nurse came out and told me that I had a son . . . and then it was an eternity before I could see him . . . When I was finally ushered into the glass-enclosed nursery, I could hardly contain the excitement I felt! There he was . . . red as a lobster with long blond hair almost shoulder length. He had a swollen fat face . . . but I could see me in his tiny little features. I stood there for a long time bursting with pride, excitement, and a feeling of explosive joy . . . That little creature behind the glass was mine! I had made him! . . . I was the creator of that! . . . I wanted to share my feelings with everyone who came into the nursery, but I held back because I knew that they couldn't possibly understand the depth of what I was feeling . . . I wanted to yell . . . scream . . . sing and dance all at the same time! As I drove home, I had the incredible feeling that I was the only person on earth who had ever accomplished such a feat . . . I didn't care about the logic of that feeling; I just enjoyed it!"

Both examples are quite antithetical in their content. Besides, one is a Sharing Monologue about a specific experience while the other shares what the actor is feeling in the moment. The entire purpose for this choice approach is to stimulate the desired emotional life and to continue to promote that life throughout the scene, if that is the responsibility.

THE OBLIGATION: To feel elated, full of joy, and as if you have just accomplished the impossible (the character of Willie Farouli in *The Time of Your Life*)

THE CHOICE: The content of the above monologue about becoming a father

THE CHOICE
APPROACH: Sharing Monologue

USING THE APPROACH

The scene in *The Time of Your Life* is the one in which Willie hits the jackpot on the pinball machine that he has been playing all through the play. He goes wild and has a monologue to Jim, which is outrageous in its elation and joy. The actor playing Willie might use the Sharing Monologue as a preparation before the scene just to elevate his excitement. He could do it as an Inner Monologue while playing the pinball machine, saving the really impelling parts of the experience for when he hits the jackpot, at which point he might use those elements to kick off the beginning of his monologue.

WILLIE: (Doing the Sharing Monologue internally: "I can't believe it, that living thing in front of me is mine! . . . I made it!! It looks just like me . . . and I did it . . . Wow, I can't believe it!")

Dialogue (not verbatim):
I did it! . . . I did it! . . . I knew I could do it! . . . ("It's mine; I'm its father . . . Nobody else on this earth has ever felt what I feel right now.") I always knew I could beat the marble game! Not that that's the only thing I want to do in my life . . . but when I set my mind to something, I do it! . . .

He goes on bragging about himself and continues to be good-naturedly full of himself. The Sharing Monologue can be the exclusive choice approach for this piece, or the actor can use it in combination with other choices and approaches. Remember, the content of a Sharing Monologue can be anything.

24. SELECTIVE ENHANCEMENT

This choice approach came to be by sheer accident. One of my students had just finished doing a monologue, and when I asked him what he had worked for, he said that he was working with "selective enhancement," meaning of course Selective Emphasis. I corrected him and went on with the critique of his work. A couple of days later, I started to think about his mistaken use of "enhancement" for "emphasis" and realized that this might be an added tool for the actor. I went through all the choice approaches in my head to see if there was such a tool in the repertoire. There was not! I thought, "Out of the mouths of babes . . ." I started to explore this possible approach. First, I defined it for myself: what was enhancement, and how could it be used as part of the creative process? I understood the technique of selecting an element of a whole object and isolating just a part of it; but enhancement meant making more of it, making it bigger, better, more interesting, more beautiful, more "anything" than it really was; in other words, enhancing it to make it more impelling or more compelling to you. In the beginning I only dealt with available stimulus, but later I took the approach into imaginary choice areas.

The approach technique for doing Selective Enhancement can be Sense Memory, Sensory Suggestion, an Inner Monologue describing the enhancements, Believability—in short, any of the choice approaches that would convince the actor of the existence of the added elements in the stimulus. Imagination plays a large part in the process, as it does in all the other choice approaches.

If you are familiar with my earlier works, you might be wondering how this choice approach differs from Endowments. It is actually quite different! Endowments is the process of putting on an object something that isn't there—creating a feature, a sound, a look in a person's eyes that didn't exist before you created it—while enhancement is the process of *using* what is already there and "enhancing" it. Take, for example, a person's beautiful blue eyes, which seem like a bottomless well of blueness. Enhancing those eyes would entail acknowledging their blueness and beauty and possibly enlarging them slightly or creating a greater contrast between the iris of the eye and the pupil and carrying that contrast into the whites of the eyes, making the blue bluer, richer, more fluidly changeable, and so on. This could all be accomplished through the sensory process or by sensory suggestion.

It is very important to note here that you must always use the object with which you are working. Start in an area that appeals to whatever you are trying to promote. If it is a threatening demeanor in a person, relate to what is there. Using what is available, start to enhance it by making it more pronounced, bigger, more prominent.

Example:

In a hypothetical love scene, the characters are holding each other very close and are seemingly very enamored of each other.

THE ACTOR: (Using the actress he is doing the scene with) She's beautiful . . .
I love her coloring . . . her hair and the way it contrasts with her
skin . . . (At this point he might sensorially create a greater
contrast between her hair and the color of her skin. He might
do this by asking sensorial questions, creating the contrast, or
he may just suggest it and respond sensorially.) The texture of
her lips is fantastic . . . It is like velvet! (Again he could create an
added element to what already exists, using the texture that is
there.) I love her scent . . . (enhancing her odor with his sense
of smell). Her face next to mine feels soft, smooth, and exciting.
(He can enhance these feelings through his tactile responses.)
Her voice is sweet and soft; it has a depth and yet a femininity
that excites me (creating an enhanced sound, making it softer,
more melodic, etc. . . .)

The actor can do this in an Inner Monologue, so no one hears his process.
The actress needn't know what he is doing.

When using an imaginary stimulus, the actor will create the object first,
using the sensory process. Then, when it exists for him, he will start the
enhancement process. It works exactly the same way as when using Available
Stimulus.

THE OBLIGATION: (Relationship and emotional)	(Mother and son relationship) To establish that relationship, the reality of being mother and son, and to feel an incredible amount of warmth and empathy
THE CHOICE:	Available Stimulus: the actress he is working with
THE CHOICE APPROACH:	Selective Enhancement

USING THE APPROACH

The actor can elect to use any approach technique that he wishes. He should
pick the most expedient one to service the obligation. Let us use as an example
the relationship between the mother and the son in *The Trip to Bountiful*. He
obviously has a great deal of love for her, while being at the same time
empathetic to her loneliness and her need to return to "Bountiful." Using the
actress in the play, the actor concentrates on the enhancement of features and
emotional traits that will hopefully stimulate the relationship responsibility
and at the same time create the sympathy and empathy that the material
requires. While playing the scene, he could do a running Inner Monologue

enhancing the elements in the actress that promote the emotional life of the scene.

Example: (Inner-Monologue approach technique)

"She's very much like my own mother . . . in essence . . . She doesn't look like her . . . but there is a similar energy . . . and quality. They say similar things . . . and sound very much alike. I see the ravages of age in her face. (Using what is there and beginning to enhance those manifestations) She has deep lines around her mouth, and they flow downward. I see the years of sadness and pain in her eyes. (All the time making everything bigger and fuller than what really exists, the actor is approaching the enhancement process by doing an Inner Monologue describing the elements involved.) I can see the loneliness in her eyes and in the bend of her body. She hurts but doesn't want me to see that hurt . . . I see her love for me . . . It shines through everything . . . I hear the sadness in every word she speaks. (At all times the actor is taking real things and enhancing them to serve his purpose.) Her hair is so white and lifeless. She seems to have lost her lust for living, and it shows in everything she does . . . in the way she gestures, moves, and even in the lack of color in her voice . . . She is so full of love though. (The actor is primarily *suggesting* all of these things, but it would probably be a more successful involvement if he responded *sensorially*.)

The actor may have to use some Endowments in order to create the relationship reality of being with his mother; however, the enhancement process might fulfill both the relationship and the emotional obligations.

Selective Enhancement can also be used in conjunction with Believability. If both actors are doing a Believability preparation in the form of an improvisation, they could do Enhancement as part of the process.

EXAMPLE OF SELECTIVE ENHANCEMENT IN CONJUNCTION WITH BELIEVABILITY

HE: You are beautiful . . . I love the way you look at me! . . . I feel as if you were making love to me with your eyes . . . (The Believability begins with Enhancement: the actress is looking at him, but without any kind of sexual feelings.)

SHE: I am making love to you in my imagination . . . and you are great! (She is also doing the enhancement process; and if they continue, they will both create the attraction and the sexual reality.)

HE: I love the way you touch me. It is so sensual . . . (He is actually creating the reality through the things that he is saying in the Believability. She is touching him, and he is responding to that touch by enhancing how she is doing it and how it feels.)

SHE: You have all the qualities I have ever wanted in a man! I love your strength, and yet you are soft and sensitive! You're not threatened by your vulnerability, and that makes me more comfortable with mine! (She is relating to a base reality here but is definitely enhancing what is there.)

This improvisation can go on for however long it takes to stimulate the desired emotional life. Using reality and Believability as an approach technique to do the enhancement process promotes the feelings and the relationship that should lead right into the scene.

25. EVOCATIVE IMAGES

For years I wouldn't even let my students use the word "image" in relation to the creative process. I have always felt that imaging was predominantly intellectual and that it did not promote reality. I felt about it much the same way as I do about thinking about a choice; it starts in the head and somehow remains there, promoting only retrospective responses that are mostly cerebral. So it is a big step for me to be using a technique that even has the word "image" as part of its name. It all started when I invented the exercise called "Fragmented Images," described in chapter 2. While exploring that technique I became aware of the impacting impulsive responses of the people who were using it. They had real emotional reactions to these images they would hook into. That, and the fact that I have been using Evocative Words as a choice approach for years, started me on the journey to exploring Evocative Images.

Like any technique, you have to use it for a while before you know if it works and if you can trust it. It is done in much the same way as Evocative Words, but instead of calling for an auditory response, it appeals to the visual sense. Just like Evocative Words, it deals with either an experience that you have had or a belief structure; but it has a wider scope and range, since you can evoke almost anything you can imagine! The technique is done by suggesting images to yourself, related to a room, a person, or an event. It isn't done in chronological order, but more like Fragmented Images, as you jump around the room or experience, suggesting the object, its size, shape, and what it might be doing. It is very important, so as not to get trapped in the head, that you encourage a sensorial response at all times. Images call forth other sensorial responses, as well as feelings, and those responses are to be encouraged! If used properly, this technique should stimulate a sense of being there or actually re-experiencing the event. Just like Evocative Words, Evocative Images stimulates a sense of the reality, and it should produce equally good results.

Example:

(The following is expressed in words so that the reader knows what images the actor sees. The actor, however, says nothing; he only evokes those images.)

(Working for a place where particular events took place) High ceiling . . . beams . . . vaulted . . . brown . . . the sun is on the ceiling . . . wood all over . . . it's warm . . . piano in the corner . . . (His responses to images) Can almost hear it being played . . . (These are his thoughts and impulses brought forth by the place.) She used to play it . . . *Born Free* . . . that's what she used to play . . . Orange carpet . . . empty fireplace . . . ashes . . . sliding glass doors . . . open, feel the breeze . . . (Responding sensorially at all times to the evocative images) Table . . . papers on it . . . books . . . her books . . . wood in the bin . . . the sun streaming in the windows . . . rocking chair . . . empty . . . no one in it . . . She liked that chair . . . curled up in it all the time . . . That little deer . . . made out of logs . . . standing there . . . bought it for her four Christmases ago . . . The sofa . . . middle of the room . . . the painting on the wall . . . it looks like a lonely place . . . in that painting . . . nice colors . . . Arizona . . . or maybe New Mexico . . . don't know . . . I like it . . . she didn't . . . The drapes blowing in the wind . . .

In this example, what I attempted to create was a place involving a relationship that was obviously over. The actor was evoking images related to that specific place, where he spent time with someone he loved. By using the technique of Evocative Images, he should be successful in creating that place. If his images create an empty room, the absence of the person he loved should stimulate the desired emotional results.

THE OBLIGATION:	To feel frustrated and unable to communicate a long-standing collection of unspoken resentments and unfulfilled desires
THE CHOICE:	The actor's own wife and the actress he is working with
THE CHOICE APPROACH:	Endowments to create his wife in relation to the actress and Evocative Images as a second choice approach

207

The play I am attempting to use as an example is *Split* by Michael Weller. It is about a husband and wife who have been incubating an enormous amount of frustration and rage, which comes out in the course of the play and brings the relationship to a climax.

USING THE APPROACH

After creating his wife in relation to the actress by using Endowments as a choice approach, the actor starts to do Evocative Images, while talking to his choice through the lines of the play:

> She's doing her thing . . . talking and not listening . . . (Evocative Images) Look on her face . . . eyes protective . . . can't-affect-me look . . . color changing . . . redder . . . mouth . . . ugly look . . . cheek twitching . . . violent set face . . . rage . . . anger look . . .

All of the above responses are in reality visual. The actor says nothing to himself. He just sees these images. He can do Evocative Images under his own lines or while she is speaking to him. Once he has created his wife in relation to the actress and they have become a composite, he can then use the "images" to create her behavior, creatively manipulating them to produce the feelings he is after.

> (Again, the words below merely describe the images he *sees*.) She's silent . . . hateful eyes . . . glaring . . . biting lip . . . standing . . . pacing . . . caged . . . arms crossed . . . tightly . . . tense . . . cutting off circulation . . . arms turn white . . .

The actress doesn't have to be doing any of the things that the actor is imaging. It is the evocative images that will hopefully create the reality. If, however, the actress is behaving in such a manner as to promote the images, it will be easier to create the reality.

In the above example, the actor was using Evocative Images as the choice approach in relation to the actress doing the scene with him. She was there, and he was relating his images to her, but Evocative Images can also be done when no one is there. The actor in the preceding example could have done exactly the same thing on an empty stage, evoking images that might have stimulated the same responses. Every actor has different sensory strengths and dependencies. Some actors are very visual, while others are more responsive in the auditory area. A visual actor will probably use this technique more frequently and with greater success. Evocative Images is yet another tool for the actor to use in his creative process of fulfilling the demands of material.

The new choice approaches give you more options, new tools that might just work in areas for which others were not quite right. To master anything, you must practice it! Use these new choice approaches in the laboratory, in your acting classes, at home, and in your rehearsals. Make them yours!

7

REHEARSING

An entire book could be written about rehearsing! There are so many variables and so much to say. *An actor must know how to rehearse!* He must know how to use a rehearsal and what to do in it. He must understand what is expected of him. If he just stumbles through, reading lines and doing the blocking, it is a wasted time; he might as well have stayed home and paced the scenes off in his living room. All too often a director and his actors will come to rehearsals without any real idea of what to do other than run the play, fulfill the blocking requirements, say the lines, get off the book as soon as possible, and pray that it will all magically come together by opening night!

The director, of course, gives "direction," interpreting the play for the actor and asking for more volume, bigger emotion, deeper feelings, and definitely more passion in the work. After each rehearsal, he reads voluminous pickup notes, which the actors copy down on their notepads—things like, "Joyce, you were blocking Harry in Scene 2. Countercross him! Peter, I can't hear you; speak up! Danny, I want more real anger from you. Don't just shout, feel it!" and so on, in a variety of equally helpful areas! Somehow the play opens, however, and the audience seems to enjoy it; everyone is very complimentary, and all the actors feel that they have accomplished the arduous job of creating something. Unfortunately, this kind of rehearsing is the rule rather than the exception. The more professional the actor becomes, the more sophisticated the terminology: the directors and actors behave and talk more professionally, and indeed the actors seem to move around on the stage more comfortably, but it is still the same. For the most part, and with rare exceptions, the rehearsals consist of repeating the lines, blocking, getting more comfortable with the other actors, making the words of the play sound real and natural, working out problems of sight lines and stage picture, and so on. But where is the creative involvement? When do the actors and the director collaborate in the creative process of producing impulsive and unpredictable reality on the stage?

Well, first of all, in order for that to happen, they must all know what they are doing; they must be craftsmen and must have a creative process! Very unfortunately that is extremely rare. I must sound just a bit pompous here, but the reality is that I am sad about the state of affairs in the theater and in films. It gives me no pleasure to know that what I have been saying is all too true! I would rather it be just the opposite, since good work, good films, good theater enrich us all. I don't mean to suggest that there aren't any; quite the contrary, there is some wonderful work out there: scores of talented people, good films, excellent plays, and so on. These are the exceptions, however, and what is so painful is that it needn't be that way. There is a process, a how, many hows, to create reality and exciting work, but for whatever reason most of the actors and directors have somehow missed learning it.

Knowing how to rehearse, either as an actor or as a director, is totally dependent on knowing what you are doing. If you have a specific creative process through which you fulfill material, then you can chart your rehearsals and make the most of each one. I have already said that there are numerous variables, related not only to process, but to medium, time, the specific director, and the other actors. Each of these parameters dictates different approaches and adjustments. Adjusting to the medium in which you are working is very dependent on your knowledge and mastery of your craft, as well as on a certain amount of technical knowledge and experience with that medium.

KNOWING HOW TO REHEARSE
IN THE VARIOUS MEDIUMS

As I said earlier in this chapter, rehearsing is a very complex involvement, and in order to cover all the ground, I would have to devote an entire book to the subject. I will, however, attempt to deal specifically with each area of responsibility.

REHEARSING FOR A FILM

Again, so much is dependent on the time involved. Usually, if you are doing a feature film, as opposed to a television film, you have a little more time to devote to rehearsing. This is entirely related to budget. In a high-budget film there is usually much less pressure on the director to move on, so he can take more time with each scene. Television always seems to be on a tight schedule, so there is less latitude in that environment.

If a film has a rehearsal period built into the budget, there will be about two weeks of rehearsals before principal photography begins; however, these will usually be devoted to the principals. the stars of the film. Since the lower-budget films rarely allow for a rehearsal period and the more expensive films usually hire name actors, the actor who has not yet ascended to those heights never gets to be involved in a rehearsal period. Most often, the only rehearsal he gets is just before he shoots the scene. He may receive the script anywhere from two weeks to one day before shooting. He must then work to fulfill his responsibility to the material and to the character, memorize his lines, know what he wants to do with them, and usually do all of this before ever meeting or talking to the director.

So you normally come onto the set of a picture having had only solitary involvement with the script. You report to makeup and, if you are lucky, work within the next four or five hours. When indeed you are called to "do" your scene, you meet the director, shake his hand, and he briefly tells you what the scene is about from his perspective. Pray to God that he sees it the way you worked on it, because if he doesn't, you have about three minutes to change your approach! After this brief orientation, you step into the set and acknowledge the other actors. The director says, "All right, let's see it!" at which time you start to "act": you say your lines, listen for your cues, and attempt to relate to the other actors and to be real.

Meanwhile, the director, with crossed eyes, takes in the action while talking to the director of photography about how he wants the scene covered. He may say that he wants more tempo, or he may ask you to stand closer to the other actor in a position that is awkward and unreal but that fits the frame beautifully. If he is satisfied with the content and action of the scene, and if it can be heard and the cameraman okays it, he calls for a "take." So you do it! Not knowing exactly what it is that you are doing, you do it anyway. If he says, "That's a print!" you breathe a sigh of relief, since at this point getting it right has become so much more important than being creative! It certainly wasn't anything like what you did at home! Now the director goes in for close-ups and other coverage of the scene, and you, the actor, must "match" for the close-up what you did in the "master," making sure that you hit the same marks taped on the floor, match your lines and movements so they are exactly the way they were in the master shot, and try to retain the same emotional energy and content as before. You do this for three or four different angles, each of which may have three, four, or five takes. Having spent two hours on a scene that might play for two minutes, you step out of the set exhausted and somewhat confused by what has just happened! Furthermore, you haven't the vaguest idea what kind of work you did.

This is not a very encouraging picture of what usually happens when you start to work in films, but it is pretty much the way it usually is. So what is an actor to do, particularly if he cares about his work? How can you do your work in such an environment? You realize, of course, that there are exceptions. Sometimes you get lucky and work with a director who is sensitive to the actors' problems and process. When that happens, he gives you more room, is more available to discuss what you are attempting to do, and is more helpful. Whatever the case, you must be prepared to work under any and all conditions. In order for that to happen, you need to do several things: first, get as much technical experience in front of that camera as possible! Know what you are doing; know how to match, move, and use the camera to your advantage; become familiar with frame lines; know how much the camera is seeing and how much freedom of movement you have in each shot. You must also know how animated you can be depending on how close the shot is; for example, if the camera is in a tight close-up on you, any large behavior will seem humongous on the screen at Radio City Music Hall! You must have complete knowledge of, and confidence in, your technical responsibilities. Just that will make you more secure and free you to do the creative work that must be done to fulfill the material. Once you know what you are doing, you can quickly assimilate the technical demands of the shot and be free to deal with the obligations of the piece as an actor. Having worked on the piece at home, you will have identified the various obligations: the relationship obligation, the emotional obligation, and any others in the scene.

The first thing you do when stepping into the set is to listen to what the director wants. Usually it is mostly technical, but sometimes he will give you some information about your character and what he would like to see happen. If that is the case, take it in and fit it into the decisions you have already made. You may have to make an adjustment in one of your choices to accommodate the quality he wants. Once you have digested his directions, quickly acknowledge the technical responsibilities, know where to move and when, find your marks and make note of them, understand where you must be to play the scene and what the camera is going to see, what amount of freedom of movement you have, and so on. Once you have accomplished that, start working for the choices, using your choice approaches to stimulate the emotional life you want to reach.

The craft process from this point on is the same as it is on the stage. You have decided, for example, that the emotional obligation in this scene is murderous rage, so you are working to create a person toward whom you really feel that way, and you are using the Endowments choice approach to create this person in relation to the actor you are working with. If you use charts in your film work, each scene will be blueprinted as to the obligations, choices, and approaches. In addition, you will also have a continuity chart, so you will always know what preceded the scene you are doing and what will follow it. *Film acting is hard!* It takes time and a great deal of commitment to become a good film actor. For years there was a kind of snobbery, which came mostly from the New York stage actors, that essentially denigrated the talent and ability of the film actor, but that would usually disappear as soon as these "stage" actors began working in film! It is impossible not to respect the people who have become craftsmen in front of that camera.

The goals do not change; they are the same when working in film as in any other medium: you want to be real, unpredictable, organic, and hopefully reach an *ultimate-consciousness* state in front of that camera. So how do you accomplish that in light of all these technical restrictions? A very important question! Some actors never answer it! As I have already said, you master the technical responsibilities of acting in film. How do you do that? You work in front of a camera at every opportunity. Take a good camera class, and stay there until you know what you are doing; do student films—you will both learn together! Take almost any film job you can get—industrials, documentaries, educational films, and so on. Don't let your ego stand in the way of your growth. Do a one-line part in a film if you can. There is no telling what you will learn from that experience. Work with your friends: get a video camera, and do scenes together. Watch films from a different perspective: look at each scene as a "take," and see what the actor does. In short, overdose on learning how to act for the camera! Once you have done all that, you can become confident that you will not go under out there. You can then devote the greatest part of your energy to the creative process, which starts with preparation—knowing what to do to prepare for a day's work on a film.

Preparing at Home

Since you will get very little time to work on the script when you reach the set, it is important to do the bulk of your work at home. Read the material, get an overview of the screenwriter's statement, the feeling of the screenplay, its essence, and so on. Understand how your character fits into the whole thing, how he affects the other people, how they affect him, and so on. Break down your responsibilities into the applicable obligations. Decide which one of them should be addressed first, and begin to explore the choices that will hopefully fulfill it. Continue to deal with each obligation until you are satisfied that you have the "right" choices and choice approaches; then work with those until you feel confident about your approach to the role.

Make sure to chart the entire process, so that when you get to the studio you know exactly what you are going to do, what you will work for, and what approach technique you will use to create the choice. Draw up charts—an obligation-choice-and-choice-approach chart and a continuity chart. Let us imagine, for example, that you have identified three obligations in the scenes that you will do—a time-and-place obligation, a relationship obligation, and an emotional obligation—and that you have decided to tackle the time and place first. The script tells you that the character is in his library, a place where he spends a great deal of time and where he feels comfortable and secure. He knows exactly where everything is and can reach for things without even looking for them. You, the actor, have chosen a place in your home that makes you feel very much the same way: your study, where you spend a lot of time, feel very comfortable, and so on. You have decided to use Sense Memory as the choice approach and can begin working to create that place immediately. Of course, you will have to wait until you are on the set to create it there, but by working with it at home, you will have done most of the preparatory work, so that you will be able to accomplish your goal much more quickly when you do work on the set.

Regarding the second obligation, the relationship, you are told that your character doesn't know the other character and that you are meeting for the first time at the beginning of the scene. You are also given the information that you feel uncomfortable and suspicious of him. Armed with all of that, you decide to use the other actor as Available Stimulus. Having never met him, you can use the existing reality and selectively emphasize anything about him that will make you uncomfortable and suspicious of him. The last obligation, the emotional, you identify as a kind of self-righteousness and anger at being put in this position. Here again you anticipate the possibility that you may be able to use available-stimulus realities on the set, such as anything that the director or other actors do or say that could violate your belief structure, making you angry and self-righteous. Or you may have to create or endow the available stimuli with behavior and actions that will affect you that way. In any case, you might decide not to try imaginary choices at home until you have had the opportunity to deal with what is there; and of course, if you cannot use the available stimuli, you can always go to an imaginary choice when you are there.

Preparation on the Set

As I said earlier, there are so many variables it is almost impossible to cover them all. Each film, each role will necessitate different preparations. I would suggest that you get there early just in case you have to work soon after you arrive. Do the customary relaxation exercises; then do Personal Inventory to see what you need as a preparation for getting ready to get ready. If, for example, you find that you need to work on your ego, pick the kind of ego preparation that will take you to the proper place. After that you may decide to work for a choice that makes you more vulnerable. If you find that these are the only preparations that you need and can do alone, make sure that you don't prepare too early, or if you do, be sure that you can reinvest in the preparations just before going on the set. At this point, you may have to deal with the actor you are going to work with. If that is the case, seek him out and see if you can find a way to do the necessary relationship work.

Getting the Other Actor
to Prepare with You

Often this becomes an art in itself! Many actors feel that they are too "professional" to do any kind of preparation before they actually step in front of the camera. Others will welcome the opportunity to prepare, run lines, or do whatever is necessary to make their work better. You have to "feel it out," see if you are working with the kind of actor who is involved with process and wants to "warm up"! If you are, do whatever is necessary to establish the reality of the relationship. Explore his features; look for the things in his behavior that promote the right impulses for you; selectively emphasize things that he says or does that make you feel what you want to feel. You needn't tell him what you are doing since it can all be done silently while making small talk. If an endowment is necessary, if you have to create sensorially things that do not exist in him, however, you will probably need more time.

If you come across an actor who is obviously not into that "schoolroom acting shit," one who "says his jokes, takes the money, and runs," you will have to subtly seduce him into working with you without his knowledge of what you are actually doing. The best way to do this is to start with a compliment: tell him how much you enjoy his work, or whatever, get him to talk about himself—all actors love doing that!—then do your work with him as he talks. While you are doing your process, he is "getting off" telling you about his life, and at the same time he is getting the value of your preparation by becoming somewhat related and involved with you—and he doesn't even know it! Of course, achieving ensemble will usually be more possible when you are working with a cooperative actor who is willing to do ensemble-type preparations.

If the obligation is a large emotional encounter and you can get the other actor to prepare with you, go to your dressing room and do some work on the choices that will precipitate the emotional life between the two of you. For example, suppose the scene starts with a violent disagreement over an issue or another person and the level of life is quite emotional. If you do some imaginary monologues talking to the other actor as if he were someone else, you could establish the impetus that will organically catapult you into the scene; or you may find an issue between you that will work as available stimulus. Whatever the case may be, use your time to get ready to work. Once you step into the set, quickly assimilate your technical responsibilities, and begin working for the choices you have decided on. Carry your preparations into the scene and go from there. As you go from take to take and setup to setup, be sure that you stay in touch with the obligations in each section; reinvest in the specific choices and approaches, and don't allow yourself to get distracted from your creative responsibilities. If possible, try to use choices that might reach into the unconscious and bring some of its life into each scene. As you gain experience with the craft, you will learn to recognize those kinds of choices.

Working with the Various Directors

Every director you will work with will be different! Each one has his own style, from no direction to fastidious attention to minute detail! Your responsibility is to know your job, to be able to do what you are asked, and to do it professionally and well. If God is good to you and you get a director who really knows what he is doing, allow him to lead you into what he wants from you. Very few directors in the world have a process that allows them to collaborate with the actor to produce organic and exciting results, but some are bright enough to recognize that you indeed do have a process, and they will clear the way for you to use it. Let them!

Most often, the director will tell you where to move and on what line, and he will give you some input on what he would like to see happen in the scene. Listen to his directions. Be clear about the technical responsibilities. Walk through the moves, make sure that you "nail down" the action of the scene, and then move into your craft process. If the director tells you something that is inconsistent with what you had planned to explore, make his direction clear to yourself, and adjust or modify your choices and approaches accordingly. The rule is that a director will most likely leave you alone if he is getting what he wants. If you are a craftsman and can function in the medium, you will have no trouble with directors. It is almost never necessary to discuss or to show your process to anyone. Unless a director specifically wants to know exactly what you are doing, it is your own business. Once in a while you will be fortunate enough to encounter an "actors' director," and if this is the case, he will most likely attempt to direct you creatively by manipulating and suggesting stimuli or affecting you in some desired way. When that happens, let go of your choice and go with where he is leading you. The most important things you need when working with any kind of director is to know what you are doing, to be malleable and open, to have confidence in your craft, and to use it!

How to Use the Brief Rehearsals You Get

Usually, all you have to rehearse a scene in a film is a few minutes, and unless there are problems with it, the director will look at it, make some suggestions, and shoot it. So you must be able to do your work fast! Unlike a play rehearsal, where you can repeat, stop, and ask questions, a film rehearsal does not give you much time. So know exactly what you are going to do in the shot! Be clear about your choice and approach. If possible, begin working before you step into the set. Be ready at every opportunity. If you don't feel right about your work in a particular take, ask the director if you could do it again, but for God's sake, learn from the last take, and use the next one. If you need another rehearsal, speak up and ask for it. It is better to use the time in another rehearsal than to waste the film by shooting it when you don't feel ready. Of course, it is important to know the difference between taking your due as a creative artist and being a pain in the butt! If you really know what you are doing, however, and you need more time, additional input, clarification, and so on, don't be afraid to ask for it. Remember that the only thing that is really important in the last analysis is what comes out on that film. You can be a "one-take Charlie" and be loved by the producer and the director, but if your work isn't good, that's all they'll remember. Beware of the trap of tension and panic. Under the pressure of a take, your work can go out the window if you begin to concern yourself with the wrong things. If you feel that pressure growing in you, stop and deal with it. Do some Personal Inventory, deal with your demons, acknowledge the distractions, and reinvest in the strongest part of your choice to "suck" yourself back into the scene. If you want to do shtik and play, do so after you have finished working for the day. While you are there, use every moment you have to prepare and exercise your craft!

A Rehearsal and Preparation Checklist for Film Acting

Home Preparation:

Read and understand the material, break down the responsibilities of your character, decide on your various choices and approaches, and work on them at home. Create a complete chart of your obligations, choices, and approaches as well as continuity chart.

Preparation on the set:

1. Get there early enough to prepare. Do the relaxation-cluster. Do Personal Inventory: find out where you are and what other preparations you need to go on to the next step; do them!
2. Take an available-stimulus inventory: find out what exists in the environment that you can use to promote your goals, and work with it.
3. Find out with whom you are working; do some preparations with them, and get ready for the scene.
4. Refer to your charts frequently so you know exactly where you are and what you must do.
5. Always be aware of the need to establish an ensemble relationship with the other actors, and decide on your choices with that in mind. Encourage ensemble preparations.

6. Understand the director, know where he is coming from, and make the necessary adjustments to get the most out of the collaboration.

7. Stay in touch with how you feel at all times; include your moment-to-moment life in the scene.

8. Use every second of the rehearsal, first to solidify the technical demands of the scene, and then to create the reality craftually.

9. Prepare for the next day. Mentally go over everything you did today, and if necessary write it down in some kind of journal. You may have to do some preparations tomorrow in order to match the emotional state you were in today. Refer to your charts, and follow the continuity. Tomorrow is not only a new day; it is a continuation of today!

10. The goal and the bonus of our work is to accomplish the highest state of inspiration and reality possible. An *ultimate-consciousness* experience is that, so remember to do *ultimate-consciousness* preparations and to make choices that will hopefully stimulate responses from the unconscious.

REHEARSING FOR A PLAY

Again, there are many kinds of plays and many levels of production, from college theater to Broadway with a lot in between! Every circumstance is slightly different, and rehearsal schedules and techniques vary with each of the many directors involved. If you get a Broadway play, the rehearsals may last anywhere from three to six weeks, starting each morning and going for a full eight- or ten-hour day. Off Broadway is similar, but as you get less and less professional, to where actors don't get paid for their work, you will find that the rehearsal schedules vary greatly. Whatever amount of time you spend rehearsing, it is very important to use those rehearsals creatively. Your process is extremely important to the outcome of your work. Unlike in film, here you do have the luxury of time to explore and experiment. Unfortunately most actors and almost as many directors do not know *how* to rehearse, so it becomes a process of repetition and acclimation. From the very first rehearsal, you must know exactly what you are doing and what you are going to do! Part of your time will be spent with the director and the other actors rehearsing either in the theater or in some other rehearsal space, but the rest of it should be spent doing your "homework."

Directors work very differently. Some may start the rehearsal process by having the actors read the play together and discussing its statements and their interpretations. Others will want to get the actors on their feet immediately. Whatever the approach, you must use each and every rehearsal. You must know what you are going to do each day. A good way to start is to see what is there! Find out where everyone is coming from. If you start rehearsing by reading the play, don't impose any concept in the reading. Read it from where you are in the moment. Listen to what the director says and what he wants, and make notes about it. Listen to, and watch, the other actors; get a sense of how they work, what they do, and what you are likely to get or not get from them. Allow yourself a wide open field to discover what is there to be addressed. Let the material carry you if it will. Often, the actor will get sucked into the current of the realities of the material, and that will be the foundation of choices he makes later on. Know what is there that might work for the obligations of your character, and identify the elements that you can relate to that will intensify the impact of these available realities. Avoid making any "final decisions" in the early rehearsals; allow yourself the time to explore the possibilities. Remember that you are a long way from performance, so don't push for results of any kind. Relate to the rehearsal period as an adventurous journey into unexplored territory.

If the director starts immediately to "block" the play, it is important that you just note and move through the blocking process. You cannot do more than one thing at a time, so don't attempt to work for any choices until you have assimilated the blocking. You will be able to organically motivate and impel yourself to move to those places later. It is extremely important to prepare before starting a rehearsal, and if the director you are working with doesn't do preparations, you must do them for yourself. Start with instrumental preparations. As the rehearsals proceed, the preparations will vary in terms of the demands of each particular rehearsal. Know what you are after, and ask yourself in what kind of place you have to be to accomplish that reality. That will lead you to the kind of preparation you need.

Early in the rehearsal process, after you have become acquainted with the interpretation and theme of the play, you will identify the various obligations: time and place, relationship, emotional, character, thematic, historic, and subtextual. The chronology of approaching these obligations should be made specific by the play.

After a few rehearsals, when you have gotten acquainted with the play and the people, when you kind of know how the director sees the play, when you have assimilated and recorded the blocking and have allowed yourself to be carried by the material, it is time to start approaching the obligations in the order of their importance and of their relationship to each other. This is a good place to start your obligation-choice-and-choice-approach chart. As you carry the book, your chart will be right there in front of you and will remind you of the responsibilities in each scene. Most often, it is wise to start with the creation of the place. This is where all the action in a scene takes place, and besides being important in terms of the way it affects the character, it is also important because it allows the actor to be someplace else than on the stage. Once he has decided to create a specific place, if he works for it in every rehearsal, it will soon become a reality, so that every time he comes on the set he will feel as if he were in that place.

After you have figured out the obligations of the play from your character's perspective, it is important that you do your homework. There is only so much you can do at home since you don't have the other actors to work with; however, you can explore certain choices, make decisions on which choice approaches to try, and work on character element obligations. From the very beginning of the rehearsal process, look for choice areas that are multidimensional and somehow connected with the unconscious. Attempt to explore your choices in your dream life. If you work on a particular choice before going to bed at night and remember to "play" with it in the sleep-wake state, you stand to learn a lot in addition to finding choices that appeal to your unconscious.

At the end of each rehearsal day, find out which scenes the director is going to work on the next day and, if he can tell you, what his emphasis will be. Once you know that, you can take it home and prepare to deal with the responsibilities of the next rehearsal.

In a sense you are doing two rehearsals: first, you are dealing with whatever the director wants to confront, and secondly, you are doing "your" work. That is not to say that you don't both want the same things. It simply means that often the director is involved in the technical responsibilities of the entire piece and gives the actor "result" directions. He tells you what he wants to see you do, how to relate to the other character, and where to move, and asks you to project, to be fuller, bigger, and so on. It is the actor's job, when working with a director who does not specifically share his process or approach, to understand and accommodate the director's wishes, while at the same time doing his own craft process to create the realities that impel the character's behavior in the play.

If nothing is chronologically more important, the best thing to start with is the creation of the place. The actor should understand how the place affects the character and how it stimulates or influences what takes place in the scene. Having identified that, he can choose a place from his own life that brings up similar impulses for him. Before the rehearsal begins, he can usually start to create his place in the rehearsal environment. There are a variety of choice approaches that he can use, the most thorough of which would be Sense Memory. He can do this silently by asking the sensorial questions and responding with the specific sense that he has questioned. If at all possible, and depending on the circumstances of the play, he might bring some personal articles from home that might promote the reality he is attempting to create. If not, he can work for them through his sensorial process. Once he has created the place and has some sense of it, he can step onto the stage and immediately be affected by his place. This frees him to go on to the next obligation.

Let's say that he has already dealt with the character obligation at home. He has worked for a specific choice that elevates his criticality, a major attribute of the character he is playing. By selectively emphasizing everything around him that he can find fault with, including every person he encounters on the street, he has piqued a critical part of himself. His attitude, behavior, and essence have become critical and judgmental. The rehearsal starts with a carping argument between the characters in the play, and as the scene proceeds they denigrate each other's character with a barrage of ugly criticism. Our actor has created a place where he lived for several years in a very unhappy marriage. Many arguments occurred in this environment. In addition, he has dealt with the character element of being a critical and judgmental person, so he steps onto the stage with two of his obligations already serviced. The rehearsal involves dealing with the relationship elements and the emotional life that evolves out of that relationship. The director has blocked the scene, and the actor knows where to sit, when to move to the bar and pour himself a drink, and so on.

In this particular rehearsal he has decided to deal with the relationship obligation, which is that of a man married to a woman that he can't satisfy. The relationship has disintegrated into constant conflict and indictment. As a choice he decides to work for his ex-wife in relation to the actress doing the play with him. His choice approach is Endowments, and the approach technique, Sense Memory. Throughout the rehearsal, he is creating his choice and also using the actress. He does his process before, in between, and under the lines of the scene.

Example:

HE: (Sitting in a chair facing the actress who is sprawled out on the sofa.) You drink too much! (Silently) *What are the similarities in her eyes?* (Responding with the visual sense) *What is the color of her hair in relation to the actress?* (Another visual response)

SHE: And you are always there to remind me, aren't you, Paul?

HE: Someone must be there to remind you what a disgusting lush you are! *How are their voices alike?* (Responding with the auditory sense)

SHE: Did you ever love me?

HE: *What is that sound she makes that I find repulsive? ... What is the depth and quality of her voice when I hear that?* No, Sybil, I don't think I ever have ... How does that hit you, darling?

SHE: You're a slob, Paul ... do you know that? ... Look at you ... You're a loser!

HE: *What does she smell like?* (Responding with the olfactory sense, attempting to re-create the odor of his ex-wife) You may be right, Sybil, but at least I'm playing the game that I'm losing!

The rehearsal continues, often with a comment or interruption from the director. As the actor navigates his way through, exploring his choice, he will discover if it is taking him where he wants to go. If he feels it isn't strong enough, or that maybe it makes him too hateful, he may make an adjustment or two with it or in relation to the actress. Knowing what the characters feel about each other, both actors start a relationship preparation before the rehearsal. They may begin with a simple, selfless "Wonder, Perceive" exercise and go into an improvisation, selectively emphasizing things about each other that create distaste, frustration, and conflict.

So for this rehearsal the actor has:

1. Worked on the character obligation (being a critical and judgmental person) as homework
2. Created a parallel place (his own living room when he was married, a place where he had similar experiences) when he arrived at the rehearsal
3. Done the necessary preparations to free his instrument, and worked with the actress on a relationship preparation to stimulate an emotional point of view toward her that parallels the circumstances of the play
4. During the actual rehearsal, worked to get a sense of his ex-wife in relation to the actress, using the available realities in conjunction with his choice. He accomplished this by sensorially doing an Endowment.

Essentially all rehearsals are handled in the same way. The difference is in the various responsibilities and obligations. The choices and approaches will differ, but the process of using the craft is the same. After the rehearsal the actor should refer to his obligation-choice-and-choice-approach chart and make the necessary comments about the effectiveness of each approach. He will decide to either keep the choice, further explore it, make some adjustments to it, or possibly try another. He should definitely listen to the director's notes before making any final decisions about where to go next with his process. Let us say that the actors have spent the entire morning on that scene, doing it more than once. The actor has had the opportunity to test his changes and adjustments. After hearing the director's comments, he should make some notes about what his next move will be in relation to that scene just in case they do not return to it for a few days.

It is very important to mention at this point that the actor must allow himself to be *irreverent* to the scene while exploring the way to ultimately fulfill it. If, while working for his choice, he finds the whole thing humorous, he must honor that and express it during the rehearsal. The creative actor must always "allow and permit" all his impulses to be included in his behavior on a moment-to-moment basis. If he attempts to service his concept of the material, he will short-circuit the reality stimulated by his choice and will end up presenting an emotional life that does not come from a real place. Depending on the kind of director you are working with, it may be necessary to explain exactly what you are doing, making sure that you reassure the director that you understand the result responsibilities of the scene. Inform him that you are both working toward the same goal but that you must have the permission to use the rehearsal to explore the stimulus that will impel you to behave as the character does, from an authentic place. You need only tell him about the irreverent exploration; it isn't necessary to expose your choices or process to anyone.

Every rehearsal is explored in essentially the same way. You identify the obligations of the scene you are going to rehearse and do as much instrumental and craft preparation as you can prior to getting on the stage. Work for the choice or choices that you have decided to explore in this particular rehearsal, and find out where they lead you. Be open to anything that affects you in the moment, and go wherever it takes you. Keep your charts and rehearsal journals current, noting the effect of everything you have explored. Make notes about future possibilities. You may try as many as eight choices in a scene before you decide on the one you want to use. Remember that's what rehearsals are for, finding the specifics that fulfill the material. If an actor or director does not use them creatively, the results will be commensurate with the loss of that opportunity. Every play brings with it its own special demands, and the actor must accommodate the special responsibilities through his process. Working with a director can be either a nightmare or a wonderful collaboration. If the actor remembers to communicate with him and has a solid process of work, they will most likely complement each other.

When doing a scene with more than one actor, you will need to establish a relationship reality with all of their characters. Sometimes, if you are fortunate, the available stimuli will suffice. There will be enough of a reality between you and the other actors to fulfill the material, but if that is not the case, it will be necessary to have choices for each and every character in the play. Use the rehearsal process to deal with that obligation, and promote the choices in your offstage relationships whenever possible. Try to get the other actors to do relationship preparations before each rehearsal. If after a fairly long rehearsal period you arrive at the choices that you are going to use throughout the play, repeatedly work for them in successive rehearsals to make them more solid and dependable. After working with a choice for a long time, you begin to discover the "triggers" in it, and it seems to stimulate results at a more rapid pace. If at all possible, encourage the other actors to do preparations. Besides the standard involvement preparations, there are also ensemble preparations. If your goal is to accomplish ensemble in the play, you must be related on that level and use choices that lead you into that kind of relating. The ensemble preparations are discussed in great detail in chapter 3 of this book. Use them!

A Rehearsal Checklist for Doing a Play

1. Read the play, either as a group or individually. See what is there, what it is about, and what kind of person your character is. Get a sense of the material, the author's intention or statement, the feeling, the ambience of the piece.
2. In successive readings, allow yourself to be affected and carried by the material. Don't rush to make choices or to identify the obligations yet. See what the words stimulate for you. It is possible that the impact of the material will suggest some of your approaches to it.
3. Make note of all the available realities when you are in the reading stage. The play will tell you what your character is like, his personality, the way he relates to the world and specifically to the other characters in the piece. It will describe his sense of life, the conflicts he has, and the ones that come to the surface during the play. It will also let you know how he feels in his environment, how he behaves, and why. All this and much more will unfold as you rehearse. It is very important that at the very earliest you explore and make note of all the available-stimulus realities that are there: the other actors and how they look, behave, and relate to you and to each other; your first impressions; the director, his personality and style; which can be an affecting impetus somewhere down the line—the place, the way it smells, looks, and the feeling of the space itself; immediate responses from the unconscious that you may not be able to explain. If you find the stimulus that piques those responses, you will be able to relate back to it.
4. Prepare before each rehearsal. Do the relaxation-cluster: relax, sensitize, and do Personal Inventory. If you are unusually tense, do an Abandonment or some other large commitment preparation. If after the basic preparations you identify further instrumental obstacles, such as feeling insulated, do a vulnerability preparation (e.g., a Coffin Monologue). When you feel instrumentally ready, you can go into the area of craft preparations. Knowing what the obligations are

for the rehearsal you are about to do, choose a preparation that will create a foundation of emotional life for the scene. For example, suppose that the character is nostalgic and sad about the way his life has turned out; you might work for a choice that takes you back to a time in your own life when things were more promising than they turned out to be.

5. Identify and understand the various obligations of the material. Know what the overall obligations are—such as your character obligation, which maintains itself throughout the whole play—and what the individual scene obligations are.

6. Decide on the chronology of obligations—what must be addressed first. For example, let us say that the character obligation is so intrusive and powerful that it influences all the relationships to the other characters. Everything that your character relates to is colored by the nature of his personality. He might be a paranoid type of person who trusts no one, so everything he relates to is tainted by his paranoia. Or let us say that the historical responsibilities affect everything the person does, says, or thinks. That will definitely make these obligations more important and determine the order in which they should be attacked.

7. Create an obligation-choice-and-choice-approach chart. It should be built scene by scene. For more detail, refer to Chapter 4.

8. Create the place. Providing that there are no other obligations that must be dealt with first, create a parallel environment before each rehearsal and while you are on the stage, until such time as you actually feel you are in that environment.

9. Do your homework. Work on each part of the play at home, explore various choices and approaches, and experiment with them. Bring your discoveries into the next rehearsal.

10. Work on the *ultimate consciousness* as part of your homework and rehearsal process. Since having an *ultimate-consciousness* experience is the pinnacle of electrifying acting, preparing to reach the unconscious should be a part of the rehearsal routine.

   (List of techniques that you can use to pique responses from the unconscious and promote an *ultimate-consciousness* experience:

   a. Create places from your own life that are rich with experiences, and relate them to the play.

   b. Use affective-memory choices that are loaded with conscious-unconscious connections.

   c. Do improvisations with the other actors relating to them as if they were other people in your life, people with whom you have deep psychological and emotional agenda.

   d. Go over the scene every night before bedtime, using your choices. Encourage yourself to dream about the work, the play, and the specific choices.

   e. Become aware of any suggestions that you get from your dreams or in the sleep-wake state.

   f. Before you start a rehearsal, do a variety of *ultimate-consciousness* preparations, such as Primal Moan, primitive explorations, "I'm Five Years Old," etc.

   g. Encourage activities and thoughts in your daily life that reflect the behavior and involvements of the character.)

11. Inventory each rehearsal after you have finished it. Go over what happened, what seemed to work, what didn't, where your choices led you, what adjustments need to be made, what comments you heard from the director and the other actors—anything that you want to remember.

12. Prepare for the next rehearsal. Find out what scene the director is going to do and what he will emphasize. Do your homework, and return prepared with your craft choices.

13. Be irreverent to the material, in order to organically explore the choices. While working with a choice through the use of a choice approach, express all the impulses that are stimulated even if they seem improper for the play. That is the way to find out where a choice will lead you. Sometimes a choice will create behavior that is so much more exciting than in your original concept!

14. Prepare with the other actors; do relationship and scene preparations before and during all rehearsals. These preparations will not only get you into each scene, but they will also establish the ongoing reality of the relationship throughout the entire play.

15. Work with your process in each rehearsal. That is what you do on and off the stage. Use the choices and approaches to fulfill the obligations of the play. Repeat the process in every rehearsal and scene until you are secure with those choices. Be open and impulsive; go with your moment-to-moment realities.

16. Establish communication with the director; be open to his suggestions and help. Let him know what you are doing so he understands when you seem to go off on a tangent.

Knowing what to do and how to use a rehearsal is what makes the difference between lucky accident and artistry. The artist sees the picture and begins the creative process to organically bring life to that image. He does this with his talent and craft. Talent without process cannot be depended upon and is usually unrealized.

REHEARSING A SCENE FOR A CLASS OR WORKSHOP

The laboratory is a great place for the actor to learn how to rehearse! It is where he can and is encouraged to experiment and fail. *An actor must have a place to fail!* The workshop is the place where he can first learn the craft and then use it in relation to material. Usually two actors will get together and do a scene from an established play. They will attempt to fulfill the requirements of that specific scene, using it as a framework in which to explore their craft. The rehearsals take place outside the workshop, usually in the apartment of one of the actors. They rehearse a few times, or maybe many times, and then bring the scene to class and do it. They are critiqued and worked with, and then they return to a new set of rehearsals, attempting to apply what they have just learned. How they use their rehearsals is every bit as important as if they were doing a play, since it is this experience that will sculpt the process they will carry into their professional life.

Ten Sample Rehearsals

The following are examples of ten separate rehearsals on a scene for a class or workshop. Again I would like to stress the number of variables and possibilities available to the actor. The craft potentials are unlimited and reach into infinity. The kinds of preparations, choices, and approaches that can be used are numerous. The interpretation is individual. An actor's emotional state varies from day to day and rehearsal to rehearsal, necessitating preparations that will confront each specific instrumental problem. What we can accomplish with these ten sample rehearsals is to create a kind of blueprint that will map out the possibilities of approach and the usage of the process. As you read each example, imagine the alternate preparations and choices available.

Rehearsal Number One

The material I have selected to use as a framework is a play called *Split,* by Michael Weller. It is a two-character play about a man and a woman who are married and live in Manhattan. He is a teacher and aspiring writer. They are both in their middle to late thirties and seem to have what on the surface is a normal relationship. As the play proceeds, we find out that there are many underlying frustrations and conflicts in the relationship and that it is truly on shaky ground. The play starts at the tail end of a disagreement they have been having.

In the first rehearsal the actors may either read the play together or come together after reading it on their own. If at all possible, they should read it together since many things come out as they do, things they might forget to discuss if they read it separately. If they can discuss their impressions and interpretations in the first rehearsal, they will have a clear understanding of what they agree or disagree on. They can then find solutions or arbitrate their differences so that these won't come up later when they might have to backtrack and waste time. If indeed they elect to read the play together, they should avoid giving it any conceptual meaning. They should read it in stream-of-consciousness fashion. If something happens and either of them is emotionally affected, they should definitely honor and express their feelings.

When they finish reading it, they might discuss it, talk about why they think the author wrote it and what he was trying to say or communicate. They could also talk about the characters, who they are and how they see them. They should discuss the subtextual behavior, the relationship between the characters, their conflicts, their frustrations and what caused them (there is a great deal of ambivalence between them), and so on. They should include all the other realities of the material, such as the place the characters live in, since later in the play they discuss whose furniture this or that is. After spending most of the first rehearsal discussing the material, they could begin sharing their feelings about their own personal relationships and explore some of the parallels or similarities, discussing the elements that they relate to and can identify with. Perhaps he sees a strong similarity between the way the female character argues and his own girlfriend, and she feels that the male character avoids conflict exactly as her boyfriend sometimes does.

After discussing the play and looking for parallels, they could read it again, stopping to clarify or define things as they go through it. At this point neither actor should attempt to define the obligations except in very general terms. They can, however, discuss their discoveries about the material, acknowledge the thrust of the piece, the author's statement or point, and some of the relationship elements. They agree that the surface behavior of the characters is a smoke screen for the real frustrations and dissatisfactions which become evident later in the play. They further agree that both characters have something at stake, and they identify it: they want a more intimate and romantic relationship and to recapture what they had at the beginning. They have drifted into that state of routine and apathy that many couples get to. They have both suppressed their frustrations and romantic hunger. The emotional life of each character changes from moment to moment, but the character element obligations can be worked on individually as well as during rehearsals.

Having spent about three hours in this first rehearsal, the actors decide to end it. It was productive, and they both feel that they have some "handles" on the piece. They decide to do about ten minutes of it as a scene.

Both actors may work some on the piece at home; however, at this point they should avoid making too many decisions about the direction they want to go in. Concepts created in the early rehearsal stages can be difficult to overcome later. Early rehearsals are for open exploration and discovery. Each of the actors might "live" with his first exposure to the material and savor the essence of the character, identifying with the realities wherever possible.

Rehearsal Number Two

The actors should begin every rehearsal with an instrumental preparation: the relaxation-cluster. Once they feel in touch with themselves, they might do a relationship preparation. There are a variety of these, and since it is only the second rehearsal, an ensemble preparation would not be necessary. However, the Observe-Wonder-and-Perceive exercise would get them involved with each other and ready to go on to the next step. Because of the relationship responsibilities of the piece—and it is definitely a relationship play—they decide to start with a personal exploration of each other. Since they will be relating to each other no matter what their choices eventually turn out to be, they must acknowledge the need to be involved and affected by each other. They could just extend the Observe-Wonder-and-Perceive exercise into a more varied exploration of each other. The objective is manifold: first, to get to know each other better, to establish a greater intimacy; secondly, to find out how they feel in relation to each other and how many different points of view evolve as they work together; and third, to discover similarities between themselves and the characters in the play, to find out what kinds of things they can use to stimulate the attraction, the frustrations, the resentments felt by the characters. They do this exploration in the framework of a wonderment exercise, asking each other things that they are curious about and expressing their feelings about each other.

Example:

HE: I wonder how you feel about me.

SHE: I was wondering the same thing . . . I like you . . . I don't know you very well . . . I think you're good looking.

HE: I like that . . . (He laughs nervously.) I like you too. Well, that's a good beginning.

SHE: Have you ever been married?

HE: No, but I've lived with people for periods of time. What about you?

SHE: Same thing. I'm living with a man now.

HE: Is it good? . . . I mean, is it a good relationship?

SHE: Yes, I think so, except . . . well, there are some problems . . . you know . . . like in the play. He gets involved and doesn't communicate, and I get angry . . . and go inside, and that festers . . . You know the trip, right?

HE: Yeah, I do . . . but doesn't every relationship have problems? . . . I mean when the honeymoon is over . . . it's over!

SHE: Are you saying that after the heat of the beginning it's just a process of maintaining?

HE: No, that's not what I mean, but it doesn't ever seem to get back there, does it?

SHE: Well, there you have it . . . that's what this play is about, right?

HE: Right. I think that's what the author is saying among other things. Do you think that you can use that? For the scene I mean.

SHE: Sure, but I'm not going to jump into choices yet, O.K.?

HE: Sure it's O.K. Why do you get so defensive when I ask you a simple question?

SHE: Well, I'm sorry if I appear to be defensive, but I would like to make my own decisions about how I'm going to work!

HE: Hey, there's an interesting parallel . . . I pushed one of your buttons, didn't I?

This exploration process may continue for as long as it is yielding good results. Both actors are finding out things about each other and establishing a relationship, as well as stumbling onto some parallel realities that they can use as Available Stimulus. After doing the exercise they take an inventory, which they share with each other.

Example of the Sharing Inventory:

HE: I feel that I know a great deal more about you. I also identify the need to do a lot more of this kind of exercise with you since I feel that we're right at the beginning of our relationship with this scene. I want to feel much closer to you. I want to be able to predict the way you'll respond and what you are going to say, and I generally want to feel much more comfortable with you. I found out that there are things that I can use in relation to you that I find sexually attractive, while at the same time I feel tentative about saying certain things to you . . . You have a short fuse in some areas! I also feel that while I can use some of the available realities between us, we don't have a history and the characters do! So I'm going to have to explore imaginary stimuli in relation to you. I think we can both use whatever conflicts we discover while working together, at least to "springboard" us into our respective choices. I would like to find something I want from you as a parallel to the scene. At this point I don't know what that might be.

SHE: I got a lot out of that exercise too. I agree that we have to do a lot more work on getting more intimate with each other! I don't feel like I really know who you are, except from class. Maybe we can do some Intimate-Sharing workouts. What do you think?

HE: Sure! Let's do that after you finish sharing, O.K.?

SHE: Fine. I think you like to control, and I have a real thing about being told what to do; and in some ways I feel I might be able to use that for the scene. I am far more independent a person than she is, and that might be a problem . . . I don't know! I find you a little remote. I think your character is somewhat remote too. What I'm trying to say at this early point is that if I selectively emphasized some of the things I see and feel about you, I could stimulate pretty heavy resentment. I agree that we don't have enough going to parallel their relationship, but I would like to start with us before jumping to imaginary choices!

After finishing the Sharing Inventory both actors launch into a very complete Intimate-Sharing exercise. (For an example of Intimate Sharing refer to Chapter 3.) This exercise should take them into a deeper relationship. If they are courageous and are not afraid to expose their innermost thoughts and feelings, they will acquire a great deal of knowledge about each other; with this knowledge come more feelings and opinions. In addition to being drawn closer to each other, they will create another vital element, and that is *familiarity!* Intimate knowledge about the actor you are working with provides an intimacy that two strangers do not reach on stage. Even if the actors are using personal choices, they are in fact talking to each other.

During the Intimate-Sharing workout, both actors talk in great detail about romantic relationships and marriage. The actress expresses a great need to have romance in her life, and while she is in love with the man she is living with, she feels that there is a large gap there. She wants much more from him and isn't quite sure how to get it. She admits during the exercise that she catches herself doing or saying things to her boyfriend that are designed to affect him, make him jealous, impress him, and so on. That's what the character Carole does in the play. The actor has also felt similar disappointments in all of the relationships he has had. Because this is such an important area, both actors decide to continue the Intimate Sharing, selectively emphasizing their own personal relationships. Each of them expresses his needs, desires, and frustrations in this area. The point of the exercise is to bring to the surface the realities that parallel those of the characters in the play.

Having spent about two and a half hours in this rehearsal, they decide to call it a day and come back the next day. The actress says that as homework she is going to consciously observe her relationship this evening, taking note of the behavioral stimuli that create the responses that are right for the scene. He says that he is going to start identifying his responsibilities and look for the obligations in the material.

Rehearsal Number Three

Since she is a night person and he is a day person, they have decided to accommodate each other by having both morning and afternoon rehearsals. This rehearsal is in the afternoon. After doing the preliminary relaxation-cluster, they share some Personal Inventory for the purpose of getting to a BEING place with each other. He asks her if she has any ideas as to where she wants to start today's rehearsal, because if she doesn't, he does! She tells him that she is open for suggestion, but that she does want to share some of the discoveries she made last evening after rehearsal number two. He agrees to start there:

SHE: It is incredible! I started watching what was going on at the dinner table. It was like standing outside looking at the two of us! When I got home I took a shower and got dressed pretty. I tried to look especially good, right? . . . Well, he came in, kissed me on the cheek, and never said a word about the way I looked or was dressed, or anything! I was pissed! . . . But instead of saying anything to him . . . I avoided my feelings and said other little sarcastic things! . . . Well, first I realized that I was hurt, then angry, and then instead of expressing it, I redirected it into what ended up as a petty disagreement about something that he told me had happened at his job. All the time I wanted him to see me! I wanted him to appreciate me! But instead of being up front with it, I did all these numbers! You see, I was afraid that if I said what I felt or asked for what I wanted, he wouldn't give it to me, so I didn't chance it. That is exactly what Carole does in the play. (The argument they have about poking the carrot is a total parallel.) So if you multiply that incident by a hundred or a thousand, you get the relationship, see?

HE: That's great . . . So how are you going to use it for the scene?

SHE: Well, I could just work to endow you with him, but I'm not ready to make that decision yet. I need more exploration.

HE: O.K., I want to start working on some of the obligations of the play, at least from my perspective. First, I would like to start creating the place. The place is always important, particularly in this play because they refer to it several times. There is that thing about the neighbors complaining about the noise. He gets bent out of shape, and they talk about getting out of the city and buying a house in the country. There is that section where they talk about splitting up and he asks her who keeps the apartment: "It was mine when we met, but you did furnish it!" he says. So I would like to create a place out of my own life experience that stimulates most of the feelings he has in his apartment. Would you like to work for a place too, or are you going to do something else?

SHE: Actually, I think that's a great idea! I'm going to use my own apartment. For one, I did furnish it, and besides, the history of my entire relationship is in this place.

So they both begin to create a place, he working for an apartment in New York where he lived briefly, she using Available Stimulus, since they are presently in her apartment. He chooses the apartment in New York because he wants to stimulate the feelings that New York brings up in him and also because at that particular time he was living with a woman that he might use as a choice for the scene. They spend about a half hour sensorially re-creating the place, while she emphasizes and selects certain objects to relate to. He suddenly starts the words of the scene, and she picks up the script and responds. He continues relating to the place while saying some of the lines, at all times expressing his here-and-now feelings through what he is saying. When they have completed the scene, they begin talking about their experience with the place. He tells her that he started the scene to see if the place had any effect on his expression, and happily it did! "I felt some of those same old feelings!" he says. "I had forgotten how trapped I felt in that place! It made me feel dissatisfied with my life . . . I'm doing more of what I want to do now, but then I was working as a waiter—which I hated—not acting, and going nowhere! Creating that place really brought all of that back, and I think it fits! . . . What about you?" She tells him that she also felt some things, although not as pertinent as his, but interesting. She felt married and doesn't understand why all of a sudden relating to her apartment made her feel that way! She did, however, feel more dependent than normally. After some more discussion about the place, they both decide to work for it at the beginning of every successive rehearsal, promising to bring some personal items every time they work in each other's place. They then agree to spend the rest of this rehearsal identifying some of the other obligations then confronting them in the order of their importance.

HE: First, I want to eliminate the things that don't need to be dealt with. Naturally there isn't a historic obligation . . . it's present day! The thematic obligation, or what the author wants to say, is exemplified in the action and interactions of the play and the characters. I don't know what the subtextual obligation is, so I'm not going to deal with it, at least not now! I think that there is a time-and-place responsibility, a relationship obligation, various emotional obligations in the section we've decided to do, and a character obligation. I have already started to work for the place; we are both in the midst of exploring the elements of the relationship; the emotional life in each part of the scene is variable and somewhat dependent on the relationship elements, so I think that I would like to start exploring the character elements. In some respects the character could be me, except that he is an avoider! I think he is conflict phobic and that he sits on his frustrations, redirecting them into his work and his other relationships, as with Jean.

SHE: I also feel that I could be this character with certain important exceptions: I'm not nearly as dependent as she is, and I think her dependence comes from some very deep insecurities and a lower sense of self-worth than I have. Otherwise I think there are some similarities in our personalities.

They both decide to reinvest in creating the place and to go into various explorations of their respective characters. She starts by doing a *litany of her insecurities* in an audible or inaudible monologue selectively emphasizing only the things in her life that pique insecurities.

Example:

"I'm not getting any younger! . . . I don't work all that often, and I would like to have children. If I'm going to do that, I'd better start soon! Only I'm not sure of my relationship. I don't know if I want to marry this guy. I'm insecure about my talent—not all the time, but often enough."

She continues this approach for as long as necessary to stimulate the level of insecurity she wants for the character element. From this point she will continue the inner monologue, taking it into emphasizing the unfulfilled needs in her relationship.

He begins his exploration of the character with a similar approach, a *litany of his frustrations* done in the same manner as hers. From there, he does a group of imaginary monologues with people in his life who make him feel helpless and like avoiding problems. He takes this into an imaginary monologue with his ex-girlfriend, who constantly forced him into conflict areas. From that point he relates to the actress and picks out the things in her that intimidate him and make him feel somewhat conflict shy. Both actors are working separately in this part of the rehearsal, but at the conclusion of their explorations they briefly inventory and share their discoveries. They both feel somewhat confused about their explorations. Her litany helped to pique her insecurities but didn't seem to make her more dependent or needy. His experiment overloaded him. He feels he did too much. However, his craftual journey did produce one very important discovery, and that is a choice he feels might stimulate the manifestations of the character elements that he wants to create: his ex-girlfriend made him feel frustrated, conflict phobic, and as if he would do almost anything to avoid those endless discussions about their life and their relationship. In addition to making that discovery, he remembered that his father used to terrify him, and during one of the imaginary monologues he was doing, he retreated into himself as he used to do. That is a fairly good character element, he thinks, so he has decided to use his father as a "preparational" choice. Being less than satisfied with her exploration, she does an "I Want, I Need" exercise with some very good results. It indeed elevates her need level.

At this point, about an hour and a half into their third rehearsal, they decide to try some of the things they have just explored by carrying them into the lines of the scene. Briefly reinvesting in the place, they then go to the litanies. He follows his with a brief imaginary monologue with his father while she silently does an "I Want, I Need" exercise, and then they go into the lines of the scene, not concerning themselves with doing them verbatim. When they finish, they both feel as if there is a foundation starting to be built for the scene. He experienced that trapped feeling stimulated by the place, as well as a tentativeness and a desire to avoid confrontation brought about by the imaginary monologue with his father. At the same time, relating to his ex-girlfriend supplied some of the relationship elements of the scene. She also had some success with her choices. Her litany made her feel more insecure, and the "I Want, I Need" exercise indeed stimulated some of her life needs; but she hasn't yet found anyone in relation to whom to be needy or insecure. At this juncture they end the rehearsal.

Rehearsal Number Four

After the preparations, they talk a little about their homework. He has done some more character exploration and found that certain people in his life, in addition to his father, make him feel conflict phobic as well as stimulating the need to redirect his frustrations into other involvements. He wants to do an Evocative-Words preparation related to about four different people in his life and an experience involving them. She excitedly reports that she has made a humongous discovery about her relationship. She has found out that if she admits that she loves her boyfriend and relates to those elements about him that support these feelings, she immediately feels insecure, needy, and dependent in relation to him. She has further identified many of the same feelings of jealousy that the character has toward her husband. All of a sudden she wanted to know about the girls her boyfriend works with! Both actors are anxious to start this rehearsal.

After sensorially working for the place, each of them does his own personal work: he does his Evocative-Words preparation semi-audibly, while she goes into the "I Want, I Need" exercise. He then starts an imaginary monologue to his ex-girlfriend paralleling the material. She also explores an imaginary monologue with her boyfriend, attempting to stimulate the love and attraction. At this point they decide to do an ensemble preparation with each other in order to get involved on a more meaningful level.

The exercise they choose to do is "You Make Me Feel." It stimulates a moment-to-moment responsiveness and dependency on each other's responses. At a point of high involvement with each other, he starts to talk to her as if she were his ex-girlfriend. She, realizing what is happening, responds to him in terms of the way he affects her, while at the same time talking to her boyfriend. At first the conversation seems only to involve the moment they are in, but as they continue, they both begin talking about experiences from their past, experiences that they had with their respective mates. It is like a Believability exercise involving their choices. Each of them responds as if what is being said is coming from his choice. To this point they are improvising; they haven't yet dealt with the lines of the play. At a crucial point, she picks up some of the words from the scene that happen to match where they are in the improvisation. The carryover is fantastic. The few lines they exchange sound exactly like the improvisation. They then stop to talk about the work. Both feel that they are on the right track for the scene. They make the entry in their rehearsal journal and chart and go over what they have done to this point. It all seems to be building on the last workout, and very naturally so.

After a short break and getting outside in the open air, they return to the rehearsal somewhat rejuvenated and even more excited. He suggests that he would like to do an Affective-Memory exercise surrounding that place and time in his life, because he was so affected just by the place that he wants to see if Affective Memory will sink deeper shafts into his unconscious. She doesn't feel the need for anything like that since her relationship is current, but she tells him that she can use the time to do some Inner Monologues to her boyfriend, going back and forth between what she gets from him and what she doesn't get in a kind of antithesis workout. She thinks it might create the ambivalence the character feels in the play. So they both work for about forty minutes on their respective approaches, then reinvest in relating to each other, again as if they were the choices; only this time she begins with "Do you remember? . . . " He picks it up immediately, and they start to talk about things that date back to their first meeting. They discuss mutual friends, restaurants they frequented, their early sexual feelings, their first argument, how jealous they were of each other, a fight he almost got into over her, and so on. It creates a nostalgic essence between them and a real affection. They continue on this road, to where the problems began. The improvisation goes on for a while, and then they decide to quit for the day. It has been a very heavy rehearsal. His Affective Memory did indeed open some capillaries into his unconscious, and he is feeling a little' shaky. The work is making her feel as though she has opened a Pandora's box in her own life. She has been challenging her feelings about her relationship, asking questions about what she really wants, where her priorities really are, and so on. Both of them are now beginning to experience the organic underpinnings of the life of these characters in this play, and they know it! Before he leaves her apartment he reminds her that there are some material realities that they have not even discussed, like the fact that these two characters are waiting for company to arrive and that there is an urgency here that has not been mentioned so far. They acknowledge the existence of these obligations but decide to deal with them in future rehearsals.

Rehearsal Number Five

At the beginning of this rehearsal, even before doing the preparations, he says he wants to do an exposure exercise out loud. Is it O.K. with her? She says, "Sure!" but doesn't understand why. He says he will tell her later. He begins:

"I feel real insecure! . . . I mean about my acting . . . I know what I'm doing, but I still feel like I'm not doing nearly enough, and maybe not even the right things! I sometimes feel that all this work is some sort of masturbation, and if I were a real actor I wouldn't need to do all this nonsense; I would just feel it, believe it . . . Isn't that what an actor is? All this "Method" nonsense . . . all it did was confuse me! . . . Last night I dreamt all night about not being able to kiss anyone . . . I mean I had forgotten how to kiss . . . Everyone was talking about how wonderful kissing was, and I had forgotten how to do it! I mean, don't you think that is significant? I woke up this morning feeling like I didn't know what life was all about, where I was, where I was going, or anything! . . . Sometimes it's a little hard to take, you know? Well, I guess that's all I wanted to say."

They both sit there for a moment, not saying anything. She breaks the silence by saying that was pretty heavy and does he know what the dream meant? He says that he could probably come up with some theories about what it meant but that he isn't really sure. He knows that if he hadn't started this rehearsal by sharing his insecurities, he would probably not be able to work today. He reassures her that he really believes in the work and that she needn't worry about his commitment, but she says that she wasn't at all worried.

They do their basic preparations and then begin working for the place. Since the rehearsal is in his apartment today, she has brought a whole shopping bag of objects from her place and begins placing them around. Each rehearsal has essentially started with the re-creation of the place, and each day it has taken less time to do it. He does some of his character preparations, the Evocative Words and the imaginary monologues, while she does an Inner Monologue dealing with all the relationships that she has had in her whole life and what has happened to them, why they failed. She later explains that the thought had occurred to her that if she could get in touch with all that failure in her romantic life, maybe this relationship would become more important to her. When they finish, they jump into another ensemble preparation, this time the five-part exercise, starting nonverbally, going to sounds, then gibberish, and finally words. He wants to try the scene as written, going moment to moment with what they are both feeling, so they do. There are some nice elements in it. They both agree that they didn't feel married or that the relationship was at stake, but that they did feel that they were somewhere else than in a rehearsal. He says that he wanted to get an idea about how all the work they had done so far was paying off.

She feels that the relationship is not yet real enough for her and that they should try something that would create a greater reality in terms of their respective choices. He responds that he hasn't made a solid decision about the relationship choice yet! That surprises her since she thought he was using his ex-girlfriend. He tells her that he is considering it, but that he has a great deal of resistance to that choice, since he has closed that chapter in his life; and besides, he wants to see how far he can go with Available Stimulus before working for an imaginary choice. She reminds him that he has already spent at least three rehearsals relating to his ex-girlfriend. He acknowledges that and says he is going to try to get past the resistance he feels with that choice. She asks him why it is such a difficult area for him, and he tells her that he feels very guilty about that relationship. It seems that she wanted to get married and he didn't! He wasn't as direct with her as he should have been, and he still feels like he wasted a lot of her time "stringing her along" as he puts it. "Use it!" she says, "It's perfect for the scene! Don't you see the parallel here? Suppose you create your ex-girlfriend in relation to me and the issue is getting married, right? . . . It's what she wants, and it's what you want to avoid . . . You see? . . . It does parallel their relationship in a way, while at the same time you have quite an agenda with this woman: guilt, anger, the need to avoid, frustration with an unresolvable issue! You see?" It all makes a lot of sense to him, and they decide to use the rest of the rehearsal to sensorially create their choices by using Endowments in relation to each other. After about fifteen minutes they begin to speak, at first with their own words and then with the words of the scene. As they relate to each other through the lines of the scene, they continue to work sensorially to endow each other with the features of their respective choices. The endowment seems to make the relationship more focused, somewhat more intense. He starts to go back and forth between the lines of the scene and his own words, saying things to her about their relationship and how she made him feel when she nagged at him. The actress begins responding to what he is saying in his own words as well as through the lines of the scene. She relates to everything as if her own boyfriend was talking to her. They do the entire scene using the Inner-Outer-Monologue technique, and when it is over, they discuss their feelings about the rehearsal:

HE: I felt great about that one! Thanks for suggesting that I confront my feelings about my ex; it really opened a door for me. I felt that because I have been carrying around all that guilt I didn't want to deal with those feelings, so when I allowed myself to feel all that, it really "dimensionalized" the relationship for me . . . Also, working with Endowments made all the difference. I really felt for the first time that she was who I was talking to.

SHE: Great! I got a lot more from you too! . . . You seemed to be looking way down into my soul. It was very intense, and for the first time I felt there was something at stake between us. I had a little trouble with the endowment process . . . I couldn't remember specific little things related to my boyfriend . . . isn't that ridiculous? Anyway, I think we should continue this approach, and I'm going to do some homework sensorially!

They both feel relieved and as if they have "broken the back" of the relationship responsibilities. He, however, brings up a really important point about the work and the parallel to real life. To this point, he says, they have been trying to create the conflict, the frustrations, and the dissatisfactions, but in a real-life situation all those things come out of what people want and don't get! So maybe they have been approaching the whole thing from the wrong direction. She immediately responds defensively to his suggestion and tells him to speak for himself! Instead of getting into conflict with her, he realizes that either she didn't understand his point or he hadn't made it clear.

HE: I think that all the work we have done to this point has been wonderful. I don't want to suggest that we have wasted our time, but let me make my point, O.K.? (She nods.) O.K. . . . I think what keeps people in a relationship is that they want something from each other that they keep trying to get! Right? (She nods.) O.K. . . . not getting what they need creates the conflict, etc. . . . and so on into their pattern of relating! So what I'm saying is that I think now we need to backtrack a little and work for whatever stimulates the needs we have in relation to our choices. If, for example, I emphasized everything that turned me on about my ex and worked for all the attractive and wonderful qualities that brought us together, the things that made me want her in the first place, then if those needs and attractions were frustrated by other behaviors and actions, I would naturally want to get back to those qualities and to the relationship we had, right? . . . so there would be a striving to change things, and that's what I think happens in real life.

SHE: Yes, you're right! I totally agree. I'm sorry I responded like that!

HE: Don't apologize! We are collaborating here . . . I think that we are going to ruffle each other's feathers from time to time, and it's O.K.!

SHE: Thanks! Yes, yes, I see exactly what we have to do here. Even though we know that they eventually split up, we should essentially work to change the outcome of the play! Except that we fail, right?

HE: Right, but we can't know or accept that . . . We have to find a way to fight for what we want from each other!

On that note they decide to adjourn and work the next day. They both agree that there is a lot to think about and work on. As homework they agree to explore some of the possibilities of stimulating these needs in relation to each other and to their choices. Before leaving, they both spend about ten minutes making entries in their rehearsal journals and charts.

Rehearsal Number Six

This rehearsal starts very quietly. Both actors seem preoccupied, and after a brief greeting they go into their relaxation preparations. Afterwards, instead of working to create the place as usual, they agree to start immediately to confront the issue brought up at the end of the last rehearsal. He has an idea about how to approach it:

HE: Let's start with an ensemble preparation, go from that into our Endowments and from there into relating to our choices at the very beginning
of our relationships. We will emphasize all the wonderful things and
talk about all of our plans together, as the improvisation proceeds, and
at some point in the relationship we can subtly sneak into the beginnings of the conflicts, dealing with the real elements that create the
frustrations. We must not fall into the trap of jumping on that, though!
Let's try to strive for the good things, O.K.?

SHE: How do we do it without getting too intellectual? I mean if we know
what we are doing, then aren't we conning ourselves?

HE: That could happen for sure! But I think that if we create a solid enough
reality we might hook into our real needs in those areas. If I could have
all the things I had with my girlfriend without all the misery, I would
still be there. So if I could appeal to those *deep needs,* maybe I would
want to strive for the relationship . . . I didn't give it up easily!

They agree to do the work and launch into an ensemble preparation
attempting to get involved with each other on a very deep level. At a point in
the preparation, they both begin to work sensorially to create their choices in
relation to each other and spend as much time as necessary to get a real sense
of them. He reminds her to make an adjustment in the sensorial process to
create her boyfriend as he looked, behaved, and dressed at the beginning of
their relationship. She acknowledges the suggestion. After about ten or fifteen
minutes of silent work on the Endowments she breaks the silence by saying, "I
love you," which impulsively brings tears to his eyes. He responds with "I love
you too." They begin to talk about things that are happening in their lives at
that time, and a lot of the conversation involves sex and flirtatious innuendo.
They laugh a lot, and there is a lot of embarrassment between them. This
encounter continues for about twenty minutes, liberally combined with Believability elements, things that may not actually have occurred at the time but
that contain enough truth to make them believable. She very subtly begins to
interject some slight dissatisfactions, which they both attempt to deal with, at
first by ignoring them, and later by avoiding some of them. However, after
about a half hour of the improvisation, the tone of the relationship has visibly
changed. Both of the characters (actors) are struggling to hang on to what was
there in the beginning. Whereas, when they started the improvisation, there
was a lot of physical contact, it has greatly diminished! He has moved away
from her and now sits facing her in a chair. He interrupts the improvisation to
suggest that they go to the scene, continuing what they are doing and adding
an Inner Monologue about what they want that they are not getting, and

including the way they feel in all these areas on a moment-to-moment basis. Without interrupting the mood they have created, they start the scene. Of course, they are being irreverent to the specific demands of the material in order to explore this choice involvement. They continue this process of Endowment (sensorially), relating to each other in an improvisational framework, subtly interjecting the elements of conflict that do or did exist in their respective relationships. Having now moved into the words of the scene, they are essentially continuing the improvisation as an Inner Monologue under the lines, relating to what they need that they are not getting, what the other person is doing that they wish he or she weren't, and so on.

Example:

HE: Line: . . . (Inner Monologue: There she goes again. Why can't she let go of anything?) Line: . . . (Please smile . . . I love you . . . I wonder if I said that to her if she'd stop this petty crap?) Line: . . . (Response to her: I love the way she smiles . . . It makes me melt . . . She's at it again . . . I don't want to listen to the same stuff again and again!) Line: . . . (What is it she really wants? . . . Is it really getting married, or is that temporary? . . .) Line: . . . (What will she want after that? . . .) Line: . . . (I hate women . . . No, I don't! . . . I sometimes hate her . . .)

This process can continue throughout the entire scene. At the end of it both actors acknowledge a kind of excitement, and at the same time both of them feel a little "overload." They take a short break, stretch their legs, and have a cup of coffee. They recap the rehearsal and all parts of the process that they have explored, feeling that this was the most successful relationship involvement that they have reached so far. He says that dealing with the early relationship indeed made him want to hold on to what was there, and that instead of working to create the conflict as actors do, he really wanted to avoid it and have everything be wonderful. He also feels that approaching the scene from this perspective piqued his unconscious need for love and romance. The life seemed to be coming from a much deeper place. "There was something really at stake for me!" he says. She agrees almost completely with him. Her experience matched his. She admits having had some of the same sexual feelings toward her choice that were there in the beginning but are not so common in the relationship now. They make some entries in their journal, add a choice to the choice part of their chart, and look at each other as if to say, What now?

HE: I really don't feel up to doing any more work, but I would like to recap and discuss some of the things that we have left to do with the scene.

SHE: Why do you want to do that? It's all in the journal . . . Do you like to hear yourself talk?

HE: No, it's not that. I just feel that if I express it out loud, put it in words, and bounce it off you, it becomes clearer; and I also like sharing everything with you!

SHE: O.K. Shoot!

HE: Well, most of the work we have done is on the relationship, and I feel really good about that! I have done some fairly good work on the character obligation, and I'm satisfied with the place I have chosen to work for. I feel that I am using you in available-reality areas, and that's good. We seem to be able to create an ensemble base every time we prepare. All of that is good. What has yet to be dealt with are the events that start the scene: our argument, expecting Jean and her boyfriend, making the dinner, the distractions, your jealousy about my relationship with Jean, your needs to resolve the argument and express what you need from me and my not wanting to deal with any of that, the feeling of not wanting them to come tonight, his relationship to teaching—and how to make that a reality for me—the way he feels about writing his book, and whatever parallel I can draw for that, etc., and so on . . .

SHE: Is that all? I mean, do you think we should get to all of that right this minute?

HE: Yeah, I know that's a lot and I know that we have only had six rehearsals, but these are the elements that ultimately have to be fulfilled, right?

SHE: Right! I don't mean to be sarcastic, but I think that we have done a lot in the time we have been working on this scene. Why don't we take it one step at a time and deal with one of those things in each rehearsal?

HE: Right! . . . We can do the scene anytime, and we will have accomplished as much as we have. O.K., I needed to do that. I'm going to do some homework on his background, draw parallels, and bring them to the next rehearsal.

With this they end the sixth rehearsal.

Rehearsal Number Seven

After a brief greeting and a cup of coffee, they begin the rehearsal. He asks for a little more time with the preparation this morning, telling her that he wants to do a longer and deeper relaxation, possibly a Logey exercise. She agrees, since she has some things she wants to explore too. Their preparations go on for about twenty minutes. Skipping the Sensitizing and Personal Inventory, he has gone right into a specific *ultimate-consciousness* preparation. Because of the work he has been doing on his past relationship, he has been dreaming a lot about it, so he has decided to experiment with attempting to sensorially re-create parts of his most recent dream. She works for her place and does some imaginary monologues with her boyfriend as preparations for getting into the scene. When they are finished with their preparations, he suggests a brief ensemble involvement to be followed by sensorial Endowments of each other with their respective choices. She suggests a different kind of ensemble preparation: Double Exposure (see chapter 3). They do about ten minutes of that, followed by "You Make Me Feel." Without discussing any of their preparations they move into the endowment process, both of them attempting to retain whatever they have accomplished in the other preparations. They work silently but very intimately for fifteen minutes, at which time he starts the scene, picking it up a little past the beginning. Continuing to work with Endowments and expressing everything they are feeling on a moment-to-moment basis, they do the ten minutes they have chosen to do in the play. When they finish, they sit looking at each other for a long moment, and then finally she says that she liked what just happened. He did too: "It seems to be taking on a variety of different kinds of life!" The conflict seemed to be there; the relationship, which they had spent most of their time creating, was real for both of them, and they agree that there seemed to be a lot at stake that last time through. He acknowledges that his *ultimate-consciousness* preparation was very important to the quality of his work this time, since he was totally unconcerned with the scene itself: "It was as if acting was secondary to what I was feeling in relation to you!" She asks him more about that preparation and after hearing the specifics says she will do one in their next rehearsal. Having skipped creating the place in favor of his other preparations, he felt that there was something missing, but he did feel as if he were someplace else. They decide to do the scene again with an Inner-Outer-Monologue approach. He suggests trying it that way because he feels that even though he was extremely involved the time before, he isn't sure that he was expressing all of his real impulses. There seemed to be a part of him which wanted to service the relationship responsibilities of the scene. So they reinvest in the Endowments, using each other at the same time, and after a few moments start the dialogue.

Example:

SHE: *Line:* . . . I feel aware that I said that line . . .

HE: (Responding to her line) *Line:* . . . I feel real positive about you . . . *Line:* . . .

SHE: (Response) I love you . . . *Line:* . . . and I really have grown to like you. . . .

HE: *Line:* . . . I'm embarrassed by that! . . .

SHE: *Line:* . . . I really mean what I just said . . .

HE: *Line:* . . . I'm beginning not to be able to separate what I feel from the lines of this play . . . *Line:* . . .

SHE: *Line:* . . . I just became aware of myself acting . . . Include it . . .

HE: *Line:* . . . You're cute, you know that? . . .

SHE: (Responds to that) *Line:* . . . I'm afraid of the conflict in this scene . . . It makes me feel like it will hurt the relationship . . . *Line:* . . .

HE: *Line:* . . . I'm not sure I understand what you just said . . . or meant by that!

This process might continue throughout the whole scene or just for part of it. Both actors should continue to work sensorially in creating their choices and at the same time express everything they feel through the lines of the scene. At the completion of the second run-through, instead of having a discussion, they immediately go into the scene again, this time verbatim. Continuing to work for their choices, he carries his moment-to-moment life into an Inner Monologue, and she encourages herself to be irreverent to the material. They do the scene a third time without taking any liberties with the lines, but including everything they feel moment to moment. Then they decide to take a break and inventory the rehearsal.

They are both very positive about what they have accomplished today and feel that the scene is growing in terms of the reality and variety of life. He mentions again that he wants to deal with some of the other responsibilities of the material, but he feels much more secure about it since he has done some homework the night before. He has found some parallels for some of the obligations and has already started to work on them. For the character's teaching he has decided to relate to a time when he had thought of being a teacher and in fact had done a semester of student teaching. He says that he did some Evocative Words related to that experience and that it really brought back some very rich memories. He has a choice for Jean, and all he has to do about it is suggest her to himself. The urgency of people coming over is easy, he says: since the conflict makes him anxious and he feels an urgency to escape from it, that might work. In addition to all of that, he has a neighbor just like the one in the play, who leaves him polite and dignified notes about how loud his stereo was the night before. He says he will work for each of these things as they present themselves in the scene so as not to overload himself with preparations. She is delighted that he has found choices for these elements and in turn confides that there is a real "Jean" in her life, a woman her boyfriend works with who is "so, so efficient . . . and so, so . . . attentive! It makes me want to vomit every time he starts talking about her. I mean, I'm not jealous . . . yes I am, damn it, but I don't want to be! Her name is Dawn, so every time either you or I say 'Jean,' I'm going to hear 'Dawn'!" They feel that they have used their time fairly well and neither wants to do any more, so they quit for the day.

Rehearsal Number Eight

Since he had the time, he did his preparations before coming over so that he could spend more time working to create the place and dealing with some of the other realities. Last night, he ran across a picture of the girl that he was going to use for Jean, and he put it in his wallet. While she does the relaxation-cluster, he does another *ultimate-consciousness* workout, this time starting with a mini Primal Moan and going into an Affective Memory concerning his relationship. She does an "I Want, I Need" workout semi-audibly and goes into an Accuse-and-Indict exercise, which is an imaginary monologue accusing whomever you are talking to of not giving you what you need.

Example:

"You never gave me the attention I needed! . . . You are always so self-involved . . . You never give me physical contact except when we make love! . . . You are just never there when I need you; you're always working . . . You're a damned Yuppie!"

They come together again, investing in the endowment process, and after a short time start the scene. She continues the "You-Never-Gave-Me" exercise in between the lines (out loud) and he gets very angry with her! It seems that he had some very important success with his primal and affective-memory involvements, and when she starts to indict and accuse him, he takes it very personally and responds with a great deal of anger. The scene takes off in that direction, with both actors mixing the words of the play with their own words. At one point it becomes so heated that he walks out of the room. When he returns, they talk about what happened. It seems that one of his ex-girlfriend's favorite expressions was "You never" and that when he heard it, it pushed all of his buttons. He admits that he wanted to strike her (the actress)—but not to worry; he has never hit a woman before in his life. That is why he left the room. They are both excited about the rehearsal and agree that they will have to stop taking liberties with the dialogue. She says that the indictment exercise really piqued her dissatisfactions and made her go after him.

They take a short break and resume the rehearsal with a parallel improvisation discussing all the other characters in the play (none of whom ever appears). They talk about Jean, using their own personal choices; they discuss how they feel about her; they talk about the neighbor downstairs, having fun with how he behaves, and about friends they had before meeting each other. Following that, they decide to do an improvisation using their own personal realities and Believability to talk about their first romantic experience with each other, the first time they made love. Both actors use their respective mates as choices and decide to take the improvisation personally. They are doing it to deal with a section of the material where the characters discuss this wonderful weekend they spent in bed right at the beginning of their relationship. They do the improvisation for about seven or eight minutes and go right into that section of the scene. It carries over beautifully! They establish an intimacy and a nostalgia that is very right for the scene. It works so well that they extend the improvisation to the whole scene. Starting from the beginning, they parallel the scene with a Believability improvisation using their own relationships. Wherever they can, they use realities that match the scene and where there isn't a parallel they use Believability to mirror the material. Throughout the entire improvisation they speak their own words, creating a parallel to the written dialogue, totally emphasizing the personal realities which match each section of the scene. At the conclusion of the improv, they start the lines, just going moment to moment with the life stimulated by the Believability, and go through the scene without working for any of the other choices. The carryover is great. They both feel that it did what it was supposed to. The work is beginning to accumulate! Feeling that they had a productive day, they end the rehearsal.

Rehearsal Number Nine

They start number nine with the customary relaxation-cluster. He does a Being Workout, and she does some in-depth Personal Inventory, after which he says that he wants about an hour to "put the scene on its feet." "We have been doing a lot of things here, just sitting around and talking. I think it's time to deal with the responsibilities of the actions of the scene, the things they do. He goes in and out of the kitchen to check dinner, she straightens the room, he makes a telephone call and talks to Jean's answering machine for a couple of minutes, they pour and drink wine, he looks for a missing wine glass, and so on. These are all things that have to be made real. So I would like to create those realities or at least explore possible choices that will make them real for me." So she starts working with the available realities of her living room and begins to straighten and clean the place up. He goes into the kitchen and, starting with Available Stimulus, attempts to sensorially create his New York kitchen. Both of them spend about half an hour working for those realities. He goes to the telephone and begins to work to create someone on the other end. His obligation in the scene is to feel discomfort at trying to cancel the dinner invitation and, when he reaches the answering machine, to compensate for not knowing what to say about why he called, by making jokes. He tries several choices, including a couple of answering machines, until he stumbles onto a good one. He had a friend in college who used to leave bizarre messages on his machine, so in an attempt to top his friend he would do the same. He works sensorially to create one of those times. Both actors then work for the odors of a dinner, a roast and potatoes. Finally they deal with creating the wine and the effect of two or three glasses on their physical state. He works for being a little high, and she responds to her exploration by giggling a lot. After about an hour they decide to isolate only the areas that they have just explored and to "walk" the scene without dealing with any of the other obligations. They start by creating the sounds and smells of the food cooking in the kitchen and go from that to creating the kitchen and then the wine. She has some burgundy, so they decide to dilute it with water and use the real thing, or at least the barest minimum of the real thing. At that point they are both working for the effects of the wine and doing the scene. They run through it twice before stopping to assess what has happened in the run-throughs.

After discussing their feelings about it, they both agree that it was awkward. Since they hadn't dealt with any of the actions and movement responsibilities before, these seemed to get in the way of their personal moment-to-moment realities, and the whole scene felt mechanical. They did, however, have some success with getting high. Neither of them feels concerned with what just happened. They agree that there is only so much you can accomplish in eight or nine rehearsals and that the relationship elements are much more important. They will continue to deal with these realities in every rehearsal from now on but will still concentrate on the relationship for the first presentation in front of the class.

After a short break they reinvest in the preparations, go into a Two-Person Being Workout (see Chapter 3), then do an available-stimulus exploration dealing with how they feel about the place, each other, and what is going on between them, what has changed since the first rehearsal in the way they feel about each other, and so on. Many changes have taken place in a little over a week. They both feel that they have somewhat of a history with each other, a variety of feelings about what they could and couldn't say to each other, the beginnings of an ability to know and predict each other's responses, and so on. They also feel an attraction and a curiosity about each other. All of these available realities could work for the scene. They have established elements that parallel to some degree the relationship of the characters, while at the same time building a foundation on which their choices could rest. They start the scene right from where they are and ease into their endowment process.

He supplements his sensorial questions with a running Inner Monologue to, and about, the choice he is creating in relation to the actress. While all of this is taking place, they both encourage an irreverent inclusion of all the distractions and all the impulses that occur. Staying with the lines as written, they express the inclusions through the emotional content of the words of the scene. They allow themselves to be affected by each other, and when that takes them on a tangent, they go with it. As they continue their irreverent experiment they begin to trick each other with their inclusions and responses. When the scene ends, they both feel wonderful. It was really fun, unpredictable, and what acting should be! She remarks that they sacrificed some of the conflict and all of the urgency in this last exploration but feels that it was O.K.! She has the idea that she might create the urgency to resolve the argument before Jean and her boyfriend arrive by using an adjustment in relation to her choice. It seems that whenever she has a disagreement with her boyfriend (her choice) and wants to resolve it, he interrupts her or changes the subject or even gets involved in another activity.

SHE: That drives me crazy, so I speed up. I get kind of manic when I feel I'm not going to be able to get my point across . . . Do you know what I mean?

HE: Sure. Do you want to try that now?

SHE: Why not?

They begin the scene again. She starts with her own words, re-creating an argument that she recently had concerning her car. He goes along with this improvisation, deliberately interrupting her as well as not listening to her. She, getting more and more frustrated, feels an intense sense of urgency to communicate. At that crucial point of frustration and urgency, she goes directly into the lines of the material, and it works quite well. Feeling too excited to end the rehearsal, they start the scene again, this time working silently for their choices. All of the work they are doing is now being done internally. They are silently doing their sensorial exploration and their Inner Monologues. Whenever either one of them feels self-conscious or conscious of his process in a given moment, he includes it as part of the behavior of the character. Whenever anything is expressed by one of them, the other is affected and responds, and in turn that response affects the first actor until the components of ensemble are realized. It seems as if the choices and the actors are beginning to become indistinguishable, and at times neither actor really knows if he or she is responding to the choice or the other actor or a combination of both. They smile at each other and end the day's work.

Rehearsal Number Ten

The actors start with their customary preparation, the relaxation-cluster, and go directly into a Being Workout, until they have achieved a BEING state. From there they move into an ensemble preparation, the five-part kind. At the point when they are communicating in ensemble terms, he suggests that they start the scene without doing any other preparation. Both continue whatever craft work they were doing, silently and unobtrusively under the lines of the scene. At the end of the rehearsal they discuss it.

HE: I just used you! I wanted to see if all the work we had done in the nine rehearsals would stimulate anything between us. I didn't work for the place, but I felt like I was there. I didn't do any character-obligation work, and yet I did have some success with wanting to avoid conflict. I didn't specifically work for my choice in relation to you. I did, however, do some sensory suggestion in the endowment area. From my perspective, I feel that a lot of the work we have done has borne fruit. I was involved with you, and I felt many of the things that the character feels about the relationship. It was an experiment to take stock of what has been accomplished so far.

SHE: I wasn't sure what you were doing, but I went with it! It felt pretty good for me too. I did some sensorial work in the endowment area, but I really feel that both you and my choice have become one. I'm not exactly sure when I'm responding to you or to him. Anyway, it was an interesting way to start the rehearsal.

The actors briefly discuss all they have done and agree that this may be a good time to distill all the choices that they have explored, paring them down to the minimum. They decide to take a few minutes to look at their charts to reassess which choices and approaches could be eliminated and which they will retain, at least for now. He acknowledges that he is ready to start getting ready, having made a mental list of what he is going to do from here.

Most of his work is going to be preparations:

· The relaxation-cluster
· A BEING preparation either by himself or with the actress
· A little character work: some Evocative Words about people in his life who stimulate a conflict phobia

He decides to combine working for the place with an Affective-Memory workout related to specific experiences he had when he was involved with his girlfriend. By doing this he will actually confront three areas of responsibility at one time: first, he will create the place; secondly, he will stimulate the parallel life of that time; and third, he will possibly pique unconscious responses through the use of Affective Memory—all of the above to be done before starting the scene.

During the scene he has decided to:

- Use available stimulus with selective emphasis in the areas that stimulate the desired results
- Do an Endowment, working sensorially to create his ex-girlfriend in relation to the actress
- Go moment to moment with everything he feels
- Deal with the realities of the material—like the cooking, the wine, the telephone call, etc.—as they present themselves

As preparations for the scene, she has decided to do:

- The relaxation workout
- A series of litanies to elevate her need and frustration levels
- An "I Want, I Need" exercise
- A love-hate antithesis related to her boyfriend
- An exercise that will make her feel insecure and dependent, to fulfill one of the character obligations
- Possibly some kind of personal inventory emphasizing her lack of accomplishment at this time in her life

At the beginning of the scene she intends to create the place by using Sensory Suggestion and then go to an Endowment choice approach, using her boyfriend as the choice in relation to the actor. She must also make an adjustment to work for him in such a way as to create an urgency to get something from him that she is not getting.

Both actors begin their preparation process. They work by themselves for about thirty-five minutes, then, without saying one word, obey a silent signal to start the scene involvement. They begin with a Being Workout, immediately followed by "You Make Me Feel" and into the first line of the scene. They work for their respective choices, honoring everything they feel and allowing themselves to respond to each other in the moment. Besides working in the endowment area, they are both doing Inner Monologues and including available realities. At those times when either of them refers to Jean or the dinner cooking on the stove, they both work for the reality by using whatever choice they decided on during the rehearsal process. In this run-through they might stop to take more time with certain stimuli, working to create the reality as they do the scene. They create the cooking odors, the smell and taste of the wine, the physical sensation after the second glass, and so on, by using Sense Memory.

They run through the scene four times in this rehearsal, each time taking advantage of what they have learned the time before, making adjustments and changes in their choices and approaches. Ultimately, after many more rehearsals, the work they do should become very simple—a single question taking the place of ten. Each actor should assimilate the reality as a result of having created the stimuli over a period of time and in many rehearsals. When they finish this tenth rehearsal, they are ready to present the scene in their class, receive critique, and go from there.

Summary of Choices, Choice Approaches, and Techniques Used in the Ten Rehearsals

Rehearsal Number One:

1. Read play together in a stream of consciousness. Avoid giving it meaning.
2. Discuss impressions and interpretations.
3. Discuss author's intentions, talk about characters, their relationships, their conflicts, etc. . . .
4. Share feelings about the parallel experiences they have had; discuss their personal relationships and how they resemble the material.
5. Reread play, stopping to clarify and define things as they go through it; discuss discoveries about the material.
6. Identify theme of piece if possible.
7. Decide how much of the scene or play will be done.

Rehearsal Number Two:

1. Instrumental preparation: Relaxation, Sensitizing, Personal Inventory
2. Relationship preparation: Observe, Wonder, and Perceive
3. Personal exploration of each other (deeper involvement than Wonder, Perceive)
   Purpose of personal exploration:
   a. To get to know each other better
   b. To establish a greater intimacy with each other
   c. To discover any similarities between themselves and the characters
4. Sharing Inventory, discussing the things they have learned about each other in the personal exploration

5. Intimate-Sharing workout
   Purpose for Intimate Sharing:
   a. To stimulate a deeper relationship with each other and create familiarity
   b. To share the selectively emphasized realities that fit the material
   c. To express needs and fears
6. Homework assignments:
   Actress: to consciously observe her own relationship and draw parallels to the scene
   Actor: to begin identifying the specific obligations of the material

Rehearsal Number Three:

1. Relaxation-cluster
2. Personal Inventory (out loud) to get to a BEING place with each other
3. Share homework assignments and discoveries.
4. Create the place (sensorially), a personal place that stimulates a relationship similar to what the characters experience in their place.
5. Start scene, working for the place.
6. Discuss effect of place on scene.
7. Identify other obligations of piece; eliminate obligations that do not apply.
8. Identify character obligations, similarities and dissimilarities.
   To confront character obligations:
   Actress does litany of insecurities.
   Actor does litany of frustrations plus group of imaginary monologues with people who make him feel helpless and like avoiding problems.
9. Inventory results of character-obligation exploration.
10. Actress does "I Want, I Need" exercise.
    Actor does Imaginary Monologue with his father.
    Purpose:
    Actress: to elevate her neediness in order to parallel character
    Actor: to feel the way his father made him feel in order to parallel the character-element responsibility
11. Run the scene using place and choices for character obligations.
12. Briefly discuss results of last exploration.

Rehearsal Number Four:

1. Relaxation-cluster
2. Discuss homework (on character-element choices).
3. Create the place.

4. Actor does Evocative Words with four different people to stimulate the conflict phobia of the character.
   Actress does "I Want, I Need" preparation to deal with character obligation.
5. Imaginary Monologues to choices
   Actor: to his girlfriend
   Actress: to her boyfriend
   Purpose: to stimulate the emotional life of the scene
6. Ensemble preparation: "You Make Me Feel"
7. Begin using their own relationship experiences, talking to each other in their own words.
8. Go into scene from there.
9. Record results in journal and charts.
10. Actor does Affective-Memory exercise to get deeper into the parallel realities and hopefully pique a response from the unconscious.
    Actress does Inner Monologue with and about her boyfriend, using antithetical approach to pique ambivalence of the relationship.
11. Both actors relate to their choices, talking to each other as if they were their choices, from a "Do you remember?" perspective.
    Purpose: to create a background for the relationship, a subtextual history
12. Discuss other reality obligations of the material.

Rehearsal Number Five:

1. Actor does exposure exercise to ventilate his insecurities, a preparation to be able to work.
2. Relaxation-cluster
3. Create the place (sensorially).
4. Actor does character preparations: Evocative Words with the same people, and imaginary monologues.
   Actress does Inner Monologue about all the relationships she has had in her life and why they failed.
5. Five-part ensemble preparation
6. The scene as written
7. Discussion of the scene, what was there and what was missing
8. Endowments in relation to each other, working for their choices sensorially, endowing each other with the features of the people they are working for
9. Scene (Inner-Outer-Monologue approach)
10. Discussion of rehearsal

Rehearsal Number Six:

1. Relaxation-cluster
2. Ensemble preparation
3. Endowments of each other (creating their choices at the beginning of their relationship)
4. Improvisation, talking about beginning of relationship, emphasizing the love and attraction (and adding believability elements)
5. Interjecting conflict into the improvisation
6. Scene, using inner monologue about what they want from each other that they are not getting (goes on throughout the entire scene)
7. Short discussion about results of improvisation and scene
8. Charts and journal entries and updates
9. Discussion about the remaining obligations as yet not dealt with, and commitment to doing homework related to those obligations

Rehearsal Number Seven:

1. Actor: Deep relaxation involvement (Logey) into:
   Ultimate-consciousness workout sensorially re-creating recent dream about his former relationship
   Actress: Creates the place.
   Does imaginary monologues with her boyfriend.
2. Ensemble preparation: Double Exposure, followed by "You Make Me Feel"
3. Endowments (both actors)
4. Scene, continuing the endowment process throughout
5. Discussion of run-through
6. Scene, with Inner-Outer Monologue expressing their moment-to-moment life and including the written words. Both actors continue endowment process.
7. Scene verbatim, working for choices and continuing Inner Monologue silently
8. Scene, third time, verbatim, with inclusion of all moment-to-moment realities expressed through the words of the scene
9. Inventory and discussion of the rehearsal
10. Discussion about choice discoveries for dealing with other obligations of material (the character's profession, other characters discussed in the play, urgency of company coming, etc. . . .)

Rehearsal Number Eight:

1. Actress: Relaxation-cluster
   Actor: Creates place sensorially.
   Does *ultimate-consciousness* workout: mini Primal Moan, into Affective Memory surrounding personal relationship.
2. Actress: "I Want, I Need" exercise, semi-audibly, into:
   Accuse-and-Indict exercise to her boyfriend
3. Endowment process (both actors)
4. Scene, going back and forth with their own words
   Actress: Continuing the "You Never Gave Me" between the lines
   Actor: Responding to the indictments with his own words and the dialogue
5. Parallel improvisation, discussing all the other characters referred to in play, friends they had before meeting each other, etc. . . .
6. Believability parallel improvisation, talking about first romantic experiences, making love, etc. . . . (Both actors use their choices to talk to.)
7. Scene, with complete carryover of Believability improvisation, going moment-to-moment with what was created by it

Rehearsal Number Nine:

1. Relaxation workout
2. Actor: Being Workout
   Actress: deep Personal Inventory
3. "Putting scene on its feet": Working to create kitchen, food cooking, dealing with movement and actions of scene, making them a reality
   Actor: Sensorially creates sound of voice on other end of telephone.
   Actress: Sensorially works for sounds and odors of food cooking.
   Both: Sensorially create taste and effect of wine.
4. Scene, twice
5. Reinvest in preparations: Two-Person Being Workout
6. Available-stimulus exploration, dealing with how actors feel about each other, the place, what is going on between them and what has changed from rehearsal number one to now
7. Scene from there, using Endowments
8. Encouragement of an irreverent inclusion of all impulses
9. Tricking each other in the framework of the scene, staying with choices
10. Repetition of scene, starting with an improvisation involving an adjustment for the actress related to the urgency in the scene

11. Repetition of scene, carrying all the work into internal involvements (sensorial exploration and running Inner Monologues, with total inclusion of all impulses and distractions within framework of scene)

Rehearsal Number Ten:

1. Relaxation workout
2. Being Workout
3. Five-part ensemble preparation
4. Scene without doing any other preparation
   Actor: Sensory Suggestion in relation to choice, plus available realities about actress established during nine prior rehearsals
   Actress: Some sensorial work in the endowment area, also using composite of actor and choice
5. Review and distillation of choices used in all rehearsals, referring to charts
6. Decide what choices to keep and use from this point on.
   Actor: Decides most of the work to be done in preparation:
       a. Relaxation-cluster
       b. BEING preparation (one- or two-person)
       c. Character work: Evocative Words and Imaginary Monologues
       d. Affective-Memory workout to create the parallel experience of the relationship he had, and at the same time create the place while hopefully appealing to the unconscious
   After starting the scene:
       a. Use available stimulus with selective emphasis.
       b. Do Endowments, sensorially.
       c. Go moment to moment with everything he feels, into scene.
       d. Deal with all realities as they present themselves.
   Actress: Decides to do as preparations:
       a. Relaxation-cluster
       b. Series of litanies to elevate her need and frustration levels
       c. "I Want, I Need" exercise
       d. Love/hate antithesis related to her boyfriend
       e. Exploration of exercises that would make her feel insecure and dependent (as character-obligation involvement)

    f. Personal Inventory emphasizing lack of accomplishment at this time in her life

    During the scene:

    a. Create place through Sensory Suggestion.

    b. Do Endowments, sensorially.

7. Silent preparations for thirty-five minutes
8. Scene, starting with involvement exercises: Being Workout, followed by "You Make Me Feel" and into material, using all their choices and inner monologues
9. Repeat scene four times, stopping to deal with various stimuli as they are presented.

These ten rehearsals form a blueprint for you to follow. The alternatives are infinite. There are endless choices, twenty-five different choice approaches, and the obligations vary with the material selected. If, however, you relate to the examples given in this rehearsal structure, they will help you to use your time very productively. Each rehearsal is filled with creative involvement, and the craft techniques are quite clear. You can use the summary as a chart. As you work with the craft, you will be able to structure your own rehearsals creatively.

No matter what medium you work in, and no matter what the technical demands or restrictions are, if you know what to do and how to do it, you will be successful in everything you do. The bottom line is *being a craftsman!*

8

THE
MAGIC OF
ACTING

Many years ago I was in Lucille Ball's workshop. We did all kinds of material there, not just comedy. It was a wonderful experience for many reasons, and I learned several things that have stayed with me since then. I remember someone asking her once: "What do you do when you're tired and out of it? Maybe you had a bad night, and the next morning you have to start a scene, on the *I Love Lucy* show, for example, where you have to be up, and excited, and full of energy." I remember her response quite clearly. Without taking one moment to think about it, she said that there were many mornings like that, when it seemed like the last thing in the world she could do was be "Lucy"; then she would walk onto the set with all those other great people, and something would happen: she would get "**THAT ENCHANTED SENSE OF PLAY**," and off she would go bouncing around the stage and off the walls.

I never forgot that. As an actor, I had experienced that feeling, never knowing what to call it but recognizing the pleasure, the excitement, and the inspiration that went along with it. When I was a young actor in summer stock, I would get to the theater early, walk onto the stage, and stand there looking out at that dark cavern that in a couple of hours would be alive with people. I would turn on the bank of lights, which created a wall of brilliance between me and that dark abyss, and I would stand there feeling the excitement course through my body. It seemed to climb up from the floor of the stage through my legs and up my body, causing the most exhilarating sensation. I felt vulnerable, invincible, gigantic, and tingly all at the same time. I knew why I wanted to be an actor; I couldn't understand anyone who didn't. Where on this planet could one experience such ecstasy? It wasn't until I heard Lucy talk about it and label it that I made the connection. It was, indeed, "the enchanted sense of play"!

I remember experiencing similar feelings as a child when I used to play pretend games with my friends—you know, the "I-must" games: "I must be the general, and you're the sergeant, and we are stuck on the ridge, and the enemy is coming up the hill. You're wounded, and I won't leave you . . ." That's what makes acting fun: acting is like playing! Unfortunately, we outgrow those wonderful years when we embraced our imagination and our fantasies. We "grow up" and become practical and responsible. We must earn a living, support a family, and climb up the ladder in order to realize "the American dream"! But isn't the dream to dream? I think that the need to play and fantasize and imagine is natural to all of us. It is a part of what talent is. Most of the time it disappears as we get older. It isn't encouraged past a certain point, and we lose that wonderful ability to "believe."

In spite of the insulation many people cover themselves with, some become actors. They come into the playground blocked, inhibited, and laden with years of obstacles that stand between them and that wonderful play state. Some of them are the very ones who advocate, "If you can act, you act!" The only thing wrong with their philosophy is that they *can't!* They spend a whole lifetime pursuing their career, never able to touch what was once there when they were children. It would be a wonderful world if we all retained that great ability to pretend and believe, but unfortunately that isn't so. The reality is that most people lose it quite early. Children have a natural ability to "play," but in some cases it is discouraged very early, and they go inside and turn off those wonderful feelings, because they know they won't be rewarded for having them. Somewhere down the line these same people decide to act. They want to feel and experience all the colors of the emotional spectrum but are blocked from a great number of their emotions. The tragedy is that most of them do nothing about it. They end up assuming, imposing, and representing real life on the stage and never reach that "enchanted sense of play." This, fortunately, is not the way it has to be. There is something that these actors can do to reach themselves. They can commit to training their instrument and mastering a process that will enable them to create reality from an exciting and emotionally colorful place. To reach the *magic of acting,* an actor must be open, available, and expressive. He must be free of restrictions, inhibitions, and self-consciousness.

THE PROCESS AND
HOW IT PROMOTES MAGIC

This is my fourth book about acting. Someone recently said to me, "You're writing another book? What more could there possibly be to say about acting?" Indeed, what more? In the twenty-eight years I have been teaching acting, I have seen many very talented actors unable to reach their talent because of the scar tissue that obstructed their instrumental availability. These same actors knew somewhere in their being that down there were the magic and inspiration that they had once experienced. So what is the answer to all of this? Is being unable to plummet into the depths and reach that well of "goodies" an irrevocable sentence? No, it is not! The problem is not in the inability to change that; the problem lies with *consciousness!* We are in the age of space travel, man has been to the Moon, but as far as theatrical conscious- ness goes, we are still sitting in the rumble seat of a Model-A Ford. We are still being taught how to *"act"* in every sense of the word. Recently I taught at a private school in the Southwest during a fine-arts festival for many private schools. In one of the sessions, a student, who admitted wanting to follow a professional career in acting, did a monologue which showed a certain sense of truth but was filled with concept and representation. He was "acting," not being honest or real. I began to work with him, using his own personal and meaningful realities as impetus for the monologue, and as a result, he did it a second time but from a very real place: it was impacting, real, and theatrical. There wasn't a person in the audience who was not incredibly moved by the life this boy had brought to the piece. When it was over, even though they were amazed at the difference, the adults as well as the students wanted to know if experiencing that reality could be harmful to the young man! (This is the nature of the consciousness that pervades even the professional theater!) I explained that quite to the contrary experience and expression were very liberating and healthy. I went into a brief discussion about the impact of repressing our feelings on the body and the psyche. I'm not at all sure that they accepted any of it, but it is nonetheless the truth! The most interesting thing that came out of the experience is that after tasting this kind of reality in an acting framework, that young man will never be able to accept the other again. While he may not at this point be able to repeat the experience without help, he knows the difference, and because of that he might seek to find the way to it again.

With this kind of limited understanding and consciousness, the training ground for the actor has been sparse. While you may be able to understand the fears of a group of high-school kids, what can you do when the same conscious- ness exists in the profession? Most acting teachers and many directors will not touch what they refer to as the psychological province of the actor. Even Lee Strasberg wouldn't listen to an actor attempting to describe his work process if it became too "personal." He would stop him in mid sentence with, "No, I don't want to hear that. Save it for your therapist!" This kind of trepidation toward the actor's instrument is what maintains the blocks that keep most actors from their real talent and from the *"magic."* It is *not harmful, but necessary,* for the actor to eliminate obstacles that stop him from being affected by internal and external stimuli. As human beings we are constructed to feel, to be stimulated, and to respond and express all the emotions that we can experience. The Church, the schools, and our well-meaning but misinformed parents teach and train us to stifle our impulses in the name of propriety and good manners. This kind of consciousness seeps into our lives, our culture, and our theater. So what is to be done? The first step is for us to become informed, to elevate our *consciousness,* and then to instrumentally strip away these inhibitions and blocks, so that we can function as free and expressive people! The actor must go into training, a training divided into two areas, his instrument and the craft. The instrumental techniques strip away and eliminate the fears and inhibitions that he grew up with. As this "instrumental therapy" proceeds, he becomes progressively more available and trusting; he is affected by a greater number of stimuli and progressively feels freer to express his responses to them. As his instrument begins to open up, as he feels and expresses more, he is in turn better able to use the natural abilities that have always been there. Having the permission to experience all human emotions, he allows himself to imagine, fantasize, believe, and play. In a sense the child who had been buried for many years under all those taboos is suddenly free to play again! All of this is accomplished over a period of time, through techniques that promote a cumulative freeing of all feelings and emotions. These techniques are discussed at great length in *No Acting Please* and *Being & Doing.* They encourage the actor to do and express things that he has difficulty allowing himself to do or feel. Once he has experienced expressing these fearful things, he progressively accepts his right to do so. If he ultimately confronts all areas of inhibition and all obstacles, he will achieve a freedom and use of his instrument that he might never have attained without that training and commitment.

Along with this involvement the actor must learn a craft, consisting of techniques and approaches that allow him to stimulate the life required by the material. It is a process of creating reality on the stage or in front of the camera. Without instrumental freedom, the actor cannot use this craft, because the techniques will not penetrate the obstacles and reach his personal reality level. Since truth can only be created from a place of truth, these two areas are dependent on each other.

Once the actor has achieved instrumental freedom, as well as some kind of mastery of the craft, the stage is set for communicating with the magical child, that part in all of us that needs no training to act! I have heard people say more than once that acting should be simple; that it should be a natural process, and that if you are talented, then you can act, but if you are not, all the training in the world will not help! Some of that is true, but the bulk of it is not! It is true that if a person hasn't much talent, all the training in the world will not change that. It will, however, teach him how to use the greatest part of what he does have! It is also true that acting is a natural thing; once the instrument is free to act, it can do so, but first we must open the doors to allow that part of us out who wants to believe and play. In order to do that with any consistency, we must have a process which will allow us to every time—a dependable process that we can count on. I have personally been accused of complicating acting with all of these involvements and techniques, but these techniques are the actor's tools. They enable him to be creative under any conditions or circumstances. Without tools there is no dependability. The actor would have to hope for inspiration and pray for the right circumstances for the child to come out and play. With these tools, however, he can create the proper environment and does not have to depend on accident in order to be able to create reality and experience the magic of acting! Without process there is no art—at least not consistently!

This entire process of work, the instrumental and craft involvements and approaches, exists for one purpose only, and that is to take the actor to his talent—to free the child so that it can fly! Every exercise, every approach is designed to pique unconscious impulses, to stimulate inspiration, and to free the intuition. That wonderful magical thing that happens to an actor when he is taken over by that flush of joy and transported to experiences that cannot even be described is a result of the preparation that sets the stage for it to happen. While it is possible to experience the magic occasionally without any preparation, it is neither consistent nor dependable. When an actor dons a costume and leaps onto the stage, enjoys every movement of his body and every word that comes out of his mouth, is transported to another time and place, and when all of that is a reality for him, there is the magic of acting! If that is what you want, and you want it to be there all the time, you must be willing to work for it, to prepare the instrument to *be,* to master a craft that stimulates the life of the play and inspires magic at the same time. To expect to attain that without preparing and working to create it is foolish. There is only one real reason for this work and that is to free the intuitive talent and reach that incredible place, the **MAGIC OF ACTING.**

THE MAGICAL CHILD
AND THE MAGICAL ACTOR

In sub-personality language, there is actually an archetype called the magical child. It is that part of us which is very aligned with the playful child energy. If it is true that the numerous facets of our personality called sub-personalities are actually forms of energy, then the child archetypes hold that child energy. We have all experienced the magical child, whether we are aware of it or not. Sometimes it is freed when we have had too much to drink; at other times it comes out when we are clowning with our friends; sometimes it bursts forth when we play with our, or other people's, children. At an amusement park, just as you reach the summit of the roller coaster ride, it may come crashing through with a scream of childish joy. It is always there somewhere, and depending on how good you have been to it, decides how often it will come out to play. "All actors are children" is a line from *Prince of Players,* which the character Junius Booth says to the owner of the theater in which he is playing. He is right! It is the magical child that does most of our acting. Without a magical child, there is no magical actor!

Besides the training process, which consists of freeing the instrument and using craft techniques that are inspiring, there are other ways to appeal to the magical child; but the first step is to identify it in yourself. Think about those times when you experienced the presence of that part of you. Ask yourself what it was that elicited that energy. What were you doing? Who were you with? The answers to those questions are among the keys to the magical kingdom where that wonderful child lives.

You must encourage yourself to play more. I mean *play*—not tennis or some other adult game—get down on the floor and *play!* Play soldier; play with toy cars; pretend that you are in the middle of the desert looking for water; turn your car into a World War II airplane; communicate with the other fighter pilots on the freeway; shoot down The Red Baron! At this point you must be thinking that I've flown off the handle, right? Wrong! I haven't lost it at all! If you expect to reach that enchanted sense of play, **YOU MUST PLAY!!!** Try to allow some time each day to encourage the magical child in you to come out and play. It might be awkward at first, particularly if you haven't done it in years, but if you do a little every day, it will not only get easier, but it will be a great deal of fun for you! I promise that after a short time you will begin to look forward to those times in the day when you can play.

Another approach to the magical child is sub-personality facilitation. This is a process I discuss in great detail in *Irreverent Acting.* If the "facilitator" can relate to your magical child, he or she may be successful in encouraging it to "come out." Whatever process you use in addition to your regular training schedule, it is important to be aware of the magical-child energy and to be consistent in appealing to it daily.

When Lucille Ball made that statement about "the enchanted sense of play," she was talking about her magical child. Why and how it just happened for her was probably the result of years of acting and doing comedy. She more than likely had conditioned a response to a soundstage environment: just walking into the set pushed her buttons and called out that magical child to play again. Of course, the fact that she is an extremely talented performer helped a great deal!

The goal of the actor is to step over that "line" into that inspired place, to be taken over by some invisible force that propels him to great heights of inspiration and creativity. The elements and ingredients that set the stage for this to happen are numerous. To reach a BEING place, where you are comfortable doing no more or less than what you feel, to be without obligations or concepts, to be free to allow yourself to experience any emotion, to pique that part of you that loves to act and play, to be courageously irreverent, to honor all your impulses, and to embrace the joy you feel when you are expressing who you are on the stage—those are the reasons to act!

THE CONTROVERSY AND MISUNDERSTANDINGS ABOUT PROCESS AND MAGIC

"The Method" has been misunderstood, maligned, and misinterpreted, even by its practitioners in some cases. Many people think that it is designed for a stark type of reality, a naturalness, and a kind of drama that lends itself to that sort of understated life. It has been called a process designed to promote and fulfill "Second Avenue kitchen drama." It is certainly not for the classics, is the contention, or even for plays with more theatrical types of responsibilities. All of that is sheer nonsense! "The Method," particularly where I have gone with it, is a process that applies to all theater, from Aeschylus to Sam Shepard. Stanislavsky didn't do Clifford Odets; he did Chekov and many other classics. The work is designed not only to stimulate the desired emotional life for the material, but to free the intuition. The fifties concept about theater, and more particularly about "The Method" in the theater, referred to a few plays of that period and to a style of acting promoted by a handful of actors who were imitated (badly) by hundreds of others who had no understanding of the process. Actually, a Hamlet leaping around the stage in his feigned madness, moving with the freedom and flamboyance of a ballet dancer, relishing and enjoying the enunciation of every word that comes out of his mouth and bounces off the back wall of the theater, is a testimonial to what is theatrical and exciting. It can also be real! The nature of an actor's behavior on stage, its size, and its theatricality are dependent on what choices he uses to stimulate that behavior. In the last analysis, when he catches fire and is inspired on the stage, it is usually because he created some impetus that stimulated that state. It is never a question of being too big or too small; it has to do with the level of reality, not with size! The unconscious is where intuition and inspiration reside. Pique the unconscious, and you open the doors to the *magic*.

THE ULTIMATE CONSCIOUSNESS, THRESHOLD OF MAGIC

The most magical experience of all is an *ultimate-consciousness* experience. When an actor crosses that line into the "never-never land" of unconscious flow, he needs nothing more but to surrender to his impulses. He is on a kind of creative autopilot. He is taken over by a force so exciting that it challenges description. Indeed, it is the ultimate magical experience. A great deal has already been said in this book about the *ultimate consciousness,* and not wanting to be redundant I will avoid restating it. However, not enough can be said about the ultimate goal of every actor, which is to reach that state where craft and conscious process are unnecessary. If you, the actor, develop your consciousness to its highest level, eliminate the obstacles related to your instrument, master the craft, and work diligently to communicate with the unconscious, you will live on the edge of the *ultimate consciousness.* Whatever the competition and the statistics of this field, once an actor experiences the magic of acting, it all becomes worth it! **THE MAGIC IS THE RESULT OF UNBRIDLED TALENT!**

If you found the information in this book valuable, you'll be interested to know that cassette tapes by Eric Morris are now available. These 90-minute audio tapes were recorded live at actual workshops and seminars conducted by Mr. Morris and are ideal for use in conjunction with his books, *No Acting Please, Being and Doing, Irreverent Acting* and *Acting from the Ultimate Consciousness*. The tapes are offered in two series, *The Craft of Acting* and *The Megapproaches*.

To receive the first tape in *The Craft of Acting* series plus a full information brochure, send your check for $9.95 plus $1.00 for postage and handling to:

> Ermor Enterprises
> 8004 Fareholm Drive
> Los Angeles, CA 90046

Money refunded if not satisfied.